Perry Marshall combines the attributes of the most calculated engineer with the artistry of a poet. If you are not following Perry's formula, you are leaving millions on the table.

—Brian Kurtz, Executive Vice President of Boardroom Inc.

Perry's methods coupled with Google AdWords offer a fast and cheap testing ground for a lot of marketing messages. He's a consummate player of this game, the smartest person I or any of my clients have ever found when it comes to Google AdWords—optimizing response for his clients, and teaching others how to do it for themselves.

—Dan S. Kennedy, author of *No B.S. Direct Marketing*

Perry Marshall is a certifiable genius in his intellect, and his understanding of far more than mere marketing.

—Jay Abraham, Founder and CEO of Abraham Group, Inc., and author of *Getting Everything You Can Out of All You've Got*

This is not a get rich quick book. What Perry and Talor prescribe is a tough look at your business, and then give you the tools to getting the right customers and creating the business you want to run. Don't expect to read this book, buy a couple of keywords and have money rolling in tomorrow. Those days are over. But, if you want to capture a sustainable, profitable niche, then this book needs to be in your arsenal.

—Rod Brant, Serial Entrepreneur, Sylvania, Ohio

I'm often asked by peers in my niche how I manage to rank so well in search engines and not go broke using Google AdWords. There are a couple of reasons—I've been subscribing to Perry Marshall's newsletters since 2003; I've read every one of his books; I listen in on all the conference calls he organizes; and finally, I *implement* his strategies and tactics. Only a fool would continue to run Google AdWords campaigns and NOT invest in, study, and implement these ideas. Just get the book!

—Jer Ayles-Ayler, AdWords User, Trihouse Enterprises, Inc.

What I love about this book is its honesty. Most of the other books on Google AdWords don't really "tell it like it is" but rather tell you what "Google would have you believe." This book is full of proven tips and tricks (even for seasoned veterans), valuable resources, and an objective attitude. I can see why Perry is the number-one quoted resource for Google AdWords.

—JASON L. MCDONALD, SILICON VALLEY, CALIFORNIA

Talor created a very successful lead generation campaign for my law practice. He is a straight shooter who understands marketing at the highest level. If you are a local business owner there is nobody you are going to get better advice from on marketing and generating leads for your business.

—JACOB SAPOCHNICK, LAW OFFICES OF JACOB J. SAPOCHNICK, IMMIGRATION LAWYERS, SAN DIEGO, CALIFORNIA

If you are a local business owner and you read this book you will be in the top 1 percent compared to your competitors when it comes to getting new customers for your business. The strategies Talor Zamir clearly outlines in this book have generated millions of dollars for businesses around the world.

—SHAUN SMITH, BLACK BELT MARKETING, PHILADELPHIA, PENNSYLVANIA

Entrepreneur MAGAZINE'S

ULTIMATE GUIDE TO

LOCAL BUSINESS MARKETING

- Capture high-quality leads from search engines in 48 hours
- Master the components of a high-converting campaign and **get the most bang for your buck**
- Utilize mobile search advertising for the greatest benefits

PERRY MARSHALL TALOR ZAMIR

Ep
Entrepreneur
PRESS®

Entrepreneur Press, Publisher
Cover Design: Andrew Welyczko
Production and Composition: Eliot House Productions

Library of Congress Cataloging-in-Publication Data
Names: Marshall, Perry S., author. | Zamir, Talor, author.
Title: Ultimate guide to local business marketing / by Perry Marshall and Talor Zamir.
Description: Irvine, California: Entrepreneur Media, Inc., [2015]
Identifiers: LCCN 2015036136| ISBN 978-1-59918-578-1 (alk. paper) |
ISBN 1-59918-578-4 (alk. paper)
Subjects: LCSH: Marketing. | Internet marketing. | Local mass media.
Classification: LCC HF5415 .M32453 2015 | DDC 658.8/72—dc23
LC record available at http://lccn.loc.gov/2015036136

Printed in the United States of America

20 19 18 17 16 10 9 8 7 6 5 4 3 2 1

Contents

Wait! Before You Read This Book . . .

Whether you are a small local business with three employees or a major player with over 100, the strategies you're about to learn have the potential to *exponentially* increase your business.

Our goal with this book is not to help you get a small bump and increase your business by 10 percent or 20 percent—not even close. What we are excited about is the potential for you to *double,* or potentially *triple,* your business (in a relatively short period of time, if you choose).

While that may sound like a bold goal, the strategies you'll learn in this book have the potential to be by *far* the greatest source of leads you've ever received on a continual basis. These strategies are not fads that might work today but not tomorrow. These are real-world, proven strategies that work right now and will continue to for many years to come.

The only difference between you and other local businesses that have been using these strategies successfully (some to the tune of millions of dollars, year after year) is that these other businesses have been educated (or maybe they hired someone who was educated) on how to implement these strategies the *right* way.

If you've heard someone talk about their experience doing something like Google AdWords, keep in mind that just because it may not have worked for them doesn't mean the strategy doesn't work. In fact, we know that thousands of local businesses are making huge profits right now with Google AdWords and other strategies you'll learn in this book.

So chances are, if someone you know has tried Google AdWords and failed, the reason is probably that they were not armed with the information and tools that they needed to make it work (the information you're about to learn in this book).

You'll also notice that search engine optimization (SEO) is Chapter 27. It is not Chapter 1. There is a very definite reason we did this. Most people start with SEO, but you should end with SEO. Do not start with SEO. Why? Because SEO takes longer to achieve than almost anything else in this book, and you need pay-per-click first before you can define your SEO goals.

The bottom line is this, if you don't implement these strategies, then someone else in your market will . . . which means *they* will be getting business *you* should have had.

If you're doing well right now without using these strategies, that's great, because it means you'll be doing even better when you do implement them!

If you're serious and ready to *dramatically* grow your business (not just a 10 percent or 20 percent bump), then you are reading the right book.

The first thing to do is get the online bonus material and resources that go with this book at www.UltimateLocalBook.com. There you'll also find a collection of supplemental material that we consider vital to this book, and you'll also get real-time notifications from us whenever there are any changes with Google for local businesses and/or other topics covered

Chapter 1

Why 95 Percent of Local Businesses Are Failing Miserably with Their Marketing

by Talor Zamir

I recently spoke with a lawyer who used to do over a million dollars a year in business. But my conversation began when he said:

> *You have to help me. These young lawyers out of law school who know how to do this internet marketing thing are taking all my business, and my business has been almost cut in half.*

He went on to tell me how he went from over a million dollars a year to around $600,000. That's no small drop in revenue, and he still had the same overhead, so it pretty much wiped out his profits.

This lawyer had advertised in Yellow Pages for the past ten years or so and had been running the same ad the whole time. The only difference was that he recently started taking out bigger ads (and paying a lot more) than he used to, but the leads have not been rolling in anymore. As a result of the big drop in leads, revenue, and profits, he got to the point where he could barely afford to do *any* type of marketing. Death Spiral.

Do you feel like you've heard this story before? Have you experienced something similar with your local business? It's not uncommon for established local businesses to find themselves in a similar situation.

Alternatively, there are many local businesses opening their doors for the first time. Opening a local business is no small undertaking, and most people don't realize all that goes into it. It means signing a long-term commercial lease, furnishing the place, hiring and training employees, registering the business, getting insurance, and on and on. Depending on what kind of business you're in, you could easily sink $100,000 before you even open your doors!

WHAT THEY DON'T TEACH YOU IN LAW (OR ANY PROFESSIONAL) SCHOOL

After you open your doors, you may ask, "Where are the clients? Why aren't new clients coming in my door?"

The cold, hard truth is you can be the best lawyer/dentist/plumber/chiropractor/etc. in the world, but if you don't have new leads coming in, then you'll be the best *broke* lawyer/dentist/plumber/chiropractor/etc. nobody ever heard of.

Unfortunately, they probably didn't teach you any marketing in school, and that's a shame, because it is the most important part of your business. Our goal with this book is to show you the most effective strategies for marketing your local business.

WHAT YOU WILL *NOT* LEARN IN THIS BOOK

This book is *not* about branding. We're not interested in any form of marketing where there is no way to measure your ROI (return on investment) and how effective your marketing efforts are.

Not to say that branding does not have its place and does not work. But branding typically costs millions of dollars, so you better have a *really* big budget if you plan on doing a branding campaign that actually gets you an ROI.

We're assuming you don't have millions of dollars to spend on advertising that may or may not get a return for your local business. And we're not here to throw a bunch of random ideas at you that may or may not work.

"REAL" MARKETING

This book is about direct response marketing. That means that you have real, measurable results and are able to track your ROI down to the penny. That is what we call "real" marketing.

We're here to show you a system that has worked for thousands of other local businesses, and we're extremely confident that, if you follow our instructions, it will work for you, too. This system has huge upside potential and could double or triple your business in less than a year.

HIGH POTENTIAL—LOW RISK

One of the biggest benefits of the system you are about to learn is that it has a very high potential upside with very little risk. Again, you have the potential to double or triple your business, however, your risk is only two or three thousand dollars to test out this method. That's a pretty good risk/reward ratio! While we can't guarantee that what we teach in this book is going to work 100 percent of the time, we will say that we have got it down to a science where it works a large majority of the time. And because this system is completely transparent and trackable, if for some reason it's not working for you, you'll be able to see very quickly that it's not, and you will be able to cut your losses.

This is about getting real measurable results and scaling a business. It is *not* about how to increase your business by 10 percent per year. Our goal is to arm you with tools that can potentially double or triple your business and give you a consistent flow of new leads coming in the door.

LIMITED BUDGET? NO PROBLEM!

This book is designed to help you grow your small to midsize local business on a limited budget with very low risk and a very high potential upside. The method you are about to learn does not require huge investments in branding or any other type of advertising. You don't have to do billboards or TV. Of course, if you are doing any of those things (and if they are working!), that's great. If your prospects are already familiar with your name, it can only help.

However, none of that is necessary, and the goal of this book is to show you how. Whether you have zero employees or a thousand, you can use this system and test it on a very low budget, see real and measurable results, and scale up massively from there.

There are countless businesses whose number-one source of leads, income, and business are the exact strategies we're going to share with you. And we are confident that if you follow our step-by-step instructions and implement these strategies, there is a very high likelihood they will work for you, too.

SEO LAST, NOT FIRST

One of the first mistakes local businesses make is focusing on Search Engine Optimization (SEO) early. This is backwards, because Paid Search generates nearly instantaneous results. So unless you want to wait around for six months, start with Chapter 1 and get pay per click right. SEO comes in Chapter 27 and it's a powerful chapter.

Sound good? Great! Let's dive in.

Chapter 2

Search Engines Are the New Yellow Pages

by Talor Zamir

I did not quite finish the story about my conversation with the lawyer I shared with you in the last chapter. After venting to me for a while about his huge drop in leads and revenue and how ineffective his Yellow Pages ads are, this was my response:

> *That's because Google is the new Yellow Pages. Twenty years ago if someone needed a plumber or roofer or lawyer or whatever, they would go to the Yellow Pages and find a business there. These days, when was the last time you've even seen the Yellow Pages? Personally, I have not seen an actual physical Yellow Pages in years.*

The point is, if you need a plumber or a roofer or a dentist or a lawyer, you're going to Google them. (*Note*: There are other search engines besides Google, but for the purposes of this book, we will focus on Google because it is, by far, the dominant search engine.) As you are reading this, your prospects are searching on Google for a business that does what you do. These are people in your local geographic area who need help with a problem you can solve, and they need that help *now*.

Will they find you there?

WHY THE YELLOW PAGES WAS (AND SEARCH ENGINES ARE NOW) THE HIGHEST-QUALITY LEADS

The reason why Yellow Pages ads were one of the most effective forms of advertising for local businesses for so many years and why search engines have now taken over as one of the most effective forms of advertising for local businesses is this:

> ***These leads are from people that have already made a decision that they need a lawyer, dentist, chiropractor, roofer, plumber, or other local business, and they are actively searching, finding, and calling* you.**

This makes them a much higher-quality lead than just about any other form of advertising.

If you have done any sort of sales or marketing, then you know the difference between "cold calling" or "cold prospecting" someone and when someone searches, finds, and calls *you*. The difference is like night and day, both in the quality of the lead as well as in the conversion rate (turning them into a paying client).

Think about it: If someone goes to Google and types in "Personal Injury Lawyer in Dallas," that means they are probably looking to hire a personal injury lawyer in Dallas *right now*.

You're not going to get a higher-quality lead than that from any other form of advertising!

In fact, the only lead that's higher quality than a search engine lead is a personal referral. If your friend says, "This is the best personal injury lawyer in the world, and you need to work with him," that would be an extremely high-quality lead which would most likely turn into a client.

However, you can't get referrals if you don't have enough clients to give you referrals! That's why it's so crucial for local businesses to constantly be bringing in high-quality leads that turn into clients for their business. Then when you treat those clients right, that should turn into referrals, which means new business that comes in for *free*. But remember, you would never have had that (free) referral business if you didn't generate the initial lead from Google.

Let's say every 10 clients generate two referrals for you, but you only have 150 clients. Then in this example you would only get 30 referrals. But if you had a constant stream of new high-quality leads coming into your business every day, and let's say you got 500 clients from that, then in this example you would get 100 referrals (free clients).

As you can see, the referral machine works in tandem with the advertising machine, but you must feed the machine (your business) if you really want to grow it fast.

WHY TRADITIONAL FORMS OF MARKETING ARE LESS EFFECTIVE

It's not only the Yellow Pages but also other traditional types of advertising and marketing that are far less effective compared to Google advertising. Let's look at the issues with some of the common sources local businesses try.

First, let's look at billboards. Billboard companies will almost always lock you into a long-term contract, and it's very expensive. They know those billboards will get stale, which is why they lock you into long-term contracts. The first month that you put up a billboard, you might get some strong, new exposure with people in the area. But by the second, third, fourth, fifth, sixth month, it's the same people typically driving by that same billboard and the effectiveness tends to drop.

Most local businesses are priced out of TV due to the high cost to produce a good TV commercial and buy the airtime. There are some lawyers, cosmetic surgeons, and cosmetic dentists who can afford it, yet even those that can afford it are receiving an extremely low ROI. These days, many people are using DVRs to record shows and skip the commercials completely.

Similar things can be said about radio, newspaper, and magazine advertising. You tend to reach the same audience over and over, so your ads go stale; you often get locked into a long-term contract; and/or have a very low ROI (if you are even able to track your ROI).

And here's what you need to understand about the ROI: Let's say you're doing a billboard, and it costs $2,000 a month. Then a six-month contract means you are on the hook for $12,000 before you even know whether it's working and you're getting an ROI or not! You're locked into a $12,000 commitment no matter what! Whereas the method we will teach you in this book is something you can test for a couple thousand dollars and, if it works, you can scale it up massively. And, if it doesn't work, your risk was only a couple grand, and you are likely to at least get something out of it.

> Remember, the best ROI and the highest-quality leads come from people who are actively searching for you.

Now, we don't want to sound like we are totally bashing traditional forms of advertising and that you should completely avoid them. If you have billboards or are running TV/radio ads already and people in your area are familiar with your name, then when they do a Google search, they'll only be more likely to click on your ad. So if you are doing billboard, TV, radio, etc. and are happy with it, then don't stop! It's only going to make what we are going to show you that much more effective.

Chapter 3

Search Engine Optimization (SEO) vs. Pay Per Click (PPC)

by Talor Zamir

I talk to local business owners all the time. As soon as I mention Google, their defenses go way up. I don't blame them. A lot of it comes from being burned in the past by online marketing companies whose results failed to live up to their promises. But there is another factor at play here: confusion.

The world of internet marketing is endlessly confusing, and the people who sell it deliberately make it worse. Marketers throw around terms like SEO, SEM, PPC, Google Maps, Google My Business, Google+, and Google Places. And those are just terms related to advertising on Google! Add in social media, email, and other forms of internet marketing, and it's enough to make your head explode!

Because of this, most local business owners are very confused when it comes to internet marketing. And when people are confused, their defenses automatically go up, and it is very difficult to get them to act (an important lesson to keep in mind for any marketing you do, by the way).

So before we go any further, we want to clear up any confusion you may have about what it is we're going to spend most of our time focusing on in this book. While we'll have a couple of guest chapters from experts, one on Facebook and one on local SEO, the majority of our time will be focused on PPC, specifically Google AdWords, because that's what we have consistently seen work best for local businesses and generate a real and measurable ROI (when done right following the strategies you are about to read).

THE DIFFERENCES BETWEEN SEO AND PPC

Now that you know that Google is the best place to reach your ideal prospects, the big question is: "What's the best way to get in front of those prospects and get them to contact you?"

There are two main ways a local business can reach prospects on Google, and it's important to understand what they are and the difference between them. The two strategies are search engine optimization (SEO) and pay-per-click (PPC) marketing.

- Local *SEO* is concerned with getting your website ranked highly in the map and organic search listings on Google for keywords related to your business. You cannot pay for placement in the organic results. Google has an algorithm that determines where each page on your site ranks for various keywords and, with local SEO, you're essentially trying to game the algorithm to get your site ranked higher than your competitors' sites for the best keywords related to your business.
- *PPC* is paid advertising on Google. PPC ads are displayed above the organic search results as well as down the right side of the search results.

Figure 3–1 on page 11 shows a screenshot from a Google search with the PPC ads, local map listings, and SEO organic results labeled so you can see exactly what we are talking about.

(*Disclaimer:* Google is continually changing the way their search results pages look, and they are constantly testing new layouts. This screenshot is what things looked like the day we took it, but it may look very different if you go to Google and do a search while you are reading this. In fact, one rumor we just heard is that Google is going to add a paid maps listings above the current organic maps results. This hasn't been released yet, but go to www.UltimateLocalBook.com to stay up-to-date on the latest strategies and news for marketing your local business.)

THE ADVANTAGES PPC HAS OVER SEO

Prime Positioning

The main thing to notice about the screenshot in Figure 3–1 on page 11 is how prominently the PPC ads are displayed at the top of the page. Usually the top three results for a local search are ads. (This is one thing that will very likely *not* change about how the search engine results page looks because Google makes most of its money from these ads.)

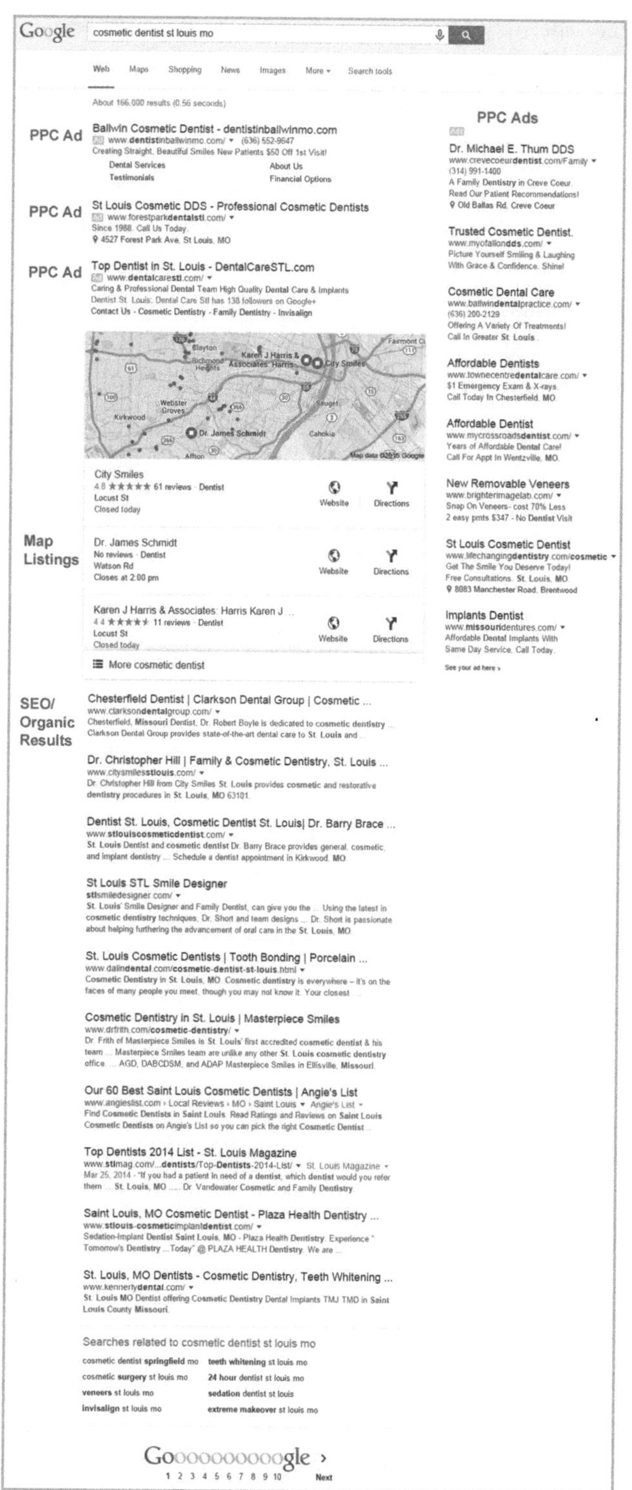

FIGURE 3-1. Google Search with PPC Ads, Maps, and Organic Results

Under that are the maps listings, and then the organic search results follow. It is important to understand that most people will click on the results at the top of the page, which, no surprise, are exactly where the ads that make Google money are positioned.

Take a look at the screenshot in Figure 3-2 that shows the "above the fold" search results. (The "above the fold" results are those you see when you first land on the page before you scroll down.) Notice how the majority of the pixels here are taken up by the paid ads. There are two map listings visible and *no* organic results. People are lazy online and will not scroll unless they have to. If they find what they're looking for above the fold, they won't go any further. Because of this, one of the main advantages PPC has over SEO is its prime positioning on the search results pages.

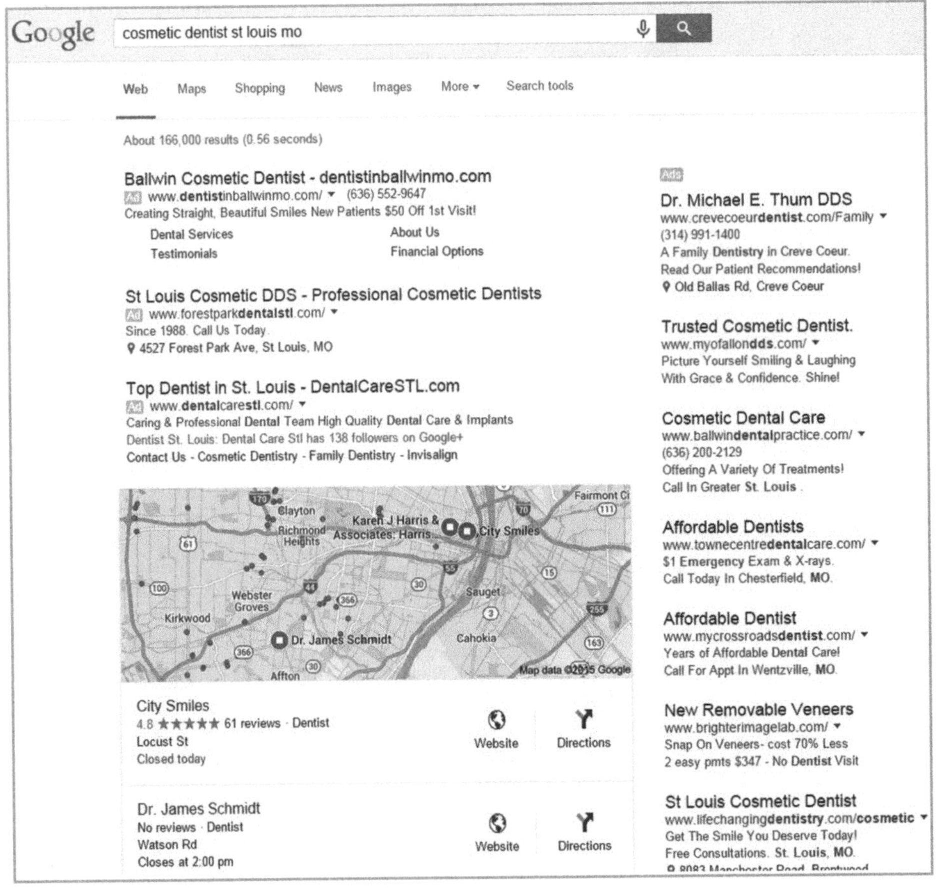

FIGURE 3-2. PPC Ads DOMINATE Above the Fold

How Patient Are You?

With PPC, you can launch a campaign and, almost immediately, your ads will start appearing on page one of Google. SEO, by comparison, is a long-term investment. You have to wait at least three to six months to typically start seeing any type of results, and in a competitive market, it could take over a year.

What this means is you can hire an SEO firm for $1,000 or $2,000 a month, depending on how aggressive you want to be, retain them for 6 months or 12 months, and yet still have no guarantee that you will be on page one or get any leads from it.

Even if you do get on page one, after a year or two of paying an SEO firm, Google may change its algorithm—and you could lose it all overnight (we've seen that happen many times).

SEO is a constant cat-and-mouse game between Google and those who do SEO for a living. It's getting harder and harder to get results, and we know a number of SEO firms that are starting to offer other services like web design or social media marketing, while others are deciding to fold up shop rather than continue to play games with Google.

If you're planning to be in business for the long term, are patient, and hire a good SEO firm, then SEO may be a very good *long-term* investment and generate a good ROI over time. Because it's a viable strategy, we've asked a respected local SEO expert, Richard Jacobs, to contribute a chapter to this book (Chapter 27). Reading this chapter will arm you with the education you need to make smart decisions about SEO and who you hire to do it for you.

You may be getting three to four solicitations a day from SEO firms telling you how poorly your website is ranking, how your horrible website is not getting you as many leads as it could be, and how they have the magic solution to get you to the top of page one on Google (we get their emails too!). The majority of these firms outsource their SEO to cheap overseas labor and mark up the costs 100 percent or more.

Please do not respond to their offers. If it sounds too good to be true, it is. Read Rich's chapter to get a solid understanding of what good SEO is all about before hiring a firm to do it for you.

Clear, Measurable Results

Another advantage of PPC is that, using the methodologies you'll learn in this book, it will give you clear, measurable results. You'll know exactly how much you spent on clicks and how many leads and how much revenue you generated in return.

You cannot get clear, measurable results like that with SEO. Google doesn't share a lot of SEO data with website owners, which makes it very difficult, if not impossible, to accurately measure how many leads you are getting from organic traffic.

In fact, one thing to watch out for is that a lot of the organic/SEO traffic you get to your site may be from branded traffic (i.e., people searching specifically for your company name). So it may look like you're getting lots of great quality leads from organic traffic, but these are people who already know who you are and would have contacted you anyway. Be sure to keep this in mind when you are trying to evaluate the results from any SEO work you do.

WHY PPC WILL BE A TOP SOURCE OF LEADS FOR A *LONG* TIME

PPC is never going away. Google is a publicly traded company with a responsibility to their shareholders to increase profits, and they are constantly rolling out new things that get more people to click on ads. Recently they rolled out new improvements, such as callout extensions (which we will talk about later) and other things, that make their ads take up more space on the page.

> *Think about it*: Google is one of the most profitable companies in the world, and about 90 percent of their revenue comes from Google ads.

Google doesn't make money on SEO. They make money on Google AdWords (the name of their PPC program). They are constantly rolling out new products for advertisers, and we found that they love local business advertisers. Why? Because your business is very relevant to searchers. If someone is searching for an injury lawyer in Dallas, Google wants people to find an injury lawyer in Dallas—they want relevant search results.

From our experience, the fastest, most reliable, and most profitable way to generate an ROI on Google comes from running PPC ads so that is what we are going to focus on in this book. You just have to make sure you're approaching PPC the right way, and we're going to show you exactly how to do that for your local business.

Chapter 4

The Dirty Little Secret Ad Agencies Are Afraid You'll Find Out

by Talor Zamir

I recently met with a big ad agency with over 60 employees that operates across the nation. It's a big, well-known internet marketing agency with Fortune 500 clients and smaller, local clients as well.

The CEO brought me in to look at their Google advertising campaigns, and after reviewing them, I told him his campaigns were a mess! This didn't come as a big surprise to him, because their clients weren't happy with their results. After discussing the issues with him, he turned to me and said, *"Listen, I just need you to keep these people happy so I can keep charging them high fees for SEO."*

His comment gets to the heart of the big secret of many ad agencies, which is ad agencies make big money off of things like SEO, video production, web design, TV advertising, and other "creative" work. This is higher margin work for them because they can charge high fees (since it is hard to measure the true value of this work) and then turn it over to their $40,000-a-year employees or outsource it to cheap low-wage workers in India or the Philippines.

Usually an ad agency starts with someone who has a lot of connections and gets a few clients. Then they hire a webmaster or a really good design person. And because the designer can make pretty pictures, they tell people, "Well, yeah. We can make a billboard. Sure. We can make you a website. Sure. We can do this."

(By the way, it is pretty easy to find people to do creative work like this for very little money. In fact, if you go to a site like Guru.com or Freelancer.com, you can probably find and hire many of the same people that the ad agencies outsource their work to and save yourself a ton of dough.)

AD AGENCY MATH

If you pay an agency $2,000 a month for SEO, they're likely making over $1,000 profit on that. While they make margins of 50 percent or more on the SEO work, if you spend $2,000 on PPC advertising, they're going to make very little money. It might only net them a couple hundred dollars a month or so, depending on how they charge, compared to SEO where they would be making over $1,000 a month from your $2,000 spend.

The agency that brought me in to look things over was making very little money on AdWords management. And, as I said before, their Google ad campaigns were a total mess. They needed to be completely redone. There were no landing pages, the campaigns were set up poorly, and the ad copy was atrocious. But the agency's attitude was: they just needed to get good enough results with AdWords to keep their clients on and keep charging $3,000 to $4,000 a month for SEO and make their high margins.

That's pretty much the big secret with many ad agencies. What most of them are *really* good at is sales, so they can try to sell you on a new website, video production, or mobile apps. It is unbelievable how much other stuff people try to sell local businesses besides the number-one thing they need.

THE NUMBER-ONE THING LOCAL BUSINESS OWNERS WANT

We know from talking to hundreds of business owners that the number-one thing they want is new, high-quality leads. And that is why we're going to focus on the number-one way to get that.

The things you'll learn how to do in this book like setting up landing pages and Google advertising campaigns is more of a specialized skill. It's *not* something that can be outsourced to a cookie-cutter person. It's harder to do, and there are much lower margins, so the ad agencies don't push this type of work as much.

If you're going to hire someone, be very careful who you hire and make sure you ask the right questions. Later in the book, we have a special guest, Adam Kreitman of Words That Click, share the questions you should ask before hiring an agency to handle PPC for you. Make sure you take his advice and go in with your eyes wide open before hiring an agency.

Every industry has its share of snake-oil salesmen, and advertising has an abundance of them. Even if you decide to hire someone to implement what you learn in this book, it's important you understand the concepts so that you avoid those who are only looking out for their own bank accounts.

Chapter 5

The 80/20 Rule: It's Not What You Think, But It's Really Profitable!

by Perry Marshall

What I'm about to share is so incredibly important, it would be criminal to not devote a whole chapter to it. It's that crucial. Master this chapter, and you'll work less, make more, enjoy greater focus, and feel less guilty about everything. It's the highest-leverage skill that exists in marketing.

The 80/20 rule, aka the Pareto Principle, says:

1. 80 percent of what you get comes from 20 percent of what you do: Small effort, big reward.
2. 20 percent of what you get comes from the other 80 percent of what you do: Big effort, small reward.

Most business owners have heard about 80/20. Most think they know what it is. But most people don't actually understand it. I was just like everybody else. I thought I understood 80/20. Turns out, I didn't understand it at all!

The 80/20 rule is one of the main reasons you are reading this book right now and not someone else's. In 2003, AdWords was brand-new, and nobody fully understood how to make it work. It was a strange beast. The 80/20 rule was how I figured out AdWords in the first place. It still is.

I experienced a huge 80/20 epiphany reading Richard Koch's classic book, *The 80/20 Principle*. Suddenly, I saw layers and layers where before

I'd only seen the surface. Eventually, I expanded on this and wrote the book *80/20 Sales and Marketing*. I'm going to give you a quick, chapter-sized sample of 80/20. Pay close attention.

BACK WHEN I *THOUGHT* I UNDERSTOOD 80/20

When I worked as a sales manager, I heard about 80/20. I printed out a sales report from QuickBooks and went through it with my calculator. Yep. Sure enough: 80 percent of our sales came from the top 20 percent of our customers, and the other 80 percent of our customers generated the other 20 percent. Dimitri was a customer who liked to call me all the time. He would always nitpick about our software, and he didn't buy much. Dimitri was near the top of my time-suck list and near the bottom of my money list. That 80/20 exercise made me realize he was chewing up time he didn't deserve. But my thinking stopped there. I didn't "fire him," I didn't think much else about it and moved on.

A few years later, reading Richard's book, a torrent of insights flooded my brain. I'm going to share them with you, and show you how to apply 80/20 to your local business so you spend way less time, get more done, sell more, and make more money.

80/20 APPLIES TO NEARLY EVERYTHING YOU CAN MEASURE IN A BUSINESS

Sources of incoming phone calls, sales commissions, number of customers, location of customers, product popularity, and the quantity of each type of product defect can all benefit from applying the 80/20 principle. The 80/20 principle applies to AdWords metrics too: keywords, impressions, ads, conversions, and web page visits. Just about every metric in this book obeys 80/20.

80/20 is a huge time saver. But that's only the tip of the iceberg.

80/20 ISN'T JUST TWO GROUPS, "THE 80" AND "THE 20"

It's actually a stunningly predictable power law that you can put on a graph. The 80/20 rule says, if you have a column of data, and you know just one or two things, like the number of items and the total, you can predict with scary accuracy how they're all going to stack up.

Here, I'll show you: Let's say the newspaper says, "Southwest Airlines, the 167th largest company in the U.S. with revenues of $15.7 billion . . ." Guess what: You already know enough to size up the entire Fortune 500, if you know how to plug that information into 80/20 (see Figure 5-1 on page 19).

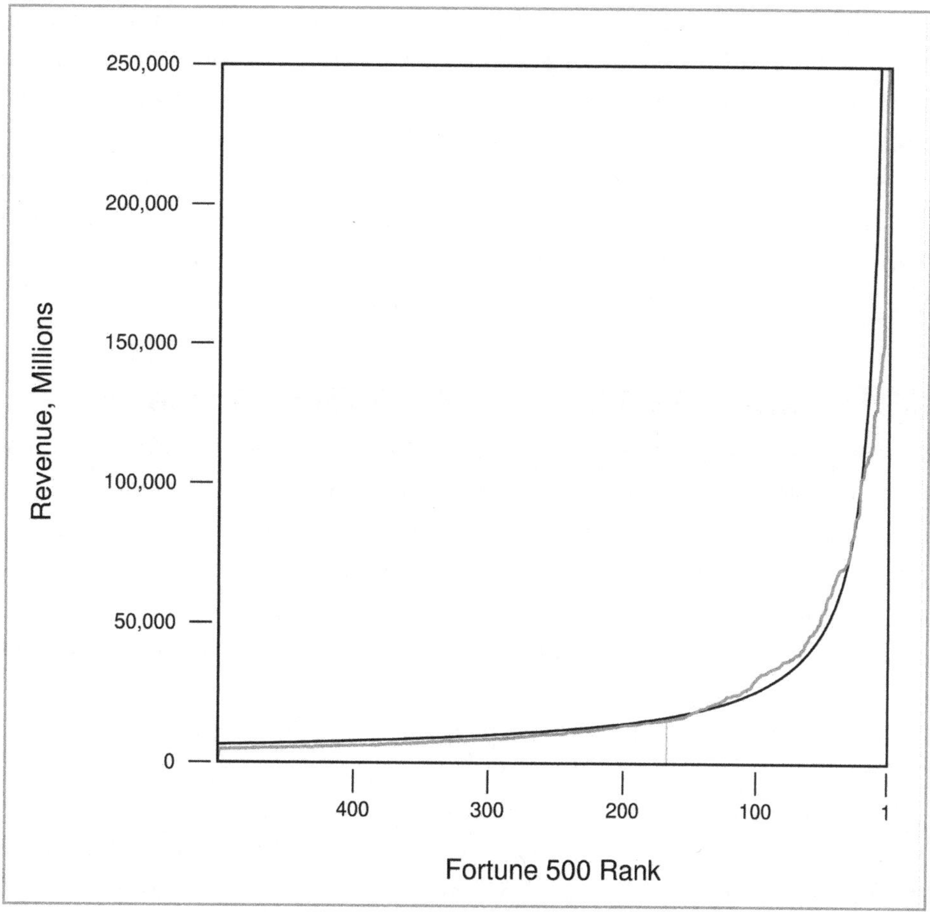

FIGURE 5-1. The Line Just to the Right of the "200" Shows Southwest Airlines Mapped on the 80/20 Curve. The Curve Shows You the Relative Sizes of all the Other Companies in the Fortune 500. You Can Compare the "80/20 Theoretical Curve" to the Actual Data (the Squiggly Line). The Two Match Up Remarkably Well. 80/20 Behavior is Incredibly Consistent and Predictable.

This is tremendously useful and very powerful for business owners. You might be leaving a million dollars a year on the table and not know it! Now in less than five minutes, 80/20 will expose holes in your product line or pricing strategy. I created a tool called the 80/20 Curve (www.8020curve.com), and it accurately predicts where you're missing opportunities.

THERE'S AN 80/20 INSIDE EVERY 80/20!

The 80/20 rule still applies to what's left after you peel away the bottom 80 percent. Not only does 80 percent of your money come from 20 percent of your customers, but 80 percent of the 80 percent comes from 20 percent of the top 20 percent.

That means 4 percent of your customers create 64 percent of your income. That's $80/20^2$. And it's still true of the top 4 percent: 0.8 percent of your customers deliver 52 percent of your income. That's $80/20^3$. And it keeps going until you run out of people.

This means you can extract huge amounts of money from tiny groups of people. The same goes for keywords, ads, or web pages. This is because 80/20 is an infinite repeating pattern. It's "fractal"—micro or macro scale—and it's the same pattern over and over. There is always an inequality, and most people underestimate how great it is.

OVERLAY MULTIPLE 80/20s—AND DOUBLE YOUR MOJO!

Not only should you get 50 percent of your business from 1 percent of your customers, but you may get 25 percent of your profits from one of your 250 products. You could easily make 10 percent more profit by pampering five big customers and fattening the margins on that one product.

The information age offers you more things to fix, optimize, and pay attention to than you could possibly attend to in a lifetime. That's why 80/20 has never been more important. You have reams of data spilling out of AdWords, etc., 24 hours a day. If you pay attention to the wrong thing, you could waste your entire life polishing turds.

To give you an idea how universal the 80/20 curve is and how many boundaries it transcends, let me show you a few quick examples. 80/20 isn't just a business rule of thumb; it's a law of nature. Let's look at how 80/20 works specifically in Google AdWords. As you saw in the examples above, the numbers "80" and "20" are not carved in stone. Sometimes it's 70/30, sometimes 60/40, 90/10, or 99/1. Keyword lists are consistently 95/5. Take a look at Figure 5-2 on page 21 and you'll see what?

This ad group has 25 keywords, but more than 80 percent of the traffic comes from two of them. Notice that the top three keywords are just match type variations of "how to write a book."

The 80/20 pattern is truly everywhere, and it radically changes how you manage your campaigns and your business. It means that most impressions, clicks, ads, keywords, ad groups, web pages, prospects and customers simply don't matter very much. It also means that a few impressions, clicks, ads, keywords, ad groups, web pages, and customers determine almost everything!

When you start, your job is to throw just enough spaghetti against the wall to see where it is starting to stick, then immediately channel your efforts into improving what's working. This is why it's so important to build your business on what people actually do and want so you're not steering a parked car.

Keyword	Clicks	Percentage of Ad Group
[how to write a book]	4,317	60.3%
how to write a book	1,452	20.3%
"how to write a book"	679	9.5%
"how to write a children's book"	142	2.0%
how to write a children's book	112	1.6%
how to write a good book	92	1.3%
free how to write a book	61	0.9%
learn how to write a book	41	0.6%
how to write a fantasy book	30	0.4%
how to write a book proposal	26	0.4%
how to write a non-fiction book	24	0.3%
how to write a children's book	23	0.3%
how to write a fiction book	22	0.3%
how to write a self-help book	20	0.3%
tips on how to write a book	20	0.3%
how to write a book in 14 days	13	0.2%
how to write a nonfiction book	12	0.2%
how to write a chapter book	12	0.2%
how to write and publish a book	10	0.1%
how to write a picture book	9	0.1%
how to write a text book	9	0.1%
how to write a business book	9	0.1%
instructions on how to write a book	8	0.1%
how to write a murder mystery book	8	0.1%
how to write a book about my life	6	0.1%

FIGURE 5-2. 80/20 Adwords Keywords Example

PERFECTIONISM CAN GET IN YOUR WAY!

People who are good at AdWords usually have a perfectionist streak. That's what makes them good at it. Your perfectionist streak likes the idea of coming up with the best possible ad, doing split tests, putting up the best possible landing page, etc. You're constantly improving, and your job is never done. You can always make it better, and that's exciting.

But perfectionism has a dark side. The fact is, if you don't ignore most of what goes on in your Google campaigns, you'll never have time to focus on the few things that are actually working.

This is true in all aspects of marketing. I know you've got a 1,000-page website and you'd love to give the whole thing a facelift. But 75 percent of your business is generated by three of those pages, so no matter what you do to the least visited 800 pages on your site, it won't make a bit of difference. You have to set hard limits on your perfectionism. Otherwise you perfect the wrong thing.

An inevitable consequence of 80/20 is that you sometimes feel like all your eggs are in one basket. While it's true there will always be a few baskets that have a lot of eggs, Warren Buffett says, "Keep all your eggs in one basket, but watch that basket closely."

THE MYTH OF THE LONG TAIL

Chris Anderson wrote a book called *The Long Tail: Why the Future of Business Is Selling Less of More*. He explained that the internet had made it possible for books that only sell 10 copies a year to stay in print forever, whereas in the old bookstore model, obscure titles wouldn't have a prayer. Those 10 copies a year, on a graph, are the "long tail"—the millions of items that receive little attention and would never make it in the bookstore.

Anderson makes a very valid point, and it's why so many tiny little tribes and niches now have a voice on the internet. The phrase long tail is very useful because it's simply the left side of the 80/20 curve.

But you must be careful about the long tail. Common wisdom is that you can get lots of traffic from "long tail keywords," using phrases such as "how to write a murder mystery book."

Frankly, that's just wrong. The phrase "how to write a murder mystery book" got eight clicks in two years (based on our keyword study in Figure 5-2 on page 21). You should try to be a big fish in a little pond, but you can't be any kind of fish in a puddle. This keyword phrase is not worth anybody's serious time or attention, and while it may add a tiny amount of incremental revenue, it's completely trivial in the grand scheme of things.

On the other hand, if you can dominate just one high-traffic, high-conversion keyword, you can generate leads and sales for years. If you can improve one keyword's ad by 10 percent, you might get a $100,000-per-year increase.

That means there's a right way and a wrong way to do "long tail." The wrong way is to just dump thousands of keywords into a campaign. The right way is to deliberately choose to be a big fish in a little pond and become the king of a small niche that has been overlooked.

There are thousands and thousands of such niches. The indicator is not that there aren't advertisers and bidders; rather, it's that nobody in a niche has a really great USP and the customers are itching for something more.

The common belief about the long tail is simply wrong. The offline world is generally 80/20, but many things online are 90/10. Ten percent of the search engines (Google, Yahoo!, Bing) get 90 percent of the searches. Ten percent of the auction sites (eBay) get 90 percent of the auctions. The internet has made it possible to sell ten copies per year of some obscure book written in 1913, but it's made it even more possible for Malcolm Gladwell to sell millions of copies of *The Tipping Point*.

Winners win big on the internet. My hope for you is that you'll be the Big Kahuna in your market, the number-one player, the alpha dog. And when you do, it'll be because you ignored the 80 percent and got the 1 percent exactly, precisely right.

SOME 80/20 RULES OF THUMB

I strongly recommend you pick up a copy of my book *80/20 Sales & Marketing* because it will take you much further on this journey. Meanwhile, here are some handy 80/20 rules:

- *One-fifth the people will spend four times the money.* If you have 100 customers who bought a $100 product or service from you, 20 of them will buy a $400 product or service and four of them will buy a $1,600 product or service. One of them will spend $5,000. The 80/20 rule virtually guarantees this will be true.
- *One percent of the work you did last year earned 50 percent of your money.* The only people who normally see this with perfect clarity are straight commission salespeople, but it's true for pretty much everybody.
- *"Average" is seldom important in Google.* Your average keyword, average ad, or customer barely matters. A few of your keywords, ads, and customers matter a lot.
- *Factors in the top 20 percent—the people and things that make the most difference—usually send signals ahead of time.* If you ask a survey question, a casual buyer will often answer with a sentence fragment. A hot buyer will talk to you on the phone for 45 minutes.

Archimedes said, "Give me a lever and a place to stand and I will move the world." With AdWords, you have a lever. With a great product and USP, you have a place to stand. Just know that 80 percent of your levers will get you nowhere, and 20 percent will make you rich.

Here are some additional tips on how to use 80/20 to your advantage:

- *Flip your daily to-do list.* You wake up and list the ten things you need to do today. You can be almost dead certain that one item is worth ten times more than the rest. Our natural human tendency is to put that specific task off until later, diverting into mundane tasks like Facebook. We humans invent devilishly clever reasons not to get that one thing done.

  Check your gut and do it—now. (Or at least after you finish reading this book.)

  If you're all-consumed with $10-per-hour busy work, you have no time to stop and ask yourself, "What salvo should I launch next week that will double sales next year?" If that question makes you squirm, good. The more disconcerting, the better. It challenges the status quo. Whatever gives you that queasy, familiar feeling of asking for a big check, that plan probably belongs at the top of the stack.
- *Make constructive use of the time you liberate.* I urge business owners and entrepreneurs to hire house cleaners and personal assistants to free themselves from mundane activities. What do you do with the extra two hours a day you free up? You could fritter it away—or go nuclear on your business strategy.
- *Perfectionism is the root of all evil.* Most of us soothe our anxieties and stay mediocre by perfecting things that don't need to be perfect. You spend 15 minutes editing that email before you press send. You clean out your car twice a week. *Most procrastination isn't doing nothing; it's doing what's comfortable and mediocre.*
- *Put "do nothing" on your to-do list.* I'm a huge advocate of the Sabbath—taking Saturdays or Sundays off. Instead of wasting time on busy work, such as checking email, everyone should create space where they pray or meditate, or simply do nothing. Your best business ideas will come when you're not working. When you're having fun doing what you enjoy doing, whether it's reading novels or tossing a baseball with your kids, that feeds your creativity.

  I learned this the hard way. I spent years with the pedal to the metal, working seven days a week. It got me nowhere because I was not doing what I needed to do most.

Choose the thing that makes you most anxious. Then head straight into the wind, because those anxieties are merely birth pangs of a larger success.

To go deeper learning 80/20, get my book, *80/20 Sales & Marketing,* which we'll have a link to at www.UltimateLocalBook.com.

Chapter 6

Google AdWords: The Greatest Innovation in Advertising History

by Talor Zamir

Not too many years ago if you wanted to do a direct response marketing campaign, you would have to rent a mailing list, write a direct mail letter, mail it to at least a thousand people, and then wait at least a few days for the responses (if there are any) to start coming in. And then you would have to wait a few weeks or a month, at least, to tally up all the results and see if there was a positive return on the investment.

If you wanted to do any split-testing (an important marketing concept we cover in Chapter 20), you would have to write a separate letter and then again wait about a month to track the results and see which letter worked best and whether it produced an ROI.

To pull this off, you were probably looking at a $3,000 to $5,000 investment, plus months of your time to get the ROI data you were looking for.

A DRAMATIC SHIFT

No longer do businesses have to chase prospects with direct response letters, phone calls, newspaper ad, etc. Now prospects chase businesses on the web. That's a dramatic shift, and one that gives local businesses that know how to leverage it a big advantage.

The best way to leverage it and get those prospects to your website is with Google AdWords. We truly believe Google AdWords has proved to be the most important innovation in advertising in the last 25 years. Here's what makes it stand apart from all the other options out there.

Reach

Google gets searched around six billion times every day. Every one of those searches represents a need, desire, or quest for information. If you can scratch the itch of even a tiny fraction of those people, you can do very well advertising on Google!

Intent

As we mentioned in Chapter 2, when you advertise on Google, you reach people who are *actively* searching for someone who does what you do. That is much different from traditional forms of advertising that are called "interruption" advertising. People aren't watching TV, listening to radio, or reading the newspaper for the advertisements. In those media, you have to try to interrupt people and grab their attention to have a shot of getting them interested enough to consider reaching out to you.

With Google, you reach people who know they need help and are in a very receptive mind-set to a business that can help them. It's the ideal time to get your marketing message in front of a prospect.

Pay Per Click

John Wanamaker, a department store owner, is famous for the quote:

> *Half the money I spend on advertising is wasted; the trouble is, I don't know which half.*

The trouble with most forms of advertising is they are nearly impossible to track and you pay a set fee. With TV, radio, newspaper, etc., it doesn't matter how many people see your ads and how many of them are interested in what you have to offer. You pay the same amount no matter what.

Not so with Google AdWords. AdWords is a form of pay-per-click (PPC) advertising, which means you only pay when someone clicks on your ad and visits your website. And, if you follow what we teach you in this book, you'll have a very clear picture of which clicks result in leads and which do not so you will be able to stop wasting money on keywords and ads that aren't producing good results.

Nearly Instant Page One Rankings

As we mentioned in Chapter 3, SEO takes months or more to start generating results, and there are no guarantees for success. With AdWords and PPC marketing, getting your ads on page one of Google the *same day* simply requires you to create an account, choose some keywords, and write some ads!

Start Small and Scale Things Up Massively

The strategies we teach you in this book don't require a big investment. In fact, we'll purposely teach you to start with a very small, targeted campaign and track your results very carefully. It's only once you see that your campaign is generating leads and an ROI that we advise you to scale up. Chapter 23 is all about how you can scale up your campaign in a big way to get more and more leads over time.

Unmatched Control

There is no other form of advertising that gives you as much control as AdWords. In your Google AdWords campaign, you can control:

- Your monthly budget
- How much you pay per click
- What search queries (keywords) your ads show up for
- When your ads are running and when they're not (You can schedule Monday through Friday 9 A.M. to 5 P.M., or you can have ads run 24/7; more on this later)
- The pages on your site visitors are directed to (landing pages)
- The ad messaging that's displayed
- How much you bid for mobile traffic (if at all)
- Your bidding strategy (e.g., maximize clicks and conversions and target a specific return on ad spend)

And this is just a partial list. This control and flexibility help make AdWords a powerful marketing platform—if you know how to use it correctly!

Geo-Targeting

The ability to target specific geographic areas in AdWords is part of the unmatched control you get but deserves separate mention here (especially since we are focused on using AdWords to promote *local* business).

In AdWords you can target entire countries (probably not relevant to most local business owners) or limit your campaign to specific states, metro areas, cities, counties, congressional districts, and/or zip codes.

You can also target a specific radius around your business so if you only want your ads to be displayed to people searching from within a 10-, 20-, or 50-mile radius around your location, you have the ability to control that. You can be super hyper-targeted with the geographic areas. If you're in a big city but have an extremely limited budget, you could even start by targeting only people that search your keywords from within a five-mile radius of your business!

Unprecedented Testing Ground

Most advertisers don't think about using AdWords for market research, but when used for this purpose, it becomes an immensely powerful tool you can use to improve all your marketing.

One of our clients, a personal injury lawyer, now has billboards that say essentially the same message as our highest-converting Google ad. Most personal injury lawyer billboards have some version of "Injured? Accident? Call the Law Offices of John Smith." They don't even offer a single benefit in their billboards!

Instead, for our client, we took the best Google ad we were running that had the message "Injured? Free Consult and No Fee Unless We Win!" Their response from the billboards dramatically increased since they started running the "winning message" based on the results of testing multiple Google ads.

Whether testing an offer, headline, potential book title, or email subject line, you can test the contenders out in AdWords (where it's cheap and easy) and let your audience decide which one they like best. Then you pluck the winning ad copy from AdWords, insert it into other advertising you do, and be pretty confident you will have a winner there too.

Improve Your SEO Efforts

AdWords can also help you when it comes to SEO. Unfortunately, a lot of people who do SEO spend years trying to optimize for the wrong keywords! An SEO analyst is going to do research on keywords and tell you which to focus on largely based on volume.

Well, if you're running an AdWords campaign and tracking conversions (much more on conversions later in the book), you might find that a certain keyword has a third of the search volume of another, but gets you five times as many conversions.

We had a situation with one of our clients where we noticed a specific local search term was getting decent traffic and conversions in their AdWords campaign. If you looked at the keyword research tools (which can be wildly inaccurate at times; more on this later in the book), they were reporting this keyword had no search traffic at all. However, because of our AdWords campaign, we knew that was not the case. With that data, we set up a separate page on the site targeting that keyword because we knew the effort was worth it.

Google AdWords is the most accurate keyword research tool around. It will give you data about keywords that you can't get any other way. If you're going to invest the time and money into SEO, you better know which keywords are worth targeting and, by using data from your AdWords campaign, you can laser-focus your SEO efforts on the best keywords for your business.

NOT AS EASY AS IT USED TO BE!

As incredibly powerful as it is, AdWords is not as easy as it once was. When AdWords started, clicks were cheap, competition was scarce, and you could pretty much throw a bunch of keywords into a campaign without thinking too much about them and you would have some success.

That is not the case anymore. Now the competition is fierce. Click costs have soared, and you have to be very smart about how you set up and structure your campaign.

Not to worry. We're going to share the strategies that can turn AdWords into your number-one source of leads and how you can generate an ROI from AdWords, even if you've tried and failed in the past.

Chapter 7

The Top Four Reasons Local Businesses Fail Using Google AdWords

by Talor Zamir

You've likely heard other business owners trashing AdWords as expensive, complicated, and ineffective. Good, let them! That just means that there will be less competition for you.

AdWords does get a bad rap in many circles, and while clicks are expensive *for most people* and the interface complex, most of the time when advertisers get bad results, they only have themselves (or those they hire to manage their campaigns) to blame.

There are four main reasons local businesses fail with Google AdWords. We're going to cover them briefly in this chapter and dig into each one in much more detail later in the book so you know how to set up and run a campaign that will give you the best chance for success.

1. NO LANDING PAGE OR AWFUL LANDING PAGE

The first page a visitor to your site lands on after clicking on your Google ad is called the landing page. A landing page is an essential part of your AdWords campaign, and a good one can instantly double your leads from AdWords (without spending a penny more on clicks).

I recently clicked on an ad for a family law attorney. You would think that would lead me to a site about family law, but instead their home page was all about personal injury law. That's *not* what I was looking for. Plus, it was an old, ugly-looking site that made it hard for me to find any information. When I finally found the page on the site about family law, it was a two-paragraph little blurb that basically said they're certified by the State Bar in family law (which don't they have to be to even practice in the first place?)

Not having a dedicated, high-converting landing page is a huge mistake. Based on experience, we estimate the typical local business website converts somewhere around 5 percent. On the other hand, a landing page that follows our template (which we share in Chapter 9) can easily convert at 10 percent to 20 percent.

Even if we assume it just converts on the low end—around 10 percent—versus the 5 percent for the typical website, you would double the amount of leads you get for the same money spent. That means for every $1,000 you spend, instead of getting 10 leads, you're now getting 20. That difference could literally make or break your month or year.

2. HORRIBLE ADS WITH LOW CLICKTHROUGH RATES

Most Google ads say basically the same thing. (And, quite frankly, they're not all that compelling in the way they say it.)

As with landing pages, a high-converting Google ad with a high clickthrough rate (CTR) can also instantly double your leads. And the best part is that Google rewards you for having high-converting ads. So not only will doubling your CTR get you twice as many potential leads, but you can also end up paying a lot less per click.

That's because Google has an algorithm known as Quality Score that determines how much you pay for clicks. In AdWords, just because you bid the most for a keyword, that doesn't guarantee your ad will show up in the top position. Google rewards relevancy. And if you can show Google your ad is more relevant than your competitors (and CTR is the number-one factor used to determine relevancy), you can end up ranking higher than your competitors, yet pay less per click than they do.

In Chapters 18 through 20, we will dive deep into the components of the ultimate Google ad and how to split-test ads in your campaign to see continual improvement and stay ahead of the competition.

3. NO CONVERSION OR CALL TRACKING

We've seen that 60 percent to 70 percent of the leads for local businesses come in the form of a phone call. Furthermore, phone call leads tend to be higher-quality leads because someone who's really a hot lead is most likely going to pick up the phone and call rather than just submit the information through a form on your website.

If you're not tracking call conversion, then you're missing out on not only 60 percent to 70 percent of your leads, but also your hottest leads. Not tracking call conversions also means that you're not going to be able to optimize your AdWords campaign well. As you'll see in Chapter 11, you can throw a ton of money away on bad clicks if you're not tracking calls and have the data that shows you which keywords and ads are making the phone ring and which ones are not.

The Dynamic Call Tracking strategy we introduce you to in Chapter 11 has been a true game changer for our clients, and very few local business owners use it. It will give you a huge advantage over your competitors in AdWords by letting them waste their budget on underperforming keywords while you laser-focus your budget on the keywords and ads that are bringing in the leads.

4. POOR CAMPAIGN STRUCTURE

With all the AdWords books, articles, and training courses available, it's somewhat surprising we even have to mention this. However, we still see AdWords campaigns every week that are set up poorly (many times by agencies that should know better) and don't even adhere to basic best practices.

One example of poor campaign structure is a single campaign that runs on both Search and Display Networks. Search and Display are two utterly different beasts, and they should *never* be lumped together in a single campaign (in fact, we urge you to avoid using the Display Network to advertise your local business, until you develop strong AdWords chops and seek additional training). Other examples include only having one ad group, having too many keywords, and going too broad with the keywords in your campaign.

Don't worry if you're not familiar with terms like Search Network, Display Network, or ad groups right now. We cover all these issues and more in Chapters 18 through 20 so you will know what they are and the right way to handle them all.

ADWORDS AREN'T PERFECT, BUT . . .

AdWords may not work all the time for every local business. There are some situations where due to high click costs, budgets, internal sales problems, or other issues that even a well-structured AdWords campaign won't generate a high enough ROI. However, in our experience that's the exception much more often than the rule. Follow the strategies in this book and those we share at www.UltimateLocalBook.com and you have a very good chance of making AdWords work for you.

Chapter 8

The Most Important Piece of the Puzzle—Your Landing Page

by Talor Zamir

We all know about the Wright Brothers. But did you ever hear the story of Samuel Pierpont Langley, the well-funded engineer and inventor who was also trying to become the first in flight? The Wright Brothers and Langley had two very different approaches that have *everything* to do with Google AdWords.

Langley focused on the engine. His assumption was that if you put a big enough engine on the thing, it will fly. So all his effort went into creating a 50-horsepower engine, big enough to get a plane off the ground.

On October 7, 1903, Langley's plane got its first test. The result? The plane immediately crashed, badly damaging the front wing. A few months later, just eight days before the Wright Brothers' successful flight, Langley tried again. This time the tail and rear wing collapsed during the attempt.

The Wright Brothers' approach focused on building a glider that could glide off a hilltop. No engine required. They focused their attention on balance and steering, and only after having a glider that worked by itself did they try to add an engine to the mix. The Wright Brothers' engine was only 12 horsepower and they built it in their bicycle shop.

You know how the story turned out—fame and glory for the Wright Brothers while Langley died a few years later, a broken and disappointed man.

What does this story have to do with marketing your local business? Quite simply it's that with internet marketing, the search engine is the motor while your website (and, more specifically, your landing page) is the glider. You can build a powerful engine that sends a lot of traffic to your website, but without a good set of wings, all the traffic in the world won't do you much good.

The lesson from the Wright Brothers is this: Build a good set of wings first and then put a powerful engine behind it. That's the formula for your internet marketing strategy that will make your business soar.

THE IMPORTANCE OF CONVERSION

Especially when you are paying per click, the conversion on your landing page is the most important part of the process. Why?

Because if you're only paying when someone clicks on one of your ads and goes to your landing page, it's the landing page that's going to make or break your campaign (we're assuming here that your keywords and ads aren't completely out of whack). So you better be darn sure your landing page(s) effectively and efficiently convert visitors into quality leads for your business.

Any pay-per-click (PPC) manager can do keyword research and get a bunch of ads set up. But many of them don't pay any attention to the most important piece of the puzzle: the landing page.

Need more convincing why landing pages are so important? If you can create a landing page that doubles your conversion rate, then you will get twice as many leads for the exact same ad spend. And the fact that most of the competition you're up against in a local market doesn't pay attention to their landing pages (or even know what one is) means you should be converting much higher than they do.

That gives you a huge competitive advantage in your market because not only will you be able to get more leads than they do for the same money spent, but you'll be paying less per lead than they are. Let's look at the chart in Figure 8-1 on page 37 to illustrate how this math works.

The chart illustrates two hypothetical AdWords campaigns. The top three rows are the same—each advertiser is spending $3,000 per month for clicks at an average of $5 per click. That gets 600 visitors to each advertiser's site each month.

The bottom three rows, however, are quite different. In the first column, Advertiser A isn't using a good landing page, so only 5 percent of the visitors to their site are being converted into leads (phone calls or contact form submissions). So each month, Advertiser A is generating 30 leads each month from the 600 visitors they're paying to get to their site.

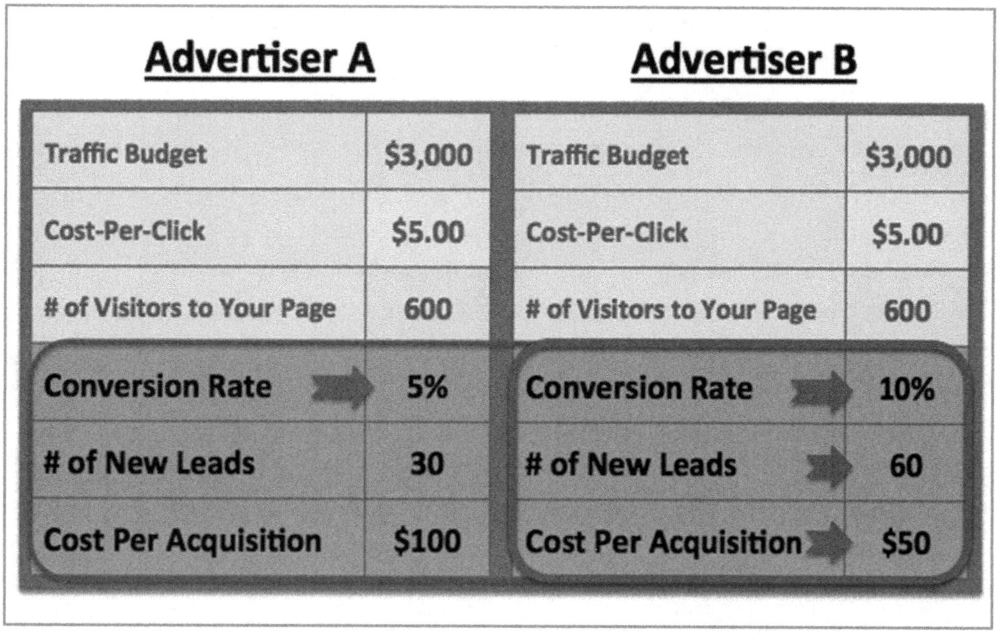

Advertiser A

Traffic Budget	$3,000
Cost-Per-Click	$5.00
# of Visitors to Your Page	600
Conversion Rate	5%
# of New Leads	30
Cost Per Acquisition	$100

Advertiser B

Traffic Budget	$3,000
Cost-Per-Click	$5.00
# of Visitors to Your Page	600
Conversion Rate	10%
# of New Leads	60
Cost Per Acquisition	$50

FIGURE 8–1. The Impact of Increasing Your Conversion Rate

Advertiser B (which is you after you read this book and know how to create a kick-ass landing page!) is converting at 10 percent, or twice the conversion rate as Advertiser A. That means 60 of those 600 visitors you are paying for each month are turning into leads for your business.

Remember this: Double your conversion, double your business.

Now here is where the magic happens. Take a look at the difference this makes in the last row—the Cost per Acquisition. Your competitor is paying $100 for each lead while you're only paying $50. This means you're going to be able to scale up more, spend more, stretch your ad spend a lot further and, ultimately, your campaign is going to be a lot more profitable.

This chart illustrates why conversion rates and your landing page are the most important part of your local business's marketing funnel. (And, by the way, while this is especially true when you're paying for clicks, conversion rate is still important whether you're paying for clicks or not.)

The landing page could be the difference between someone who spends a few thousand dollars on Google ads and decides "Yeah, this isn't working for me" and someone else who's getting leads for half or one-third the cost because their great landing page is able to scale up and add millions of dollars in revenue to their business.

WHY YOUR LANDING PAGE WILL CONVERT BETTER THAN YOUR WEBSITE

You may be thinking, "But I already paid a really awesome web designer to create a beautiful website for me. Everyone tells me how much they love it. Why can't I just send the Google ads traffic to an existing page on my site? Why do I need to create special landing pages?"

Good questions. Here is why you should not use your current website:

First, maybe you hired a designer who created a truly beautiful site for you, but most web designers are not schooled in the science of conversion. So while your website may have beautiful images, make great use of color, use a fancy slider at the top of the page (which research shows usually kills conversions, by the way), that does not mean it's going to convert well. In fact, most of the "pretty" sites we encounter do not convert well at all. Even though they may be pleasing to the eyes, they typically do not have most of the components that a landing page needs to do the most important job a landing page needs to do: *generate leads for your business*!

The other reason you do not want to use your current website comes down to psychology. Sheena Iyengar is a psycho-economist at Columbia Business School. In November 2011, she gave a TED Talk titled "How to Make Choosing Easier" which has been viewed over 1.6 million times. In her talk, she shares the results of an experiment she did as a Stanford grad student at a local grocery store. This grocery had no shortage of options for consumers—250 kinds of mustards and vinegars, over 500 different kinds of fruits and vegetables, and more than 24 kinds of bottled water. She loved going to the store but noticed that she never bought anything and wondered if having too many choices had something to do with it. So she got the store manager to agree to let her do an experiment with jam (of which the store had 348 varieties to choose from).

She set up a tasting booth near the front of the store and tested what happened when they had 24 different flavors of jam to sample versus just six varieties. What she found was that more people stopped at the tasting booth when there were 24 different kinds of jam compared to when there were six available for tasting. However, of those who stopped at the table when there were 24 kinds of jam to choose from, just 3 percent ended up buying jam. When there were just six kinds of jam on the table, 30 percent of the people who stopped ended up buying a jar. Doing the math, people were six times more likely to buy when they had six jars to choose from versus 24.

ONLINE ADD AND ONE-DECISION MARKETING

People have what we call "online ADD." Basically, if you give them too many options (as in the jam experiment), they get overwhelmed and won't make a decision.

Your job (and the job of your landing page) is to keep them focused on the action you want them to take. And for most local businesses, that action is to pick up the phone and call you (or, as a backup if they are not able to call, enter their information into a contact form on your landing page) for a free consultation.

The whole premise here is that for local businesses, the best first step to get people into their sales funnel is to give a free consultation (lawyers), free quote (mortgage brokers), free estimate (home contractors), free initial evaluation (chiropractor), etc. So if your goal is for people to contact you for a free consultation, then you want to stick to what I call "One-Decision Marketing."

That means your landing page should not have any links at the top or down the side of the page. In fact, if it were up to us, there would be no links on the landing page, but we need to include some to keep Google happy (more on this in the next chapter). The point is you do not want any distractions on that page. Your goal on the landing page is to put your best foot forward, give the biggest benefits that you offer, and keep visitors completely focused on why and how they should contact you.

> One-Decision Marketing is about giving a visitor one decision to make when they hit your landing page.

This is also why you do not want to give away too much information on your landing page. You want to strike a balance where the page is not too short, but not too long. Too short, and you risk not having enough content on it to keep Google happy and/or not giving people enough information to make the decision to contact you.

Too long hurts you too. We once created a landing page for a personal injury lawyer, and they insisted we include a Q&A from the attorney, which answers a lot of the common questions potential clients have. Even though we had a proven and highly successful landing page template for personal injury attorneys, this attorney insisted I include his Q&A transcript at the bottom of the landing page because he felt my template did not give people enough information. Adding this Q&A made the landing page twice as long.

When the campaign launched, the attorney was not happy about the amount of leads he was getting for the money he was spending. I convinced him to let me do a test where we got rid of the Q&A section and just stuck with the shorter, proven template. Once the Q&A was gone, conversions on the page dramatically increased, and he got a lot more leads for the money spent. The issue with the long Q&A is that it answered everybody's questions so they didn't need to call anymore!

THE GOAL OF YOUR LANDING PAGE

Your landing page's job is not to answer all the questions a potential prospect may have. Its job is to give prospects the biggest benefit(s) as to why they should contact you.

What you are shooting for is that, within one minute of hitting that landing page, your prospects are easily able to consume all the information they need to make a decision to contact you or not, which means you need it to focus on your best benefits (which should be in your headline, sub-headline, and bullet points).

You may be thinking, "Wait a minute. I offer a lot of different services and need the option to let people know everything we can offer them and sell more to them. A relatively short landing page with no navigation at the top or side won't let me do that."

That's great, but we are talking about AdWords and lead generation. The goal of the landing page for a local business is not to make the sale. We do not recommend mentioning price or trying to sell people into a service from your landing page. Let your staff handle all the cross-sells and upsells once they get a prospect on the phone or preferably in your office.

The goal of the landing page is to get the phone call.

Remember, people have online ADD, which is truer now than ever, since somewhere around 40 percent of searches for local business are being done from mobile devices where attention spans are even lower than on desktop computers.

Give them the big benefits. Put your best foot forward. Let them know why and how to get in touch with you. That is what your landing page needs to do. No more. No less.

In the next chapter, we will share our landing page template with you so you can see all the components a successful landing page needs.

Chapter 9

How to Make Landing Pages that Convert Curiosity to Cash

by Talor Zamir

Now that you understand why a good landing page is so essential to your success, let's look at what a high-converting landing page looks like.

We are going to share a template that we have used successfully in a number of different local business niches. Before we do, however, it is helpful to take a quick look of what you *do not* want your landing page to look like.

EXAMPLE OF A DREADFUL LANDING PAGE

Figure 9-1 on page 42 is from a law firm and is the actual landing page they were sending traffic to from AdWords (names are changed out to protect the guilty!).

Let's look at why this landing page falls short:

- *There is a lot of wasted space at the top.* The part of a website you see when you first land on it (before you scroll) is called the "above the fold" section of the site. It is *the* most important part of a landing page because it is all most people are going to see of your site. Because this is such important real estate on your site, you need to make the most of it. This page does not. The above-the-fold space

FIGURE 9–1. Example of an Awful Landing Page

is dominated by a fairly thick header (containing only the firm name and navigation links) and a huge photo (photos are fine on a site, but not when used like this).

- The big issue on this page is *there's nothing above the fold that conveys value or is helpful to someone trying to figure out what this firm does, how the firm can help them, etc.* It is a complete waste of the most important real estate on the page.
- *If you wanted to contact this firm to get more information, how would you do that?* You could click the "Contact Us" link in the navigation bar. But, remember, people are lazy. They do not want to click, scroll, or swipe any more than necessary. By not having a call to action with phone number and/or form on this page to make it as easy as possible for prospects to contact them, this firm is missing out on a lot of potential leads.
- *Even if there was a phone number on this page, why would you want to contact this firm?* What reason do they give you to pick up the phone and call? If you answered "none," you are spot on! This page has no call to action on it, which is a big mistake. You want to tell people *why* they should contact you and *how* they should do it.
- *The copy on this page is just horrible.* It's all about the firm and essentially just lists their practice areas and the main locations they serve. Clearly this was written by someone who had SEO in mind and wanted to get this site ranked higher in the organic search results by stuffing relevant keywords on the page (by the way, listing a bunch of service areas and locations like this does not work for SEO). Website and landing

page copy should be focused on the benefits you offer your clients. You want to talk more about them and how you can make *their* lives better.

The lawyer who used this website is the perfect example of an advertiser who will spend a few grand on AdWords and then say, "Yeah, I tried that AdWords thing, and it didn't work for me." And that's a shame, because it didn't have to turn out that way. Using a better landing page, like one based on the template we are about to share with you, this lawyer could have had much better results.

THE LOCAL BUSINESS LANDING PAGE TEMPLATE

This template we are sharing with you is the result of years of testing and millions of dollars in ad spend, and has proved successful across dozens of different local business verticals.

If we were looking to give away a free report or were running an ecommerce site, we probably would not use this template. This is just what we have found works the best for local businesses looking to get their phones ringing.

Let's take a look at the template in Figure 9-2 and then walk you through each part of it so you understand why it works so well and can use it effectively for your business.

Header

The header is the section at the very top of your site. It should be relatively narrow because you do not want it taking up too much of the all-important above-the-fold space at the top of your site.

There are just two things to include in the header: your logo, which goes on the far left side of the header, and a call to action, which goes on the far right side of the header.

This call to action should be in a fairly large font so it stands out and people can read it easily. Almost always for a local business we have the business's phone number here.

However, do not just put the phone number up there. Add a specific call to action above the phone number to give people a reason to call you. We recommend something like "Call Now for a Free Estimate/Consultation/Quote."

Video or Image?

Under the main headline, on the left side of the page, we have a video or image. (This video or image could go either above or below the main headline. We have tried it both ways, and it does not seem to make much of a difference in conversion rates.)

The strategy for the image or video is pretty much like it is for the rest of the landing page. Put your best foot forward. You simply want something that looks professional and helps convey the benefits you offer.

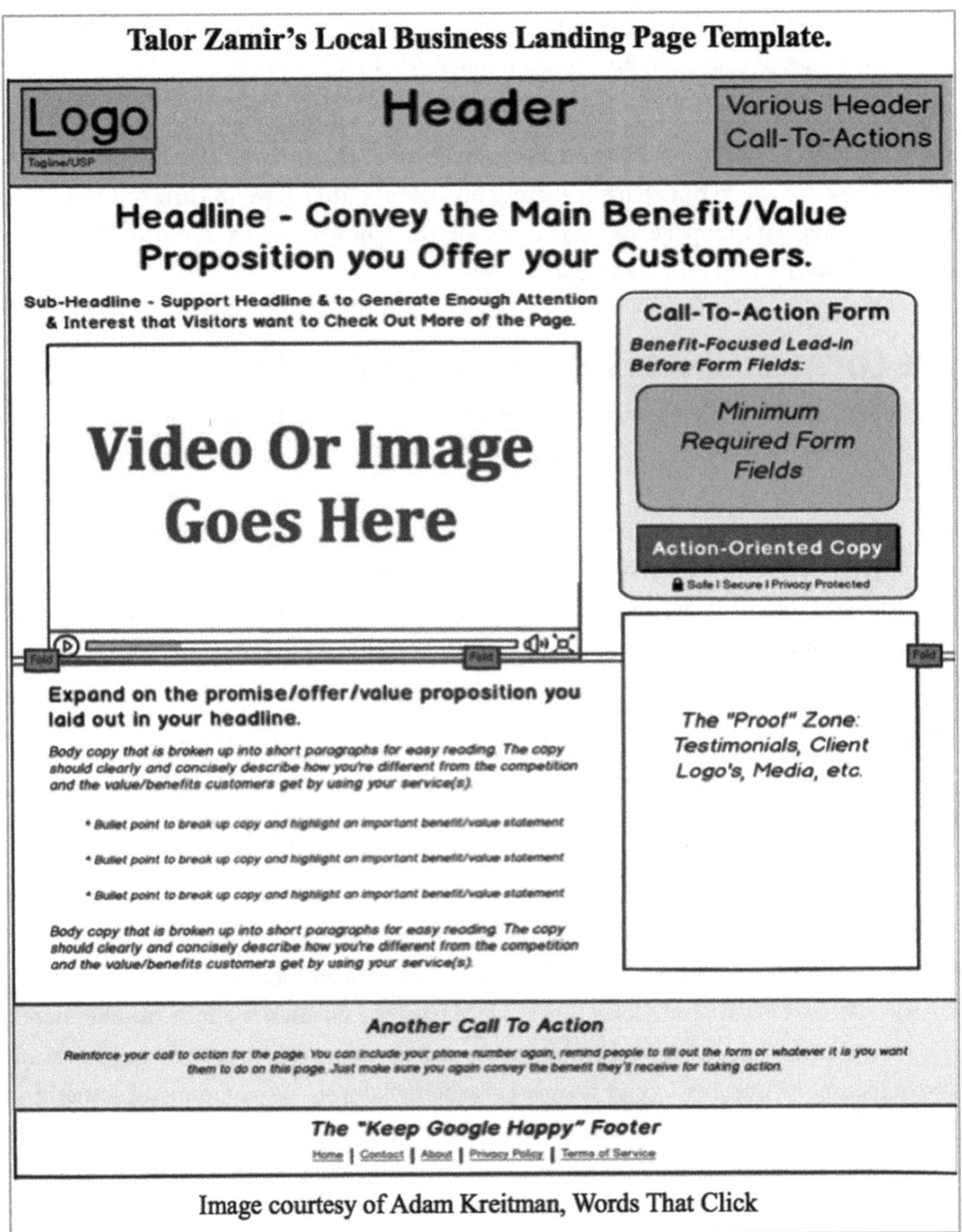

Image courtesy of Adam Kreitman, Words That Click

FIGURE 9–2. The Local Business Landing Page Template
This Landing Page Format Consistently Gets Killer Results for Almost any Business and Will Consistently Get You More Leads for Less Money than any of Your Competitors. This In Turn Enables You to Show Up at the Top of Google, Affordably, So You Get Plenty of Traffic.

For a video, keep it on the short side: around a minute or a few minutes at the most.

For the image, make sure it's relevant to your business. Ideally it's a photo of you/your staff looking happy or one that visually shows the benefits your clients get from using your services.

Headline/Subheadline

Hands down, the headline is the most important copy on your landing page. It's so important because it's going to be the most read copy on the page and will largely determine whether your prospects will pay attention to the rest of the page or simply hit the back button.

There is no shortage of detailed information out there on copywriting and creating headlines. Most of them require you to think really deeply about this, come up with a customer avatar, think about a lot of theoretical stuff, and come up with 100 ideas, etc. A lot of this information is really helpful; we are not dismissing it at all. But our goal in this book is to make things as simple and straightforward for you as possible.

Obviously we can't write your headline for you. You will still have to do some thinking about this, and at least come up with a list of your best benefits and main selling points. However, we are going to share a headline template that has proved to be successful on a number of landing pages we have created for clients.

Proven Headline Formula for Local Business Landing Pages

Here is the headline and subheadline template:

Would You Like to... (Insert Benefit 1, Benefit 2, Benefit 3)

If the answer is "YES," then call us now for your free consultation and learn...

Let's look at a few examples and then discuss this formula in more detail.

Here's one for a title loan company:

Would You Like Fast Cash in 15 Minutes or Less With No Credit Check at the Lowest Rates in Las Vegas AND You Keep Your Car?

If the answer is "YES," then call us now at (888) 555-5555, or come visit us at (location address).

For a mortgage broker:

Would You Like to Refinance Your Home to Today's Low Rates and Lower Your Monthly Payments Even If You Owe More Than Your Home Is Worth?

If the answer is "YES," then call now for your free consultation where you'll discover...

You can use one, two, or even up to three benefits in the headline.

One of the keys to the success of this headline template is putting your prospects in "Yes" mode, which, psychologically, makes them more likely to take you up on your offer.

Look how this works for the mortgage broker:

Would you like to refinance to today's low rates? "Yes."

Would you like to lower your monthly payments? "Yes."

Would you like to refinance even if you're upside down? "Yes."

At this point, your prospect has yes, yes, yes going through their mind, so you are getting them in a "yes" state of mind. That is why we follow up with *"If the answer is YES . . ."* to build off them being in that state of saying yes, and then we follow up with a call to action. That call to action leads into the promise of learning/discovering the biggest benefit you offer prospects.

There is no shortage of potential headlines you can use on your landing page. And, certainly, feel free to test different headlines to see how they perform. We have just found this template works really well, so if you want to shortcut the headline writing process, we would recommend you stick with this formula that we know works well for local businesses.

Body Copy/Bullet Points

This section goes under your headline and subheadline and expands on the promise/offer/value proposition they started.

Most people are not going to read all your copy; they are going to skim it. So a few short paragraphs are all you need along with three to five bullet points. Bullet points are a list of short, punchy sentences that convey the main benefits/key points that prospects should know about your business.

Again, keep things short, sweet, and focused on the main benefits you offer your clients.

Let's shift from the left side of the landing page to the right side.

Contact Form

Not everyone who lands on this page is going to call. So for those who do not want to call, the landing page should have a contact form where they can submit their information.

The form should have a clear call to action at the top that reinforces why they should contact you and what benefit they will receive for doing so.

For the form itself, only ask for the information you absolutely need from a prospect. For a local business, that is generally a name, email address, phone number, and an optional "comments" field where they can enter any comments, questions, etc., they have.

The more fields in the form, the less likely someone is going to fill it out. Studies have shown that adding just one additional field to a form can reduce conversions by 50 percent! So do not ask for information you really do not need like city, age, income, mother's maiden name, etc.

Keep it as short as possible. (As a local business, though, definitely require a phone number because we have found that people who only enter a name and email address tend to be lower quality leads. Plus, you want to be able to call and follow up with them.)

You can also get creative with the button that a visitor needs to click to submit their information. You can use a generic "Submit" button or a more action/benefit-oriented button such as "Get Free Estimate" or "Get Free Consultation."

The "Proof Zone"

The space under the form is a great place to demonstrate your business's credibility. We call it the "Proof Zone" because the information here should help prove to your prospects that you are a credible and trustworthy business.

How do you do that?

One common way is to provide some testimonials from happy clients. Having these testimonials in the form of a video or audio clip is very powerful. Though, if you do not have those, a text testimonial with a photo is the next best option.

With testimonials, the more specific they are and the more they reinforce the main benefits of your business, the better. Here is an example of a lame testimonial:

> *"These guys are great. I'm really happy with them."*
>
> —Joe

Compare that to this testimonial:

> *"Following my car accident three years ago, I'd experienced nearly constant chronic back pain. I tried physical therapy, pain meds, and a few natural remedies, and nothing helped. I visited Dr. Smith after a friend recommended her, and I'm glad I did. After six visits, I'm moving better than I have in years and am virtually pain free!"*
>
> —Joe Williams, Seattle, WA

If you have testimonials like this one, use them!

If you do not have testimonials, there are plenty of other ways to demonstrate your business's credibility. These include using logos of media outlets you have been featured on, logos of well-known clients, and/or special recognition/credentials/awards your business has received from industry/business organizations.

Under the main content on the page, we end up with two more sections at the bottom. We'll cover those next.

Another Call to Action

At the bottom of the page, below the fold, reinforce your call to action. Put your phone number there again so people do not have to scroll up to find it (remember, people are lazy!). And again remind them of the benefit they will receive for taking action and contacting you.

Tiny Links Needed at the Bottom of Your Landing Page

As we mentioned in the last chapter, if it were up to us, there would be no links on this landing page because we want people focused on the *one* action we want them to take. However, since we are advertising on Google, we need to keep them happy and follow their rules. And to satisfy Google's terms and conditions, there need to be a few links on the page.

We place these, in a very small font, in the footer at the bottom of the page. The bare minimum you need to include here are links to a privacy policy, terms and conditions, and a contact page.

We are not attorneys so are not going to advise you on what your privacy policy and terms and conditions need to say. There are plenty of templates available for both of these online that you can check out.

The contact page is so Google knows you are a real business and should include both your phone number and your physical address.

You can see more examples of landing pages as well as download the "Local Business Landing Page Template" at www.UltimateLocalBook.com.

WHAT YOU SHOULD *AVOID* ON YOUR LANDING PAGE

Now you have the template and the information you need to create a landing page that will put you ahead of virtually all your competitors. Before we move on, however, there are a few things you should be sure to *not* do on your landing page.

The first is you do not want to try to make a sale. The traffic coming from Google AdWords are going to be people who do not know you from a hole in the wall, so they are going to have their guard up at first. If you try make a sale, you are going to turn off most of these people, and your conversion is going to be very low. Plus, if you are selling a high-end service, you are simply not going to close a $45,000 kitchen remodel or a $2,000 retainer for a DUI case on your landing page.

Second, do not try to answer all your prospects' questions. Remember, the more information you provide, the less incentive they have to contact you. The landing page should cover the biggest benefits you offer your clients and provide just enough information for them to want to pick up the phone and call.

You need to get people on the phone and/or meet with them in person, and that is what your landing page should be designed to do.

Third, do not half-ass your landing page and just throw something up really quick. The landing page needs to look nice and clean. This means having a nice logo, a professional-looking image or video, and proofreading your copy so the page doesn't have any typos or grammatical mistakes. Look at the page as if you were a prospect for your business, and make sure the page is conveying the professionalism and image you would expect.

Fourth, do not go negative. A lot of top copywriters/direct marketers talk about how you should hit prospects over the head with the pain points they are experiencing. In fact, one of the most common copywriting formulas is Problem/Agitate/Solve, where you highlight the problem they are having, agitate it by talking about all the pain and suffering having this problem causes, and show how your product/service solves the problem and associated pain. A lot of people swear by this, and it does work. However, if you are not an experienced copywriter, you can get into a lot of trouble trying to pull this off. Negative talk can trigger undesirable thoughts/ideas in your prospects' minds.

So our advice is to avoid the negative and focus on the positive. Stick to the benefits of what you can do for them, why you are the best in your field (if you are), and why they should call you over other professionals in your field. This is the safer, more effective route to go.

And, finally, there are certain types of businesses and claims that Google does not like. Among them are:

- "Business Opportunity"-type claims, where you say you have the secret to helping your clients make millions of dollars
- Multilevel marketing (MLMs)
- Affiliate marketing
- Miracle-cure-type products like goji berries and raspberry ketones
- Bold health claims (we've even had issues with a legitimate local CrossFit gym that had a landing page featuring a video of a client who had experienced dramatic weight-loss results)

Basically you want to avoid hyped claims. Most local businesses don't have problems, but you should be aware of these things to avoid having your ads rejected by Google or having your account suspended.

Now you have a blueprint for creating a high-converting landing page. But how do you know if it is working? The answer comes down to conversion tracking, and that is what we are going to cover in Chapter 21.

First, we have a special guest chapter from USP (unique selling proposition) and AdWords expert Bryan Todd. What you're about to learn fits in perfectly with what we just covered.

The first step to launching your lead generation campaign is to get your new landing page online as soon as possible. So our recommendation is to read the next chapter on USP, then start creating your landing page *now* while this is all fresh in your mind.

If you are not technical, we recommend hiring a webmaster to put your landing page online and not waste time trying to do it yourself! (We also have a "Local Business Landing Page Generator" that you can learn more about at www.UltimateLocalBook.com).

Chapter 10

Increase Your Conversion and Dominate Your Niche with a Killer USP!

by Bryan Todd, president of Perry S. Marshall & Associates

Michael Strickland of Boulder, Colorado, runs a company that ships cars across the country. He enrolled in one of our training courses, a hands-on, first-click-to-first-sale marketing funnel improvement lab. Like many people who take this course, he assumed we were just going to go "ninja" to the nth degree on Google ads.

Sure, we did that, but on the first live small group session, I asked him, "Michael, what is the reason why I should ship my car with your company instead of every other company out there?"

Michael didn't have a solid, meaty answer. Sure, he ran a good company, and they delivered quality service. But it was a deer-in-the-headlights moment, because he didn't have a definitive answer.

My response was, "Michael, you must create a great answer to that question." So we started building his unique selling proposition (USP) together. Two weeks later, Michael emerged with a powerful new USP and his "Damage Free Guarantee," which you can see on his website today at www.ShipACarDirect.com.

That was the tipping point of Michael's business. His sales doubled in six months. Yes, all his experiments and optimization of Google ads were helpful and necessary. But his landing page and ads didn't light on fire until his USP was solid. Once he had a terrific answer to "why should I buy from you?" customers started responding, and the business went supernova.

The business ventures that fail the fastest in the marketplace are the ones that have no USP. The businesses that have their USP crisply and clearly defined acquire customers and grow.

WHAT IS A USP?

It stands for Unique Selling Proposition. It's the "thing" that makes you unique in the marketplace—it's what customers can get from you that they can't find anyplace else. You can also call it your "value proposition."

Having a clear USP gives you a strong response for these questions:

- How are you unique?
- In what way are you different from your competitors?
- Why should I buy from you, rather than from someone else?
- Why should I care about you or anything you sell?

The term came from Rosser Reeves (1910–1984). He was a pioneer in the use of TV ads, and he wrote *Reality in Advertising*, one of the most sought-after classic advertising books of the last century. (Try finding a physical copy of Reeves' out-of-print book anywhere for less than $100.)

His message on USPs was simple:

Your ad needs some way of clearly saying, "Buy this product or service, and you will get this specific benefit." Your promise should be one that your competitor cannot or does not offer.

Your promise has to win over new customers. A USP is worthless if it doesn't convince people to buy from you.

Now I'm going to give you a method for defining *your* USP. And I'm going to give you a simple approach for how to test elements of your USP in your Google ads and landing pages to find what gets you the strongest response.

THE SIX ESSENTIAL ELEMENTS OF A POWER USP

Any time you're communicating with a prospect, you can appeal to any one of these, or all of them together:

1. You're unique because of the buyer you serve.
2. You're unique because of what you sell.
3. You're unique because you have an unusual angle.
4. You're unique because of what your product/service does not do.

5. You're unique because of the time frame you offer.
6. You're unique because of your product/service guarantee.

How many of these elements are already true of you? Or: What can you change, shift, or alter in your business so that any or all of these elements become true of you?

We'll explore these one at a time, with examples of how each one might look in a Google ad.

You're Unique Because of the Buyer You Serve

Your business gets traction when you zero in on a niche. Maybe you target people of a specific demographic—a certain age, gender, income level, or religious or political leaning. Or maybe you solve a specific kind of problem—a rare health issue or a peculiar type of software malfunction. Maybe you cater to a particular hobby.

In extremely rare cases you could be unique because there's no limit to who you serve. For example:

> *"My hiring and recruiting system is unique because it works for virtually any position in any business, anywhere—from the ecommerce business in the U.K. to the information marketer in Chicago to the nursing station in the Australian outback."*
>
> —Nancy Slessenger, Vinehouse.com

Test the unique buyer approach in your ads. Whether you serve a unique demographic:

Meet Singles Your Age. We're an over-50 dating site made for older singles. beyond50.com

Or you focus on a unique niche:

Proven ROI Web Design Results. Accountable website design uniquely for ecommerce businesses. TrueROIwebdesign.com

You're Unique Because of What You Sell

Do you offer a service where others only offer a product? Do you offer a product where everyone else is selling services?

Are you the thing for sale, as a skilled technician, consultant, coach, or performer? Are you the entertaining or compelling personality that makes the business what it is?

If so, beat your drum. Having a story to tell will instantly separate you from the herd. Perry initially made a name for his business by telling his unusual story:

> "How an Inexperienced 29-Year-Old Punk Ignored All the Usual 'Marketing Wisdom'—Grew a High-Tech Business 2,000 percent in 4 Years, and Sold It for 18 Million Dollars!"

Test the "unique thing for sale" in your ads. Here are some examples. A product for sale, instead of a service:

Clogged Drains? Skip the plumber. Fix the problem for good. This ships in 24 hours. XYZdrainmagic.com

You for sale, with a unique story:

Social Media Done Right. Canada's only social media expert running his own 8-figure business. CAmediapower.com

You're Unique Because You've Found an Unusual Angle

There are so many "angles" you can use to separate yourself from competitors. Here are just a few:

- You promise a unique and specific outcome.
- You have a noteworthy track record.
- You have an unusual level of quality.
- The experience of doing business with you is one-of-a-kind.
- You offer a unique payment plan.

This ad celebrates a track record:

Iron-Clad Backup. A record 7 years without a system failure. Reliability you crave. ABCbackupsystems.com

You can use acronyms and proprietary labels for products you sell and methods you use that get results. That approach always gets people to sit up and take notice. This business owner does just that. Try testing a similar concept in your ads:

Jazz Mandolin Made Easier. Unlock the "mystery" of jazz with our one-of-a-kind FFcP method. JazzMando.com

You're Unique Because of What Your Product/Service Does NOT Do

We call these "negative promises," and they can be just as powerful as positive ones.

Maybe there's some unwanted ingredient or feature your product doesn't have. Maybe there's a bad result you prevent. Maybe your product avoids cost or waste and saves time and money.

This example ad captures the "negative promise" concept perfectly. Try testing one like it for your business:

Reduce Carpal Tunnel 50%. No office visits. No physical therapy. No painful surgery. CTStherapySolution.com

You're Unique Because of Your Offer's Time Frame

You can promise results within a set amount of time or for a set amount of time. The question is, how specific can you actually get? The more explicit you are, the better your ads will perform.

Fast Corn Relief. Corns gone in 5 days or your money back. Easy-to-use kit. CornsSolvedForGood.com

Install 1 MegaFilter and keep your home free of pollen & allergens for 6 full months. SuperMegaFilter.com

Ads that use specific number symbols perform better. It's practically an ironclad law. There are two reasons why: 1) The brain processes number symbols faster than written words, and 2) numbers make your message specific.

Prospects love promises that are specific, clear, and unmistakable.

You're Unique Because of Your Product/Service Guarantee

Give your offer an "or else"—a penalty to you if you don't deliver. Or you could refund your customer's money, replace your product, or redo your service.

Here is an example:

I Get You the Right Hire—or I redo the entire recruiting process, any time within 1 year. vinehouse.com/recruitment/

The more ballsy and specific you make it, the more your prospects will sit up and take notice:

- Double your money back
- Triple your money back
- Your money back plus $1,000
- We'll refund your money and pay our competitor to come in and give you a replacement.

Combine your "or else" with a specific time promise, and your message has power. How's this for a specific, ballsy promise?

Our Plumber Comes on Time. If we're not on time, we pay you $5 per minute late, up to $300. BenjaminFranklinPlumbing.com

Ultimately the offer your ad and landing page describe is more important than the words you use to describe it. What does your customer get by calling you for a free consultation? And how fast do they get it? How fast will it make a difference in their life? This deserves serious thought, and most of all, serious experimentation!

■ ■ ■

Bryan Todd is a writer, marketer, and USP specialist in Lincoln, Nebraska. He's worked in both Europe and Asia and has spent most of his career teaching—from foreign language and world history to advanced testing methods for the internet. He has worked with clients in dozens of industries, from health care and book publishing to manufacturing and computer software. You can also watch a free in-depth 80/20 USP video presentation by Bryan Todd at www.UltimateLocalBook.com.

Chapter 11

Why You Must Track All Conversions on Your Landing Page

by Talor Zamir

Marketing is an investment. Dollars in, dollars out. Much like stocks and bonds. Most local business owners don't think of it this way . . . but you should.

You decide to invest your money in the stock market and build your retirement nest egg. Whether you hire a financial planner or invest on your own, every month you expect to get a report that details how much money you have in your account, the specific stocks and mutual funds your money is invested in and, over time, whether your investments are increasing or decreasing in value.

These reports give you the information you need to make smarter decisions about your investments. If there are some investments that are not performing well, you may decide to sell them and invest in something else. Or, if your whole portfolio is underperforming, you can fire your financial advisor (or yourself!) and find someone you think will do a better job.

Marketing *is* an investment.

The monthly investment reports provide the transparency and accountability you need to make smart decisions about your money.

MOST LOCAL BUSINESS ADVERTISERS ARE FLYING BLIND

The trouble is most local business advertisers are flying blind when it comes to marketing. Most have no clue what part of their marketing is generating an ROI.

A big reason why is that tracking conversions can be a challenge for local businesses.

In the internet marketing world, a conversion is simply when a visitor to your website performs the desired action you want them to take. For most local businesses, that action is going to be filling out a contact form or, more likely, calling the business. In fact, we find that about 60 to 70 percent of the leads for a local business come via phone calls.

Unlike an ecommerce site that sells products online (where conversions can be easily tracked), in most situations, a visitor to a local business's website isn't going to complete the transaction right then and there. Your prospects usually first have to call or fill out the contact form and speak to someone. The sale happens later on (usually when they come into your office for a "free consultation").

This has historically been a huge problem for local business owners when it comes to measuring the effectiveness of their advertising. It used to be near impossible to track calls to your business from Google AdWords so you could accurately track and measure the results of your advertising and which keywords are generating the calls.

There have been call tracking options available for a number of years, but we are not talking about having a unique tracking number on your website. (That will only give you an idea of the overall number of calls you got for the money spent. While it is better than not doing any kind of call tracking, it is not good enough.)

TRACK CONVERSIONS WITH DYNAMIC CALL TRACKING

Dynamic call tracking systems push call data back into Google AdWords and tag them as a conversion. So for each keyword and ad, you'll be able to see not only data like cost per click, total number of clicks, clickthrough rates, etc., but also total number of conversions, conversion rates, and cost per conversion.

> Dynamic call tracking enables you to look in AdWords and see exactly which keywords and ads are making your phone ring.

Using dynamic call tracking lets you see this data clearly for every keyword and ad in your campaign. It also lets you see if your campaign is performing better on mobile devices than desktops or vice versa so you can adjust your mobile bids accordingly (more on this later).

Having this data makes a huge difference in being able to optimize and improve your campaigns over time. Here is an example.

A Case Study

One of my clients is a personal injury lawyer in a very competitive city where click costs are extremely high (by the way, personal injury is probably the local business niche with the highest cost per click).

In his Google AdWords campaign, he spent over $2,900 on one of the most obvious and popular keywords for personal injury lawyers (see Figure 11-1). However, because we were using dynamic call tracking, we knew that even though the keyword was getting clicks, it generated zero conversions—not one call or contact form completion from our landing page!

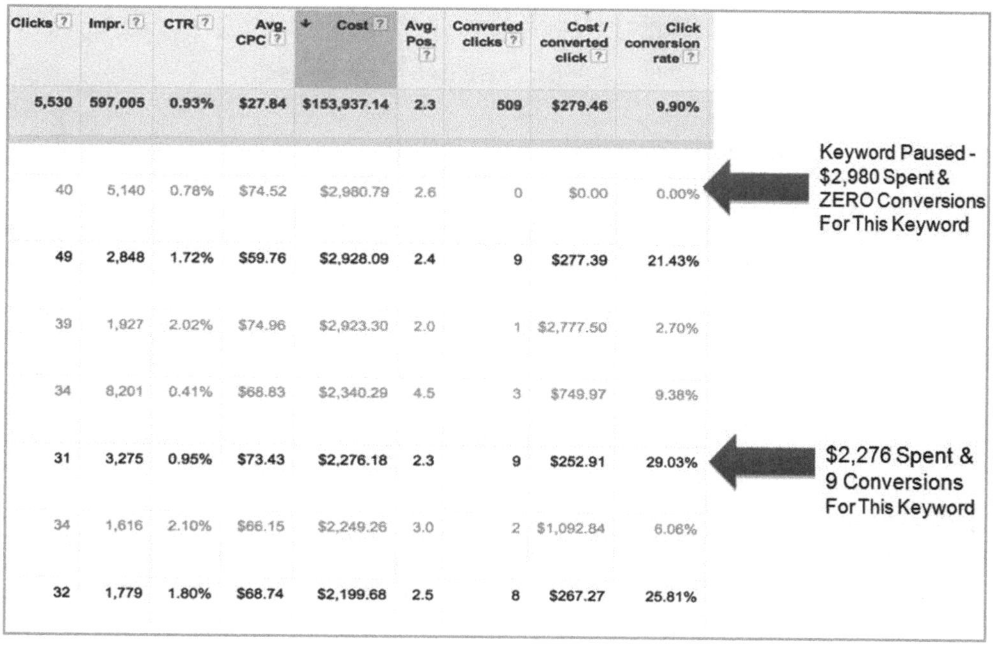

Clicks	Impr.	CTR	Avg. CPC	Cost	Avg. Pos.	Converted clicks	Cost / converted click	Click conversion rate	
5,530	597,005	0.93%	$27.84	$153,937.14	2.3	509	$279.46	9.90%	
40	5,140	0.78%	$74.52	$2,980.79	2.6	0	$0.00	0.00%	Keyword Paused - $2,980 Spent & ZERO Conversions For This Keyword
49	2,848	1.72%	$59.76	$2,928.09	2.4	9	$277.39	21.43%	
39	1,927	2.02%	$74.96	$2,923.30	2.0	1	$2,777.50	2.70%	
34	8,201	0.41%	$68.83	$2,340.29	4.5	3	$749.97	9.38%	
31	3,275	0.95%	$73.43	$2,276.18	2.3	9	$252.91	29.03%	$2,276 Spent & 9 Conversions For This Keyword
34	1,616	2.10%	$66.15	$2,249.26	3.0	2	$1,092.84	6.06%	
32	1,779	1.80%	$68.74	$2,199.68	2.5	8	$267.27	25.81%	

FIGURE 11-1. AdWords Conversion Tracking Stats

Meanwhile we had other keywords that were getting leads for $252 per conversion. You can press "pause" on any keyword. By pausing the keyword that was costing a lot of money but not getting any conversions, we were able to dramatically improve the profitability of the campaign. That way, the client's budget was only being used on the highest-quality keywords that were getting the lowest cost per lead and the best ROI.

With dynamic tracking, we've also seen that, in some niches, mobile works really well. For example, in many legal niches, mobile costs per conversion are much lower than they are for desktop computer searches. The screenshot in Figure 11-2 on page 60 shows how the cost per conversion for mobile traffic is about half of what it is from computers.

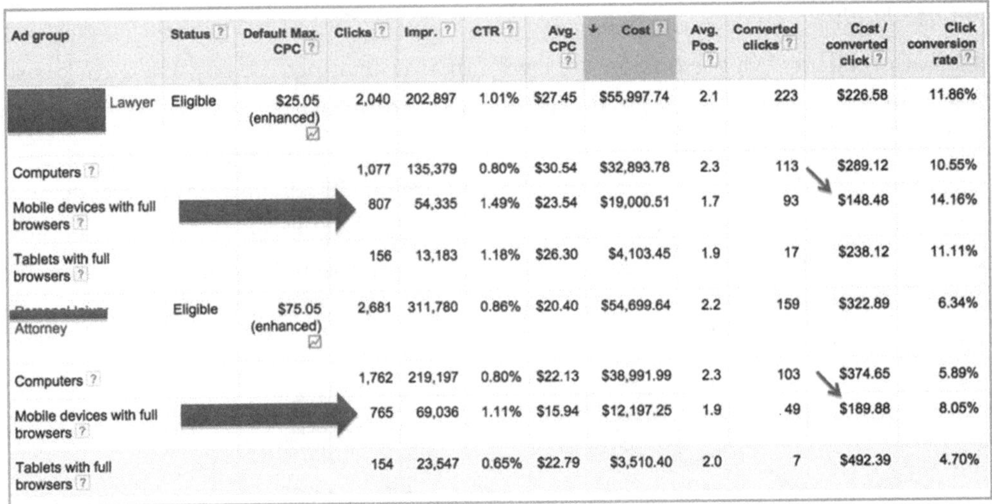

Ad group	Status	Default Max. CPC	Clicks	Impr.	CTR	Avg. CPC	Cost	Avg. Pos.	Converted clicks	Cost / converted click	Click conversion rate
Lawyer	Eligible	$25.05 (enhanced)	2,040	202,897	1.01%	$27.45	$55,997.74	2.1	223	$226.58	11.86%
Computers			1,077	135,379	0.80%	$30.54	$32,893.78	2.3	113	$289.12	10.55%
Mobile devices with full browsers			807	54,335	1.49%	$23.54	$19,000.51	1.7	93	$148.48	14.16%
Tablets with full browsers			156	13,183	1.18%	$26.30	$4,103.45	1.9	17	$238.12	11.11%
Attorney	Eligible	$75.05 (enhanced)	2,681	311,780	0.86%	$20.40	$54,699.64	2.2	159	$322.89	6.34%
Computers			1,762	219,197	0.80%	$22.13	$38,991.99	2.3	103	$374.65	5.89%
Mobile devices with full browsers			765	69,036	1.11%	$15.94	$12,197.25	1.9	49	$189.88	8.05%
Tablets with full browsers			154	23,547	0.65%	$22.79	$3,510.40	2.0	7	$492.39	4.70%

FIGURE 11-2. AdWords Conversion Tracking Stats by Device

Very few local businesses are doing this sort of call tracking. Instead, I estimate that over 90 percent of local businesses advertising on Google are blindly spending money for keywords and ads that are unprofitable. The worst part is that they never know it because they don't have a conversion call tracking system set up. They don't realize that they could potentially double or triple the ROI of their campaigns (and their business).

With this data, we may increase the amount we bid on mobile devices to get as many conversions as possible, at a solid cost per conversion. In some other niches, however, mobile traffic may not convert as well so we'll adjust the bids for mobile devices down.

You need to optimize your campaigns for conversions, *not* clicks.

GETTING STARTED WITH DYNAMIC CALL TRACKING

Now that you understand the importance of dynamic call tracking and how it can make a huge difference in the profitability of your campaign, let's talk about how to set it up.

At the time of this writing, we highly recommend using a third-party call tracking service. The cost to set up conversion tracking, in our opinion, is very cheap, especially when you consider the ROI you get from pausing nonperforming keywords. Go to www.UltimateLocalBook.com to get our most up-to-date recommendations for the top third-party AdWords conversion call tracking companies for local businesses.

Google has also released its own tracking feature called Website Call Conversions. This service is free to AdWords advertisers, although, currently, it is only available in select countries, the U.S. being one of them. (*Note:* At the time of this writing, the Google service is fairly new and clunky, and we do not recommend it. Until we fully test it out for an extended period of time and it is bug-free, we recommend paying the modest fees for a third-party conversion call tracking company. This will save you hassles.)

Another issue with Website Call Conversions is you are not guaranteed a tracking number with your local area code. This is a big deal for a local business! We have found local businesses get higher conversion rates when they use a number with a local area code instead of a toll-free number. So, unless Google changes things and can guarantee you a tracking number with a local area code, we would be hesitant to use this service because we do not want to end up with a toll-free number.

Which brings us to the option of using a third-party company for dynamic call tracking.

This is what we have been using with our clients, and we know it works well.

The costs are pretty reasonable (around $40 a month, depending on your call volume) and worth the investment. These services have local numbers available in the U.S., Canada, and a few other countries (depending on the company you use—get the most updated list at www.UltimateLocalBook.com). They also work with all traffic sources, so if you decide to expand from Google to Yahoo! and Bing (which runs through Microsoft Ad Center), or Facebook, you will be able to track your calls on those platforms as well.

An additional benefit of these services is that you get some nice features, such as recordings of your incoming phone calls so you can quality check them. The services that use call tracking also include a call recording feature so they can see how their team is answering the calls and if they are losing business from mishandled calls. (This is particularly helpful if you are not the one answering the phone!) Good services provide call logs, etc. Google's free option does not have this.

TRUE CAMPAIGN OPTIMIZATION

Most local business AdWords advertisers, because they don't track call conversions, simply do not have the conversion information that lets them optimize their campaigns effectively.

Let's say you start an AdWords account, and after the first 30 days or so it is about at break even. You have gotten some leads and made some money, but you have also spent some money, so AdWords is not generating much of a return, if any.

If you are not tracking all your conversions, you won't know which keywords are performing well and which ones are not. Therefore, you would not be able to make many adjustments to your campaign, so you would probably always be at break even. Eventually you might give up thinking that AdWords is not going to work for your business. This has happened to thousands of local businesses.

Whereas if you *are* tracking all conversions, using the information we just shared with you, you could pause the keywords that are not working (or reduce the bids on them) so your campaign becomes more profitable over time.

Many times in lead generation, if you can break even or even lose a little money in the first few weeks of a campaign, that's OK. Why? Because if you have the conversion data, you will be able to optimize and get a positive return on your investment once you are able to pause your losers and let your winners run!

Hardly any of your competitors are doing this—and as we like to say, "The one-eyed king rules the land of the blind!"

Chapter 12

How to Find the Best Keywords to Start With

by Talor Zamir

"If content is king on the internet, keywords are queen."

—Ken Giddens

Keywords are the foundation of your AdWords account. You have to be sure to have the right keywords in your account so your ads show up in front of your ideal prospects who are searching for you on Google.

While keyword research can be a highly complex, time-consuming process, we want to make things as easy as possible for you. So we are going to suggest that you do not go too crazy with your keyword research. In fact, for a local AdWords campaign, our advice is not to cast too wide a net when it comes to keywords, especially when you are starting out.

Especially for those used to doing keyword research for SEO purposes, this may sound like bad advice. For SEO, it is necessary to do comprehensive keyword research and come up with a list of hundreds or thousands of keyword variations for a business.

That is not what we recommend for a local pay-per-click (PPC) campaign. In fact, when you are starting out, before you even open any of the keyword research tools that are available (which we will cover in the next chapter), we want you to do the following.

WHAT WOULD YOUR IDEAL CLIENT TYPE INTO GOOGLE?

Think of your ideal prospect and ask yourself, "What would my ideal client type into Google to find a local business that does what I do?"

Go with the obvious keywords and write them down. And that is it! You have just done your initial round of keyword research. It may be a small list, but that's good. You want to at least start your campaign off by focusing on your best, most targeted keywords.

Here are some examples from a few local business niches that will give you a clearer idea of what we mean by the "best, most targeted keywords."

For a cosmetic dentist, there are a handful of keywords that describe what you do, including:

- cosmetic dentist
- cosmetic dentists
- cosmetic dentistry

In addition, there are variations of the specific products/procedures you offer like veneers, dental implants, crowns, etc.

For a chiropractor, the most targeted keywords are ones like:

- chiropractor
- chiropractors
- chiropractic

You will also want to combine these keywords with the name of the main city (cities) you serve. For example, "Chiropractor Lake Tahoe," "Reno cosmetic dentist," and "personal injury attorney in Seattle."

You may be thinking, "Hold on a minute. I'm a chiropractor and help people who have back pain, sciatica, neck pain, and more. Why shouldn't I bid on keywords that include those words?"

Especially if you are on a limited budget, you do *not* want to start out bidding on a keyword like back pain because it is too broad. There are people with back pain who could be good prospects, but you don't know what someone who types "back pain" into Google is looking for. Are they looking for a back brace, a back pain cream, or some other option to get pain relief?

> Start with only your best and most targeted keywords and expand from there.

Also, for broad keywords like this, you are going to be competing against national advertisers who sell back pain cream, back braces, etc. That's generally going to mean more competition and higher click prices. Not that a local business can't outcompete national competitors, but it is a harder battle to win, especially when you are starting out.

That is why we recommend sticking to the specific targeted terms. If you are a chiropractor and someone types "chiropractor" in Google, you know they are searching locally for someone who does exactly what you do.

You can always add more keywords later. But, initially, you do not want to blow through your budget because you have too many keywords, and the less relevant keywords steal clicks and budget away from your best, highest-quality keywords.

So let your best keywords lead the way. Then, after a couple of days, if you are not getting enough clicks, you can always add more keywords to the mix. Only at that point (returning to the chiropractor example) should you consider adding keywords like back pain, neck pain, sciatica, and other broader keywords.

One of the big mistakes we see with advertisers and consultants is they start off way too broad with their keywords. So they end up blowing through the budget and do not get a good number of leads.

Here is another example of how going too broad can hurt you:

If you are a mortgage broker, it seems obvious to bid on the keyword "mortgage broker," right? However, the mortgage brokers we've seen have the most success are those who focus on a *specific type of refinance.* For example, one of our clients specializes in HARP refinancing. So we bid on keywords like "HARP refinance," "HARP loan," and "HARP mortgage," then created ads that referenced HARP refinance. Those ads lead to a landing page that was all about HARP refinance, the benefits of a HARP refinance, and why you should call them now for a free quote.

> In general, the more specific and relevant the keyword, the higher quality it is going to be and the more likely it will turn into a lead.

Again, the more specific you can be in your targeting, the better. So, if you are a mortgage broker, ask yourself, "What are the two best types of refinances that I can help people with?" and focus on those to start.

Bottom line with keywords is we would rather you start your campaign with your top 20 or 30 keywords, instead of 200 or 300 keywords, and build from there.

THE SECRET TO KEYWORD RESEARCH FOR LOCAL BUSINESSES

Here is the secret to keyword research for local businesses: There really is no secret. The keywords you should use are pretty darn obvious. Do not overcomplicate matters.

When someone is looking for an immigration attorney, what are they going to type into Google?

Immigration attorney, immigration lawyer, or some close variation.

It is unlikely you are going to uncover a magical keyword that no one has ever thought of before (because if no one has ever thought of it, then probably no one is typing it into Google). So for local business search marketing, keeping things simple and targeted is the way to go.

Chapter 13

Advanced Keyword Research

by Talor Zamir

I've got a friend named Brad who used to work in a huge railway switching yard in Western Nebraska.

To most people that would be the most bleak, dead-end job imaginable. But what was going back and forth right in front of him every day? Thousands of tons of commodities—corn, wheat, soybeans.

Watching what came through and which way it was going, one day he realized he could calculate what big companies like ConAgra were anticipating in the commodity markets and play the market accordingly.

One guy merely lays bricks; another builds a wall; another builds a cathedral. There are always easy opportunities sitting right in front of you that you haven't seized yet.

As you just discovered, simply brainstorming a list of keywords will get you most of the way there when it comes to local keyword research for pay per click (PPC). However, there are times when you may want to do more advanced keyword research before setting up your campaign. Like my friend Brad who saw his railyard job as a leg up on futures prices, you might want to look below the surface and see what's *really* going on.

In this chapter, we will be sharing tools you can use to find additional keywords for your campaign, whether just to make sure you did not miss any obvious ones in your initial brainstorm or you are in a situation where your campaign is going well and you are looking for ways to expand from your initial keyword list.

We are going to lay out two options for you: one free, one paid. One that uses Google's keyword data. One that lets you "spy" on the keywords your competitors are using.

USING GOOGLE'S FREE KEYWORD PLANNER

If you have an AdWords account, you have access to Google's Keyword Planner. If you enter one or more keywords into this free tool, it will generate a list of related keywords.

Along with the keywords, it shows you how many times each keyword is searched per day/week/month, a suggested bid, etc. For the most part, we'd recommend ignoring this data and focusing on the keyword variations it generates and which variations you think your ideal prospect would be typing into Google.

Here are the basics on how to use the Google Keyword Planner:

- You'll find the Keyword Planner under the Tools tab in your AdWords account (see Figure 13-1).
- Once you select the Planner, chose "Search for new keyword using a phrase, website, or category" option under the "Find new keywords" section (see Figure 13-2 on page 69).
- Next, enter a few seed keywords that describe your business (i.e., chiropractor, kitchen remodeling company, divorce attorney) into the "Your product or service" box and click the "Get ideas" button (see Figure 13-2).

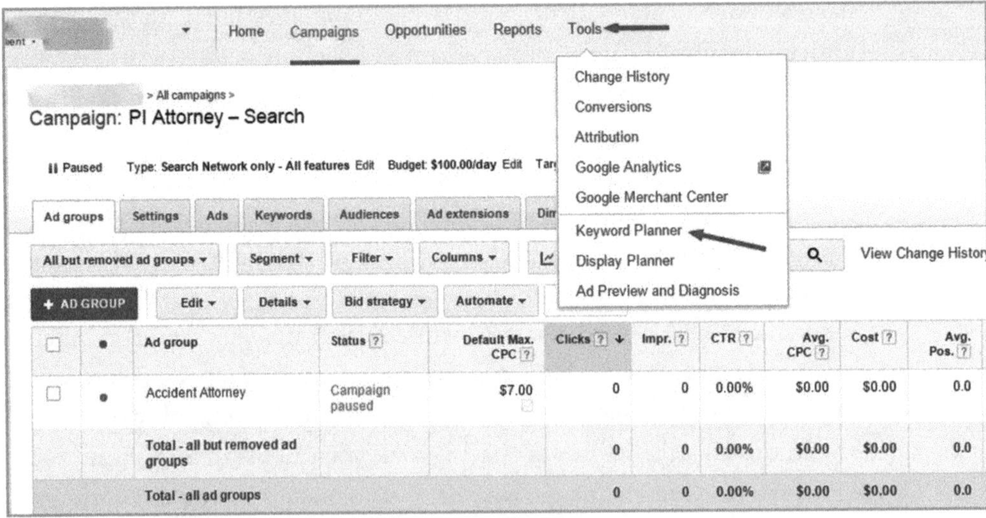

FIGURE 13-1. The Keyword Planner Is Under the Tools Tab and Gives You Access to Hugely Valuable Market Data, 24/7.

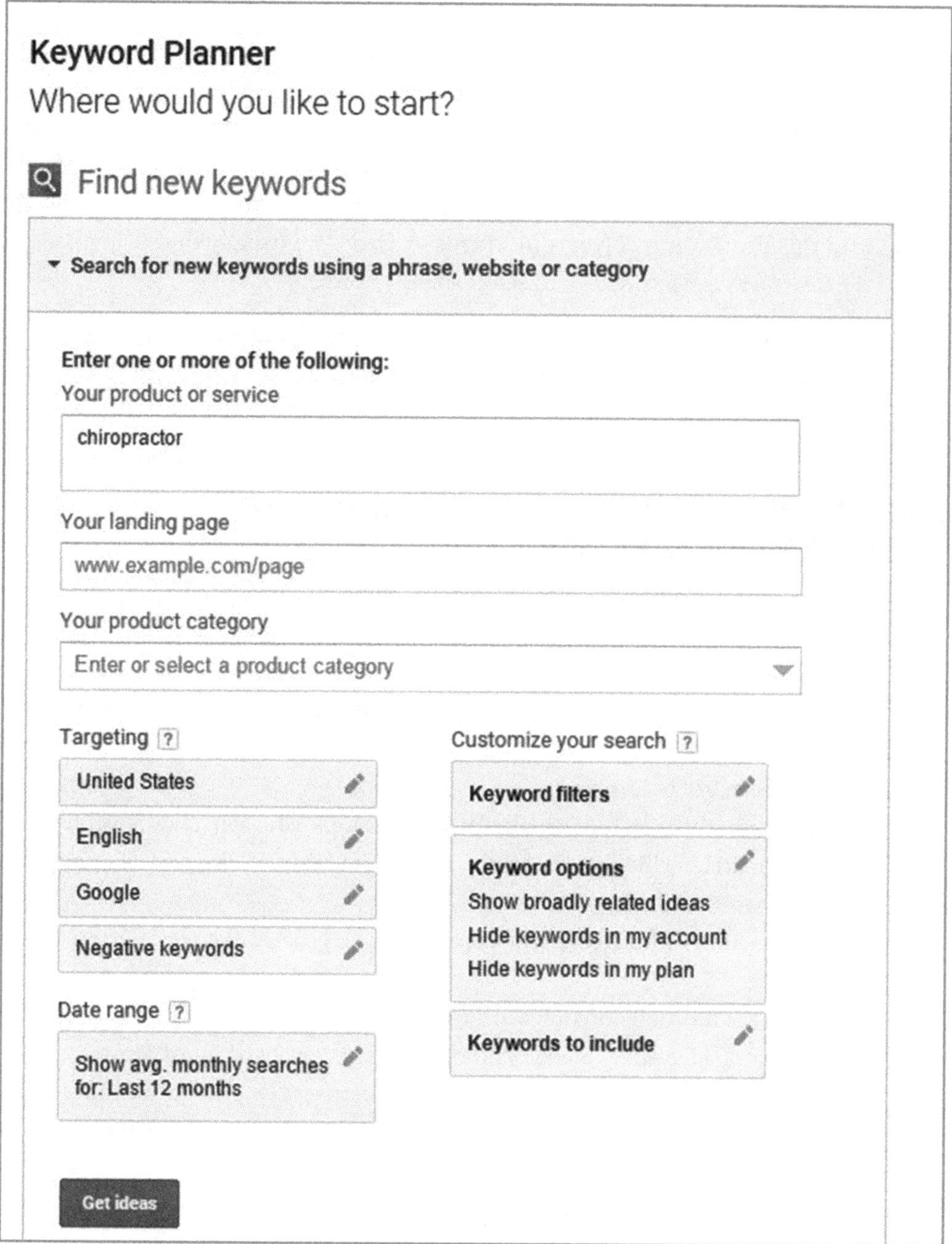

FIGURE 13-2. Finding New Keywords with the Keyword Planner

There are filters and targeting options that can help you refine your search. You can play around with them if you'd like but, for now, we recommend ignoring them.

- The Planner defaults to showing you the "Ad group" ideas tab (see Figure 13-1). This can be helpful for coming up with keyword ideas and ways to segment your campaign into ad groups (more on ad groups later). For now, click over to the "Keywords" ideas tab and look through the list of keywords for good candidates to add to your campaign.
- You can either scroll through the list on the screen in AdWords or you can download this list and then open it in Microsoft Excel (we usually find using Excel is the easier way to view, sort, and select the keywords).

That covers the essentials on how to use the Keyword Planner. The list it spits out can be helpful; however, there is another way for doing advanced keyword research we prefer to use.

HOW TO SPY ON YOUR COMPETITORS TO FIND THE BEST TARGETED KEYWORDS

Spy tools give internet advertisers the ability to "spy" on what their competitors are doing. These tools can provide helpful information for both SEO and PPC.

On the PPC side, they will show you a list of the advertisers whose ads are showing up for a given search term. Then you can investigate each advertiser more in depth, seeing what ad copy they use, the landing pages they are sending their traffic to, and a list of keywords they are bidding on.

These tools are not free but usually offer free trials you can take advantage of. Go to www.UltimateLocalBook.com to see an updated list of the top "spy on your competition" services available.

Each tool functions a little differently, but here is a general overview of how to use them.

First, type in the most obvious keyword that describes what your business does. This will give you a list of advertisers who are bidding on that keyword in AdWords.

Next, click on some of the names of the top advertisers to get more details about their campaigns. What you are most interested in seeing is the list of search terms their ads have been showing up for.

Figure 13-3 on page 71 is a screenshot of the results for an immigration attorney in one of these tools.

As with the Google Keyword Planner, there is some additional information you will get for each keyword in the list. And, as we advised with the Google Keyword Planner, just ignore them. Your main purpose is to use your head to find keyword variations for your ideal prospects.

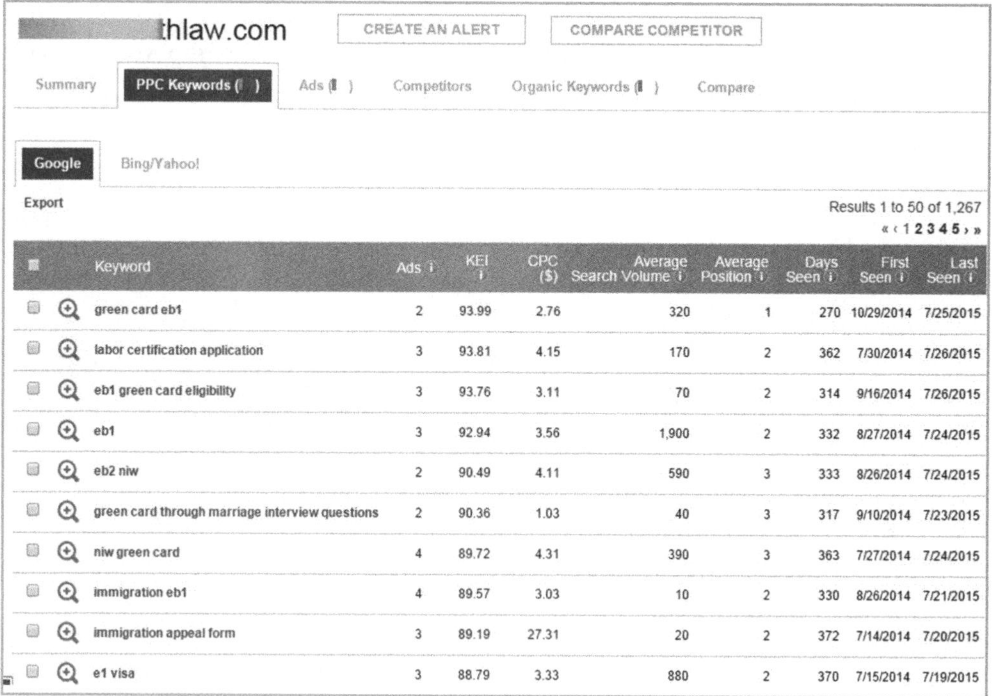

thlaw.com | CREATE AN ALERT | COMPARE COMPETITOR

Summary | PPC Keywords ( ) | Ads ( ) | Competitors | Organic Keywords ( ) | Compare

Google | Bing/Yahoo!

Export

Results 1 to 50 of 1,267

« ‹ 1 2 3 4 5 › »

Keyword	Ads	KEI	CPC ($)	Average Search Volume	Average Position	Days Seen	First Seen	Last Seen
green card eb1	2	93.99	2.76	320	1	270	10/29/2014	7/25/2015
labor certification application	3	93.81	4.15	170	2	362	7/30/2014	7/26/2015
eb1 green card eligibility	3	93.76	3.11	70	2	314	9/16/2014	7/26/2015
eb1	3	92.94	3.56	1,900	2	332	8/27/2014	7/24/2015
eb2 niw	2	90.49	4.11	590	3	333	8/26/2014	7/24/2015
green card through marriage interview questions	2	90.36	1.03	40	3	317	9/10/2014	7/23/2015
niw green card	4	89.72	4.31	390	3	363	7/27/2014	7/24/2015
immigration eb1	4	89.57	3.03	10	2	330	8/26/2014	7/21/2015
immigration appeal form	3	89.19	27.31	20	2	372	7/14/2014	7/20/2015
e1 visa	3	88.79	3.33	880	2	370	7/15/2014	7/19/2015

FIGURE 13-3. Keyword Research Tools Give You Insightful Competition Data that Shows You Which Keywords Are "Easy Money" and Which Ones Are "Difficult Money."

A few tips for using spy tools:

- Look at the search terms lists of three to five advertisers. That is pretty much all you will need to generate a comprehensive list of potential keywords to include in your campaign.
- If you download the search term lists into Excel for each advertiser, combine them into a one main Excel file, sort them alphabetically, and pay attention to the terms that show up on all (or most) of the advertisers' lists. These are likely the best, most targeted keywords in your market.
- You do not have to just search for advertisers in your city. For example, if you are a chiropractor in a smaller city, do some research on what the top chiropractors in Los Angeles, Chicago, or Houston are doing. Those big cities are much more competitive, and the AdWords advertisers really have to have their act together to be profitable, so look at their search terms lists (and, obviously, if they're bidding on the keyword "chiropractic clinic in Houston," you would change that to "chiropractic clinic in {your city name}" for your campaign).

That covers it for doing keyword research for your local business. However, before you add any keywords to your AdWords campaign, there is a vitally important concept to understand: match types. And we are going to look at them in the next chapter.

Chapter 14

Keyword Matching Options: Dodging Google's Stupidity Tax

by Talor Zamir

In his book *Swim with the Sharks without Getting Eaten Alive* (HarperBusiness, 2005), author Harvey Mackay tells the story of buying an envelope company. Shortly after plunking down the money and becoming CEO, he found himself in a devilishly difficult business where it was flat out impossible to make money.

Only after an enlightening conversation with an industry veteran did he find out that *all the profit in the envelope business comes from selling scrap paper that falls from the cutters onto the floor in manufacturing.*

Dang.

Keyword matching options are kind of like that. And picking the wrong options is worse than throwing the scrap paper away when you were supposed to sell it. Sometimes it's like burning your factory down.

Simply selecting the right keywords is not enough when it comes to AdWords. Before you add any keywords to your campaign, you will need to get familiar with the concept of keyword match types. These are very important because the match type for each keyword in your campaign determines which search queries (i.e., the actual words people type into Google) can trigger your ads.

If you do not manage the match types for your keywords the right way, your ads can show up for all sorts of search queries that are not related to what you do. So even if you did an awesome job selecting your keywords, not using the right match types will kill your campaign.

UNDERSTANDING KEYWORD MATCH TYPES

Here is an overview of the different keyword match types you can use in your AdWords account.

Broad Match

Broad match keywords are those you add to your campaign without any additional characters around them (as you will see later in this chapter, the other match types are designated by things like quotes, plus signs, and brackets). *Adding a bunch of broad match keywords to your campaigns is one of the biggest mistakes advertisers make in AdWords!*

Why?

Because when you add a keyword as a broad match keyword, your ad will appear if Google *thinks* that what someone typed is similar to your keyword. Only in very rare circumstances will we ever use broad match keywords. The reason is that broad match is *really* broad. With broad match, you are leaving things up to Google to decide which search queries are similar to the keywords in your campaign. And Google's idea of what searches are similar to your keywords may be very different from your own.

Google "Match Type Stupidity Tax"

For example, we have seen campaigns for a solar panel company that had the broad match keyword "solar panel" in their campaign. Their ads frequently appeared for searches about the solar system (and people researching the solar system was *not* the market this company was trying to reach).

When you use broad match keywords, you are giving a lot of control over your campaign to Google. That is not the position you want to be in—you *want to be in control of your campaign!*

Using broad match can result in getting a lot of bad clicks. And, remember, when you are starting out, it is very important to keep it a very targeted campaign focused on your best keywords. Otherwise, you can end up paying for a bunch of bad clicks and not get many leads because your budget is being wasted on irrelevant search terms.

To keep your campaign focused on the best searches, stick with the other match types that we are about to cover.

Exact Match

Exact match keywords are those that you add to your campaign surrounded by brackets like this:

[chiropractor]

[chiropractic]

What this tells Google is that you only want your ad to appear if someone types *exactly* and *only* what you have inside the brackets. (Note that Google will also show your ads for plurals and misspellings of your exact match keywords—exact match is not *exactly* exact match!)

Let's say one of your keywords is:

[chiropractor in Reno]

Essentially someone would have to type "chiropractor in Reno" for your ad to appear. If they typed in "chiropractor in Reno NV," your ad would not be triggered for your exact match keyword.

Exact match is great because it means you are getting very targeted clicks, and you pretty much know exactly what word(s) someone typed in to trigger your ad. We always use exact match keywords in all our campaigns and highly recommend you do the same.

Phrase Match

Phrase match keywords are surrounded by quotation marks in your campaign like this:

"chiropractor"

"chiropractic"

For phrase match keywords, your ads appear if someone types in a search term that includes the phrase that is in quotations. (Again, as with exact match, Google can show your ads for plural and misspellings of your phrase match keywords.)

Let's look at the example of the phrase match keyword:

"Reno chiropractor"

For this keyword, your ad can show up for the search terms "Reno chiropractor in Nevada" or "best Reno chiropractor" because both search terms include the same phrase—"Reno chiropractor"—that you have as your phrase match keyword. However, your ad would not show up for the search term "chiropractor in Reno" because the words "Reno chiropractor" do not appear in the same order as they do in your phrase match keyword.

Phrase match is another great match type to use, and we highly recommend you use it in all your campaigns along with exact match.

Broad Match Modifier

Broad match modifier keywords are created by putting a plus sign in front of each word like this:

+chiropractor +Reno

+chiropractic +Reno

For broad match modifiers, your ads can appear if someone types *any* variation of your keywords. Here is an example for the Broad Match Modifier keyword:

+chiropractor +Reno

With that keyword in your campaign, your ad would show for any Google search that contains *both* the word "chiropractor" and the word "Reno"—in any manner. Here are just a few of the potential search terms your ad could show up for:

- best Reno chiropractor
- chiropractor in Reno Nevada
- find a chiropractor in Reno
- chiropractors in Reno NV

Because these search terms contain both "Reno" and "chiropractor" (including plurals and misspellings of those words), they will trigger ads for the broad match modifier keyword above. For broad match modifier, it does not matter what order the words appear in the search query; they just have to be in it somewhere for ads to get triggered. However, the search term "chiropractor in Nevada" would not trigger an ad for that keyword because it does not contain the word "Reno."

We generally use a combination of exact, phrase, and broad match modifier keywords in our AdWords campaigns. However, when you are starting your campaign, you may want to stick to just exact and phrase match and see what happens after the first couple of days. Then, if you need/want more traffic, you can add broad match modifiers.

SHORTCUT FOR GENERATING KEYWORD MATCH TYPES

Instead of manually adding brackets, plus signs, and quotes to all your keywords to come up with the different match type variations for each for your keywords, you can shortcut the process.

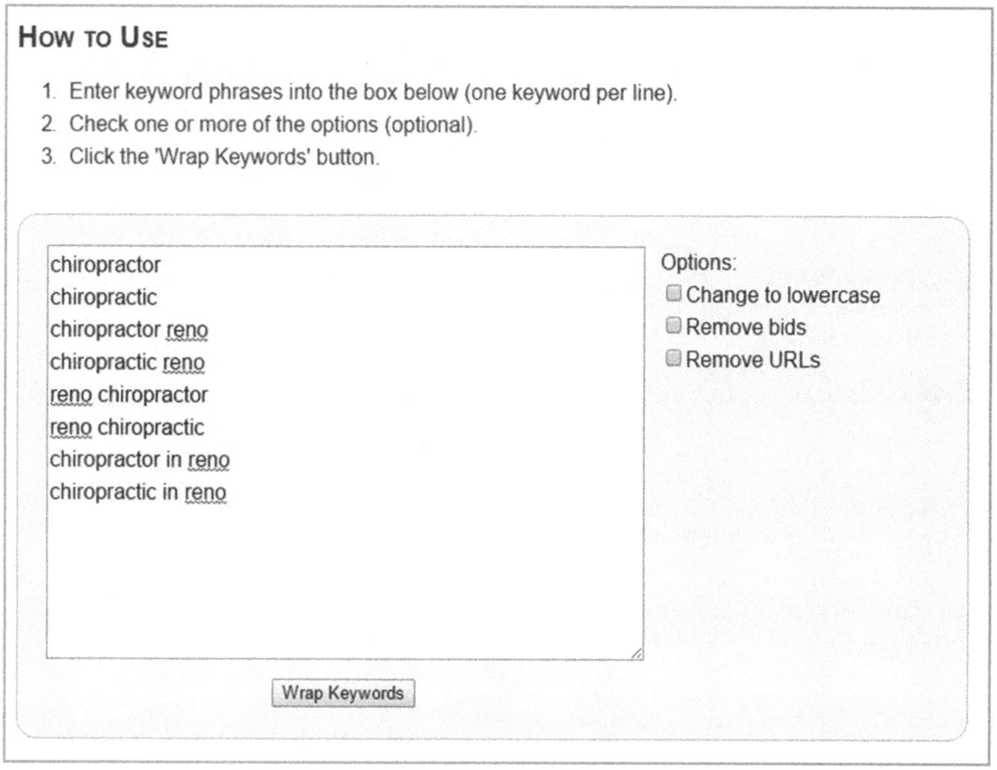

How to Use

1. Enter keyword phrases into the box below (one keyword per line).
2. Check one or more of the options (optional).
3. Click the 'Wrap Keywords' button.

chiropractor
chiropractic
chiropractor reno
chiropractic reno
reno chiropractor
reno chiropractic
chiropractor in reno
chiropractic in reno

Options:
Change to lowercase
Remove bids
Remove URLs

Wrap Keywords

FIGURE 14-1. AdWords Wrapper

We use a free tool at http://AdWordsWrapper.com to make this quick and easy. When you go to the site, you enter a list of your keywords in the main box of their "Google AdWords Keyword Tool." Then simply click the "Wrap Keywords" button, and the tool does the rest. (See Figure 14-1.)

It will generate different keywords lists with every combination of match types for your keywords. So if you only want phrase and exact match keywords, just copy the keywords in the "Phrase" & [Exact] Match results box. (See Figure 14-2 on page 78.)

Want the three match types we recommended using above? Simply copy the results from the +Modified +Broad, "Phrase" & [Exact] Match box into your campaign–and you are done!

If you have a number of keywords in your campaign, this tool will especially save you some serious time over manually setting the match types for your keywords.

NEGATIVE KEYWORDS ARE REALLY IMPORTANT!

A negative keyword tells Google that if a negative keyword or phrase in your campaign appears in the search query, you *do not* want Google to show your ads. Negative keywords

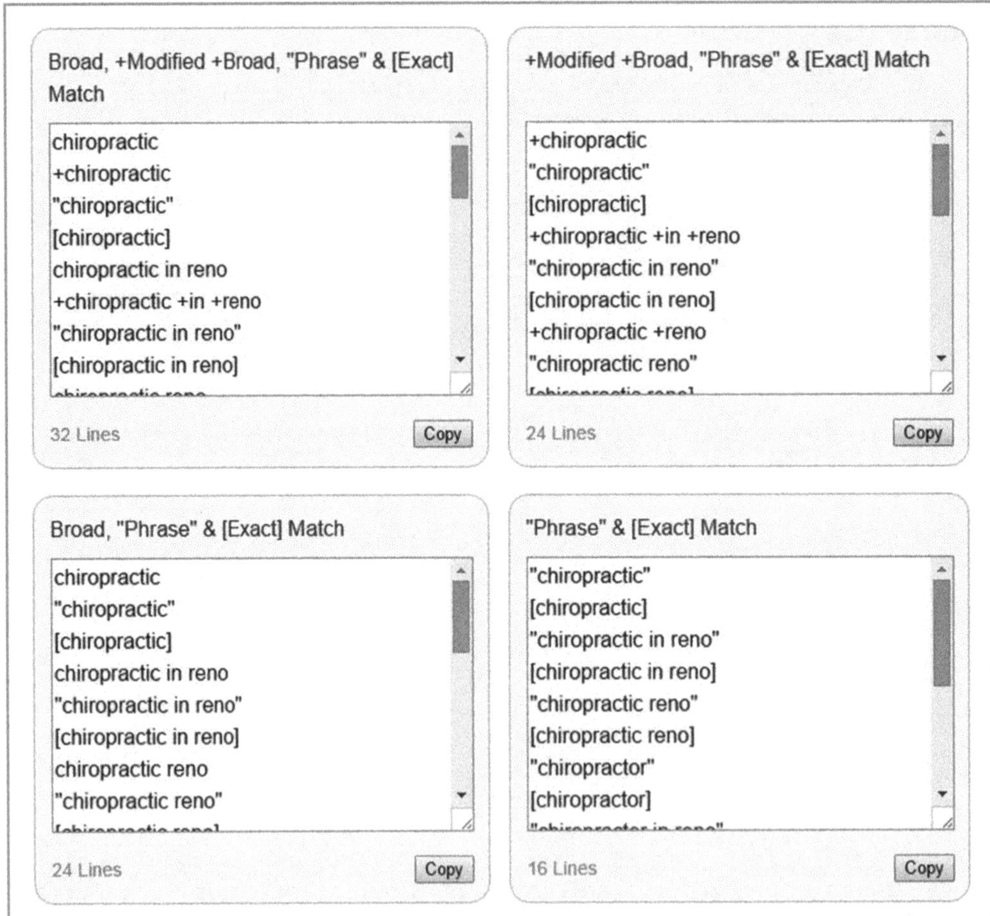

FIGURE 14–2. AdWords Wrapper Match Types You Can Use

are a big deal. Please pay close attention. Many times people bid on keywords like "roofer" and they don't realize that their ad is showing for "roofer jobs" which drives down click-thru rates and drives up cost.

For example, if you add the word "free" as a negative keyword to your campaign, any time a searcher includes that word in their search query, your ads will *not* show. So while you may have the word "Atlanta chiropractic" in your campaign, if someone typed in "free Atlanta chiropractic clinic," your ad will *not* appear since you have "free" as a negative keyword.

If all you are using is exact match keywords in your campaign, negative keywords are not important. However, as soon as you start expanding to phrase and broad match modifiers, you will want to make sure you have negative keywords in your campaign.

Some of the common negative keywords to add to a campaign for a local business include free, job, salary, career, photo, picture, game, how to. (Be sure to add both *singular* and *plural* versions of all your negative keywords!)

To add negative keywords, go the Keywords tab in your campaign and scroll to the bottom of all your "regular" keywords. There you will find the link to the section where you can add your negative keywords. (See Figure 14-3.)

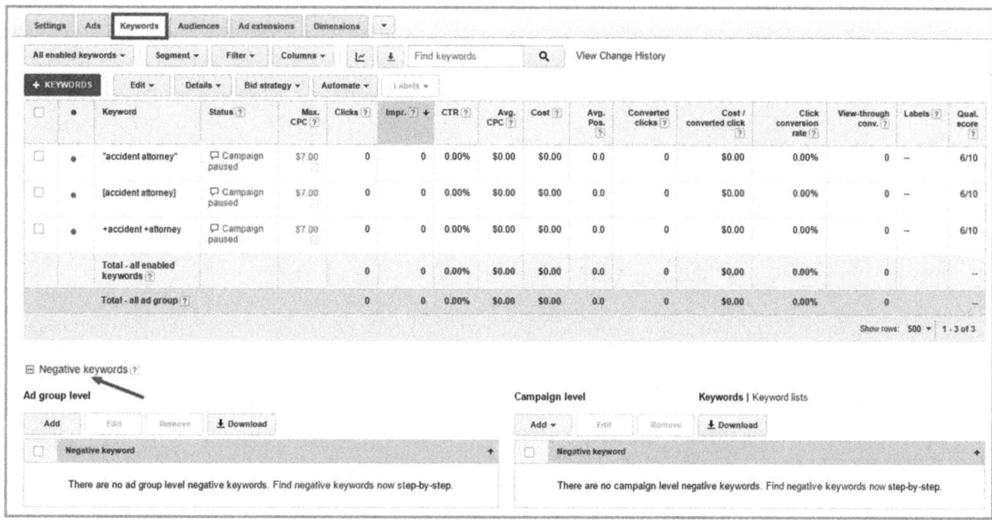

FIGURE 14-3. Negative Keywords Tab

You can add negative keywords either at the ad group level or the campaign level. Typically, you are going to be only adding negative keywords at a campaign level, so we will stick with that in this example. You add campaign negative keywords on the right side of the screen, so under "Campaign level," click on the "Add" and select "Add keywords." (See Figure 14-4.)

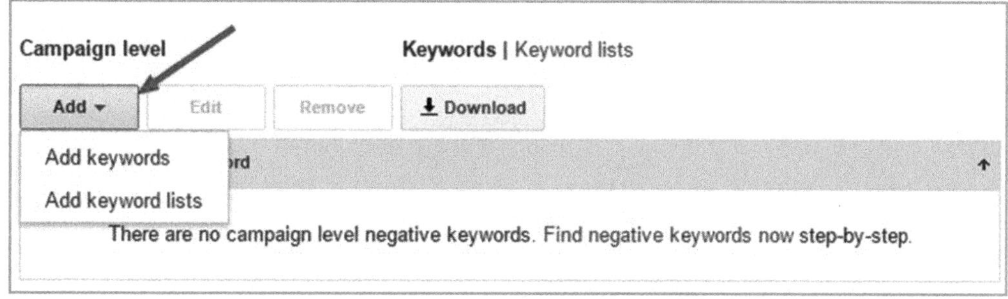

FIGURE 14-4. Adding Negative Keywords

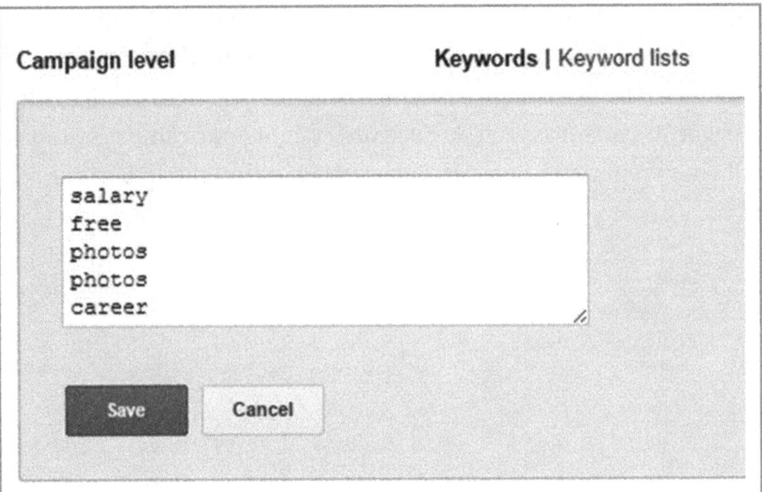

FIGURE 14–5. Negative Keywords List

Next, enter your keywords into the box and click "Save." (See Figure 14-5.) And that is all there is to it.

Now that you have all your keywords picked out and have assigned them the match types you want, it is time to get them organized. Organizing your keywords is one of the keys to success in your campaign and is the topic we cover in the next chapter.

Chapter 15

Breaking Out Your Keywords into Ad Groups

by Talor Zamir

The following scenario is one of the most common (and fatal) AdWords mistakes, and almost all beginners make it.

You own a sporting goods store. Your store carries all types of sports equipment, including golf balls, tennis rackets, baseball gloves, and lacrosse sticks. If you start an AdWords campaign for your store and someone types "golf balls" into Google, would you want them to see an ad that mentions tennis rackets, baseball gloves, or lacrosse sticks? Of course not!

In fact, you really don't even want them to see a generic ad about how great your store is. What you do want them to see is an ad that specifically mentions golf balls. Taking this even further, ideally, if they type in "Titleist golf balls," they should see an ad that announces "Titleist golf balls," and when they click on that ad, it should go to the page on your site that shows your selection of Titleist golf balls. Here's why.

THE PSYCHOLOGY OF SEARCH

As you are building your AdWords campaign, keep in mind there is a psychology involved with people searching online.

The search process starts with a need, desire, or quest for information that pops into the searcher's head. That represents the most important thing in the world to the searcher at that moment in time. This need, desire, or quest for information leads them to type a particular search query into Google.

Now here is the really important part: *The more closely the words and messaging in your AdWords ad mirrors what is going on in the searcher's head, the more likely they are to click on it.*

To take it a step further, the more closely the words and messaging on your landing page matches the words and messaging in your ad, the more likely you are to get the conversion.

Because of this, the concept of *segmentation* of your AdWords campaign is critically important to your success.

People are lazy. If they've just searched for Titleist golf balls and they land on your home page where they do *not* see anything resembling a golf ball, they will not hunt all over your site seeking for what they want. They'll just click the "back" button and jump onto someone else's site. You need to do the work for them!

In AdWords, segmentation is where you group closely related keywords and ads together so you can show searchers the most relevant ads when they search. You control this in AdWords by using ad groups. Ad groups are how you ensure that the searcher looking for "golf balls" on Google sees an ad for your store that specifically mentions golf balls in the ad copy.

STRUCTURING YOUR ADWORDS ACCOUNT FOR SUCCESS

At the highest level of your AdWords account, you have your campaigns. Campaigns share common budgets, settings, etc. What you do not want to do in AdWords is dump all your keywords into a campaign, write one or two ads, and let things run. Instead, you want to create multiple ad groups within your campaign. Ad groups are closely knit groups of keywords that share their own set of ads.

Here is an example using a campaign for a personal injury attorney in Reno so you can see how this works. For this fictitious campaign, we are going to break keywords up into four different ad groups.

The first is an "accident attorney" ad group, and it has the obvious keywords you would expect someone searching for an accident attorney to type into Google. These would include keywords like:

- accident attorney
- accident attorneys in Reno
- auto accident attorney Reno
- Reno car accident attorney

In this ad group, you would have at least the exact and phrase match version of each keyword and maybe modified broad match as well (this applies to all four ad groups).

We will name this ad group "Accident Attorney" when we create it in AdWords (so we can easily tell what types of keywords are in the ad group) and add all our "accident attorney" related keywords to it. Because the keywords are variations of "accident attorney," we recommend using the term "accident attorney" in your ads along with the city name, ideally in the headline.

Here's an example ad you could use for this ad group:

> **Reno Accident Attorney**
> {INSERT BIGGEST BENEFIT}
> Free Consult 24/7 * Call Now!
> awesomerenoattorney.com

We will get into what it takes to write great ads in Chapter 18, but for now, just understand the concept that you want your ad copy for each ad group to be highly related to the keywords in the ad group.

The second ad group for our fictitious personal injury attorney is for "accident lawyer" keywords, so we will create a new ad group named "Accident Lawyer" and have keywords like:

- accident lawyer
- accident lawyer in Reno
- auto accident lawyer Reno
- Reno car accident lawyer

Because we want things to be as congruent as possible between the keywords and ads, we will change the headline of the ad to specifically use the term "accident lawyer" like this:

> **Reno Accident Lawyer**
> {INSERT BIGGEST BENEFIT}
> Free Consult 24/7 * Call Now!
> awesomerenoattorney.com

The third ad group we create will be named "Injury Attorney" and will contain keywords like:

- injury attorney
- personal injury attorney
- personal injury attorney in Reno
- Reno injury attorney

And the ad will be:

Reno Injury Attorney
{INSERT BIGGEST BENEFIT}
Free Consult 24/7 * Call Now!
awesomerenoattorney.com

The fourth ad group we create will be named "Injury Lawyer" and will contain keywords like:

- injury lawyer
- personal injury lawyer
- personal injury lawyer in Reno
- Reno injury lawyer

And the ad will be:

Reno Injury Lawyer
{INSERT BIGGEST BENEFIT}
Free Consult 24/7 * Call Now!
awesomerenoattorney.com

Why create separate ad groups for attorney and lawyer keywords? It goes back to what we mentioned before about having your ad messaging match the search term your prospect types into Google as closely as possible. If someone is searching for an attorney, show them an ad that says "attorney" in it. If they are searching for a lawyer, show them an ad that says "lawyer" in it.

> Again, the *more* congruency between your keywords and your ad copy, the *more* likely you are to get the click and, ultimately, the lead.

In the next chapter, we are going to walk you through the process of setting up your campaign. Before you do that, however, we recommend creating a document (using a text editor or Microsoft Word is easiest) where you have all your keywords—match types variations of each keyword included—for your campaign listed and broken out into ad groups. This will come in handy as you build your campaign, which is what you are about to do next.

Chapter 16

Build Your Google AdWords Campaign from Scratch

by Talor Zamir

All the details that go into an AdWords campaign may seem daunting. But once you've gone through the process, you'll probably agree that few things took so little time to set up yet made such a profound difference to your flow of customers, your sales volume, and your bottom line at the end of every month.

It's time to set up your AdWords campaign. (Make sure your landing page is online first.)

If you do not have an AdWords account yet, that is going to be your first step. Head over to www.google.com/adwords and follow the instructions on setting up an account.

(Google changes this process frequently, so we are not going to take you step-by-step through account setup. However, at the time of writing this, Google makes you set up your first AdWords campaign as part of the process. We would rather you follow our instructions below for setting up your new campaign because we find it is easier to pick the right settings, enter keywords, and ads the way we have it outlined below. So, if Google still makes you set up a campaign when creating your account, just breeze through it for now and set a budget for this campaign, which you won't be using, at $1. Then as soon as you finish setting up your account pause *the campaign and create a new one following our process below.)*

WARNING: *DO NOT* USE ADWORDS EXPRESS!

During the setup process, Google may recommend that you set up an AdWords Express account because you are promoting a local business. *Do not* use AdWords Express. This is *not* the same thing as the kind of Google AdWords campaign we have been talking about here.

Basically AdWords Express is a stripped-down version of AdWords that Google created to make setting up an AdWords campaign as easy as picking a budget and writing an ad. That may sound appealing, but with the information we are sharing with you in this book, you will be much better served by following our formula to set up a Google AdWords campaign the *right* way.

AdWords Express takes most of the control out of your hands and gives it to Google. This is like putting a German shepherd in charge of the ham sandwiches. With AdWords Express, you do not get to choose your keywords, match types, how much you pay per click, etc. All that is 100 percent up to Google! And when you give that much control over your campaign to Google, you are just asking for trouble.

You want to be in control of your campaigns and make sure you are bidding on the keywords that make the most sense for your business, paying what you want to pay per click, etc.

So if Google gives you the option of signing up for AdWords Express, no matter how nicely they may ask or how appealing they may make it sound, *do not sign up for it!*

Got it? Good!

CHOOSING THE RIGHT CAMPAIGN SETTINGS

Let's dig in and set up your first campaign—the right way! For this example, we are going to set up a campaign for our fictitious personal injury (PI) attorney in Reno that we started creating ad groups for in the last chapter. While the example is for a PI attorney, the steps, settings, and strategies are identical for any local business. So if you are not a PI attorney, just plug in your own keywords and ads while following along, and you will be good to go!

Campaign Type

In your AdWords account, go to the "Campaigns" tab, and click on the big red button to add a new campaign (see Figure 16-1 on page 87).

Once you click on that button, you will have a few options about what kind of campaign you want to set up. The option you want to select is "Search Network Only" (see Figure 16-2 on page 87).

FIGURE 16-1. You Create a Campaign by Going to the "Campaigns" Tab and Hitting the Create Button

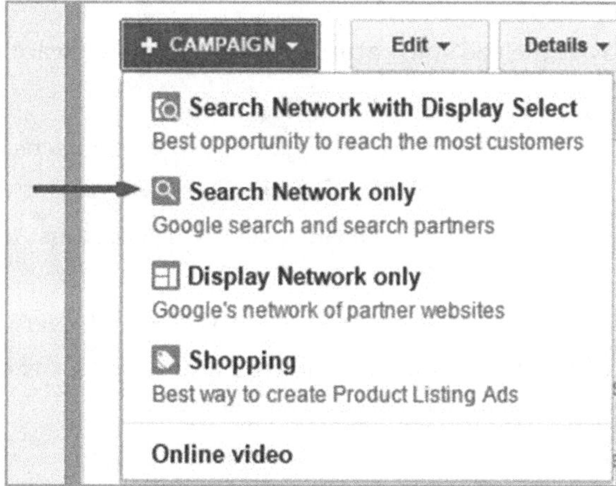

FIGURE 16-2. You Want "Search Network Only" When You Create a Search Campaign

Google does indicate the "Search Network with Display Select" is the "Best opportunity to reach the most customers." But your goal is not to reach the *most* customers (especially when starting out). Your goal is to reach the *best*, most targeted customers.

In addition, the Display Network is a very different beast than Search Network and should be handled very differently. If we decide to use the Display Network for a local business (which is very rare), then we will set up a new Display Network-only campaign so that we keep our Search Network traffic and Display Network traffic separate. The keywords, ads, etc., you use in Search Network campaigns are very different from the ones you use in a Display Network campaign, so you do not want to combine them.

The Display Network is very difficult for a local business to get good results from, so we recommend you do not use it and stick to the Search Network. Search is going to bring you the most high-quality traffic to your site.

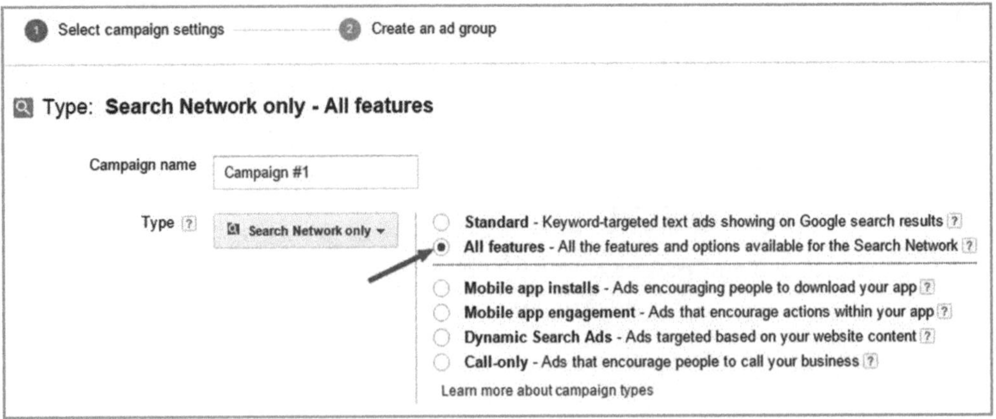

FIGURE 16-3. You Need All Features Available on the Search Network

Once you choose "Search Network only," you'll end up on a screen where you choose a number of your campaign settings. The first thing you will want to do is select the "All features "option so you have access to all the features and options AdWords has to offer (see Figure 16-3).

For a local business, you *always* want to choose "Search Network only" and "All features" so you have a Search campaign running and have all the options available to take full control over your campaign.

Campaign Name

Next, it is time give your campaign a name in the "Campaign name" box. We recommend giving your campaign a descriptive name so if you set up other campaigns down the road, you can easily tell which campaign is which just by looking at the name.

For this example, we will give the campaign the name "PI Attorney—Search" so we know it is a Search network campaign promoting our personal injury law firm.

Networks

The next option you have is to choose the Networks your ads will run on. The default (which has to be checked) is the Google Search Network. This makes sure your ads run on Google (which is kind of the point here, so you definitely want that option!).

The other option, which is checked by default, is "Include search partners." We usually leave this checked as well (as in Figure 16-4 on page 89).

What this means is that Google will show your ads on other search engines like AOL and Ask.com that do not have their own PPC programs, so they partner with Google to display AdWords ads on their sites.

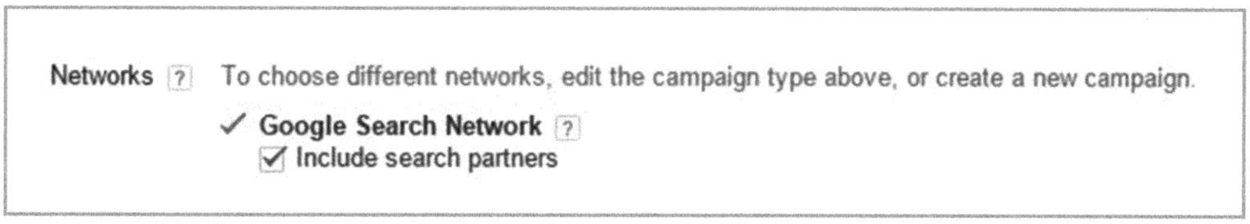

Networks ? To choose different networks, edit the campaign type above, or create a new campaign.
✓ Google Search Network ?
☑ Include search partners

FIGURE 16–4. Go Ahead and Include Search Partners When You Select the Search Network

Devices

For a Search campaign, there is nothing to set here so just skip this one for now.

Locations

This is where you choose the geographic area you want your ads to be displayed in. Google defaults the location for your new campaign to "United States and Canada," which for a local business, is probably not the option you want.

There are a few different ways you can set this up. All of them, however, start with you selecting the "Let me choose . . ." option (as in Figure 16–5).

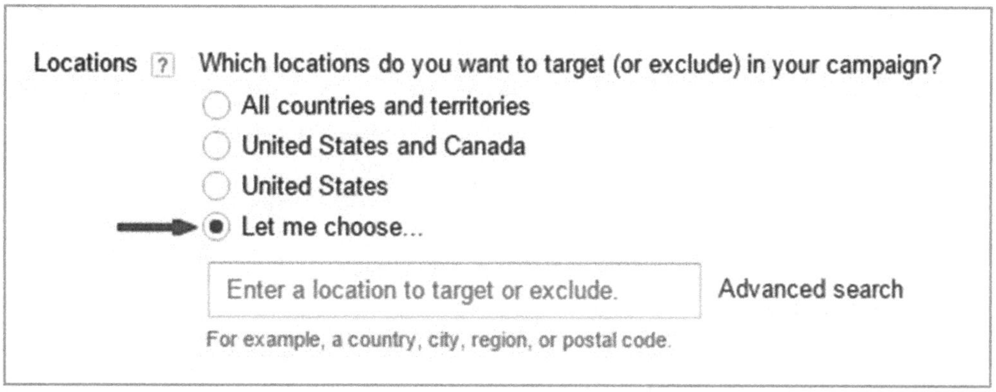

Locations ? Which locations do you want to target (or exclude) in your campaign?
○ All countries and territories
○ United States and Canada
○ United States
● Let me choose...
Enter a location to target or exclude. Advanced search
For example, a country, city, region, or postal code.

FIGURE 16–5. You Will Want to Specifically Choose the Geographies You Advertise In

You can enter a city in the box below "Let me choose . . ." So, for example, if you enter "Reno" into the box, you will see the city of "Reno, Nevada, United States" as the top option. However, if you look down the list (as shown in Figure 16–6 on page 90), you'll see another option: "Reno NV, United States." This is the Nielson MDA region for the Reno area. This option includes the city of Reno as well as all the surrounding towns that make up the Reno media market. If you select the former option, your ads will reach an estimated audience of about 297,000 people. Target the entire DMA settings from ?

Networks ?

Devices ?

Locations ?

Matches	Reach ?	
Reno, Nevada, United States - city	297,000	Add | Exclude | Nearby
Renovo, Pennsylvania, United States - city	1,000	Add | Exclude | Nearby
Reno County, Kansas, United States - county	51,000	Add | Exclude | Nearby
Reno, Ohio, United States - city	5,000	Add | Exclude | Nearby
Reno, Pennsylvania, United States - neighborhood	4,000	Add | Exclude | Nearby
Locations that enclose: Reno, Nevada, United States		
Washoe County, Nevada, United States - county	338,000	Add | Exclude | Nearby
NV-2, Nevada, United States - congressional district	477,000	Add | Exclude | Nearby
Reno NV, United States - Nielsen® DMA® region	535,000	Add | Exclude | Nearby
Nevada, United States - state	6,950,000	Add | Exclude | Nearby
United States - country	185,000,000	Add | Exclude | Nearby
Related locations		
89502, Nevada, United States - postal code	155,000	Add | Exclude | Nearby
Paris, Texas, United States - city	39,000	Add | Exclude | Nearby
Parker County, Texas, United States - county	188,000	Add | Exclude | Nearby
96109, California, United States - postal code	11,000	Add | Exclude | Nearby

reno   Advanced search

For example, a country, city, region, or postal code.

FIGURE 16-6. Google Gives You a List of Possible Matches When You Type in a City Name

region, however, and you will have a much greater reach, with an estimated audience of about 535,000.

To add one of these target areas to your campaign, just click the "Add" link next to the option, and it will be added to your campaign. Which one you select depends on your business. If you are an attorney who works with people all over the Reno metro area, then the larger DMA region is a a good choice here. However, if you are a dentist in the city of Reno itself and patients usually don't travel far to come to your office, then just targeting the city of Reno is a good choice.

There are a couple of other options for geographic targeting that we recommend for local business owners when starting your campaign. One option is to target specific zip codes or towns in your area where your ideal prospects are likely to live and/or work. To do this, enter the name of the town or zip code into the box below "Let me choose . . ." and add one (or a few) to your campaign.

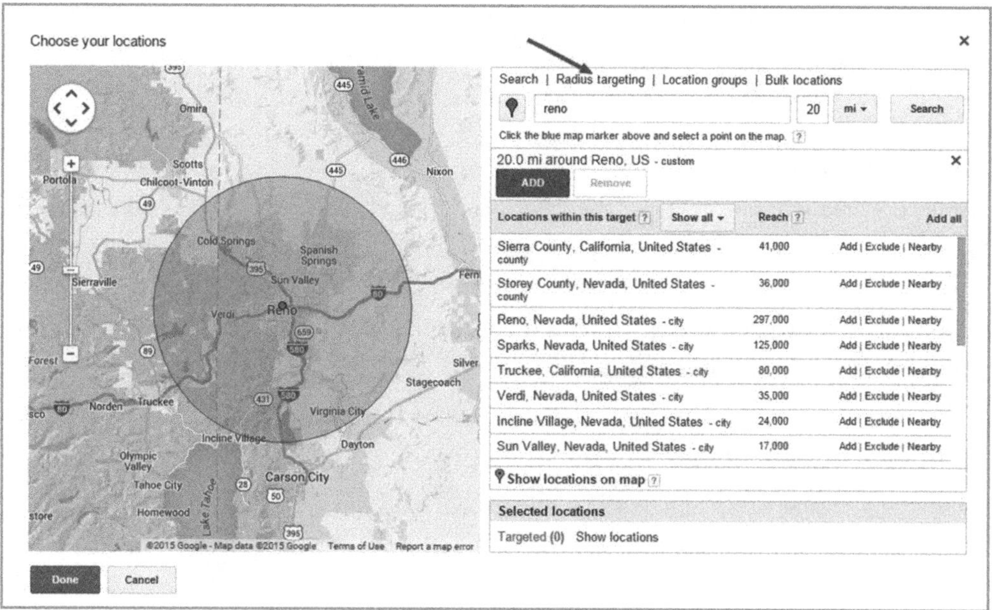

FIGURE 16-7. Radius Targeting Lets You Advertise to Everyone within a Certain Distance of a Specific Address or Postal Code

The other option is to target a 10- to 20-mile radius around your business's location (you can choose what size radius you want to target—it does not have to be 10 to 20 miles). To do this, click on the "Advanced search" link next to the "Let me choose . . ." box.

On the Advanced screen that pops up, click on the "Radius targeting" link as shown in Figure 16-7.

In this screen, you can type a city name or, even better, type in your specific business address in the box at top and then select the radius you want to target. The map will then show you where your ads will appear. In the example above, I used the city of Reno and want my ads to appear in a 20-mile radius around it. Once you define your radius, click the red "Add" button to add the targeting to your campaign.

We like targeting a 20-mile radius around a local business's location. As our recommendation has been with other parts of your AdWords campaign, like keywords, the reason is because the best strategy is to start *small* and very *targeted*. (Keep in mind if you are in a heavily populated area like New York City, you may only want to target a five- or ten-mile radius.)

Especially if you have a business where clients come to you, it is better to stick closer to your physical office location when targeting. Most clients are not going to drive 50 miles to come see you. The people who live and work closest to you are generally more likely to do business with you.

Again, start narrow and focused; you can always expand the targeting area once your campaign is up and running. Once you select your geo-targeting settings, click "Done" and it will take you back to the main Settings page.

Advanced Location Settings

Under the area where you chose the locations your ads will run, there is an option for "Location options (advanced)." Starting out, we recommend you select the second option under "Target," which is "People in my targeted location." (See Figure 16-8.) This tells Google that you only want your ads to be displayed to people in the geographic area you selected in the previous step.

Location options (advanced)

Target ? ○ People in, searching for, or who show interest in my targeted location (recommended) ?
● People in my targeted location ?
○ People searching for, or who show interest in my targeted location ?

Exclude ? ● People in, searching for, or who show interest in my excluded location (recommended) ?
○ People in my excluded location ?

FIGURE 16-8. The Location Options Menu Lets You Choose Whether to Target Just People Who Live Near You, or Also People Far Away Who Are Interested in Your Area (e.g. a person in Las Vegas searching for a jewelry store in Reno)

The default option is "People in, searching for, or viewing pages about my targeted location (recommended)." The way this works is if you are a personal injury attorney in Reno and someone in Miami types "injury attorney Reno" into Google, they could potentially see your ad. Your ad could also be shown to that person in Miami if they had been researching a trip to Reno. Because they showed "interest" in Reno, Google can show your ad to them, even though they are not in Reno and did not specifically search for an injury attorney in Reno. The safer option is to change this setting to "People in my targeted location." (Is someone in Miami searching for a personal injury attorney in Reno really an ideal prospect for your business? Maybe . . . or maybe not. Are you likely to get visitors from out of town?)

If you get good results with your campaign and want to expand, you can always change this setting back to the default option. But, again, because we want to be as highly focused and targeted as possible to start, we recommend selecting "People in my targeted location" because they are the ones most likely to become your clients.

For the "Exclude" option for advanced location options, leave Google's recommended choice as the default.

Languages

We usually do not mess with this. For most of you, stick with the default setting, which is English.

Shopping Channels

These do not apply to local businesses, so you can ignore this setting.

Bid Strategy

For the "Bid options," under "Basic strategy," select "I'll manually set my bids for clicks" (Google defaults to the option of having *them* set your bids for you!), as shown in Figure 16–9 on page 94.

The default bid is the maximum amount you are willing to pay for your keywords. We are going to cover bidding strategies more in depth in the next chapter, so, for now, just enter any number here.

The budget is where you set how much you are willing to spend on clicks each day. The amount you enter here is largely up to you. Here are a few things to keep in mind, though:

We are doing this because you want to be in control of what you bid for your keywords, not Google!

- The budget you set here is a *daily* budget. So if you are willing to spend $3,000 per month on AdWords, divide $3,000 by 30 to get a daily budget of $100.
- You will never spend more than your daily budget over a 30-day period. However, on any given day, the actual amount you spend may be more than your daily budget. If this happens, do not worry. On other days, you will spend less than your daily budget, so everything evens out.
- Setting your budget too low may work against you because your ads will only appear a small percentage of the time people type your keywords into Google. This also means that it will take longer to get meaningful data and decide if your campaign is successful or not.
- This is a starting point. You can always adjust your bids higher or lower any time.

A lot of people ask us how much they should budget for their AdWords campaign. There is no easy answer to that question. Part of it, at least initially, is to start with a number that will let you sleep at night. The other part of it is we are teaching you how to start a very tight, focused campaign so we recommend you budget enough to get as many of those targeted clicks as possible.

Under the "Delivery method (advanced)" setting, we recommend you switch this to "Accelerated," which means Google will show ads more quickly until your budget is reached. You do not want to miss out on potential clicks if you get a lot of action earlier in the day and then Google puts the brakes on things to spread your remaining budget out over the remainder of the day.

We are also going to set an ad schedule that will determine the times your ads run (we will cover that soon). With an ad schedule in place, we recommend your ads run using the Accelerated delivery method.

With all that said, Figure 16-9 is what this section for bidding should look like, though your numbers may be different.

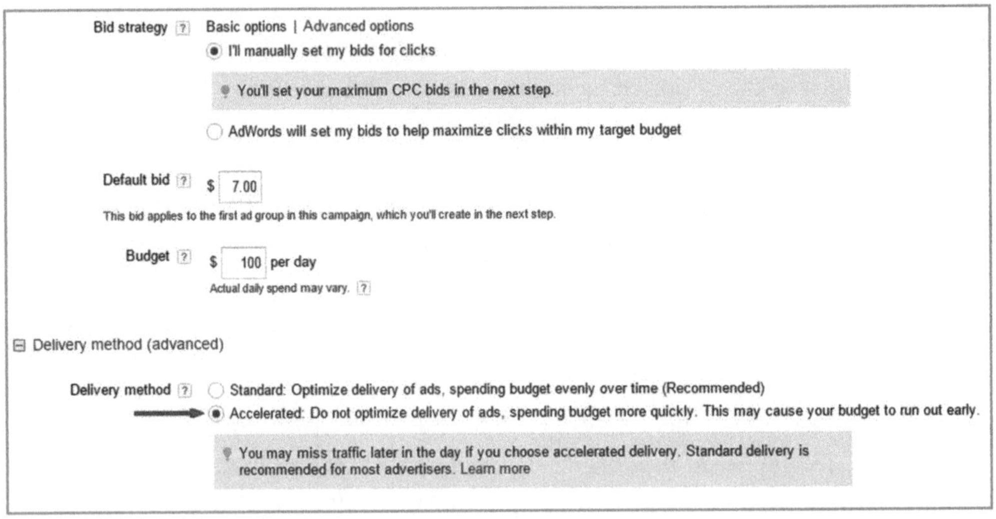

Bid strategy ? Basic options | Advanced options
I'll manually set my bids for clicks
You'll set your maximum CPC bids in the next step.
AdWords will set my bids to help maximize clicks within my target budget
Default bid ? $ 7.00
This bid applies to the first ad group in this campaign, which you'll create in the next step.
Budget ? $ 100 per day
Actual daily spend may vary. ?
Delivery method (advanced)
Delivery method ? Standard: Optimize delivery of ads, spending budget evenly over time (Recommended)
Accelerated: Do not optimize delivery of ads, spending budget more quickly. This may cause your budget to run out early.
You may miss traffic later in the day if you choose accelerated delivery. Standard delivery is recommended for most advertisers. Learn more

FIGURE 16-9. In the Bid Strategy Menu, Choose to Set Your Own Bid Price for Clicks!

Ad Extensions

Ad extensions are very important to have in your AdWords account. In fact, they are so important that we are giving them their own chapter! For now, just skip over the ad extensions, and we will give them the full attention they deserve in Chapter 19.

ADVANCED SETTINGS

There are a couple of things to pay attention to in the Advanced Settings section: ad scheduling and ad rotation.

Ad Scheduling

As we have mentioned before, a high percentage of the leads from local AdWords campaigns come via phone calls. When those calls come in, you want someone there to answer the calls and be available to talk with the prospect immediately. **Having a competent live person answer your phone is *critical.*** You never want to spend money on ads if when people call, they go to voicemail. Your prospects will probably just hang up and call the next ad (your competitor), and your ad money will have been wasted. So we recommend you only run ads when there will be someone to answer the calls or if you have a 24-hour answering service that is trained in handling the calls and taking down all the potential client's information.

The way you can control the days and times your ads run is by using ad scheduling, which is listed under the "Schedule: Start date, end date, ad scheduling" option in the advanced settings. All you do is select the days and times someone is around to answer the phone. This will make sure those are the only times your ads run. So for example, if your office is open Monday through Friday, from 8 A.M. to 6 P.M., you set things up like you see in Figure 16-10, making sure to check the X next to Saturday and Sunday to remove those days from the schedule.

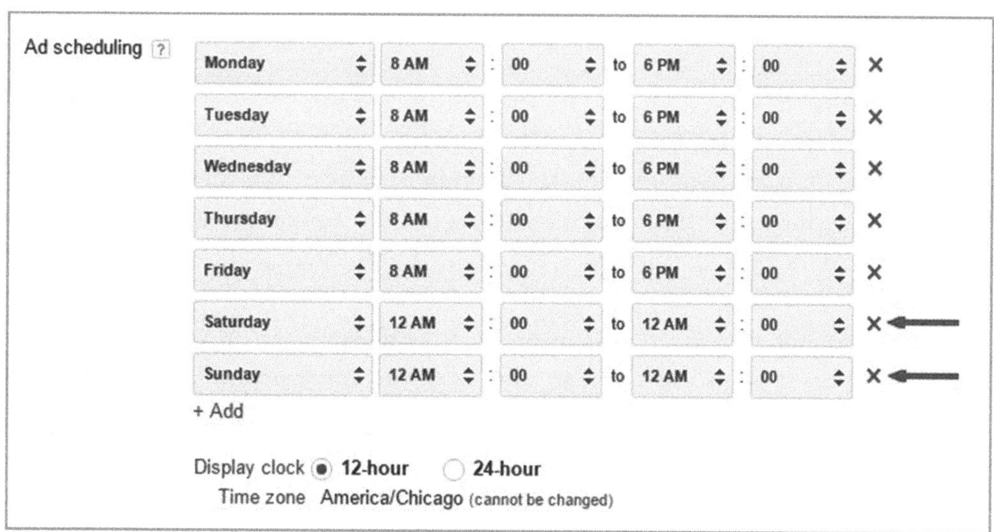

FIGURE 16-10. The Ad Scheduling Menu Lets You Advertise Only When Your Phone Is Being Answered

You can get even more advanced than this if you want. If your secretary takes an hour lunch break from noon to 1 P.M., you can set a schedule where you ads run from 8 A.M. to noon and then from 1 P.M. to 6 P.M.

Ad Rotation

Every ad group in your campaign is going to have at least two ads in it (we will discuss ads more in an upcoming chapter). How Google handles the rotation of

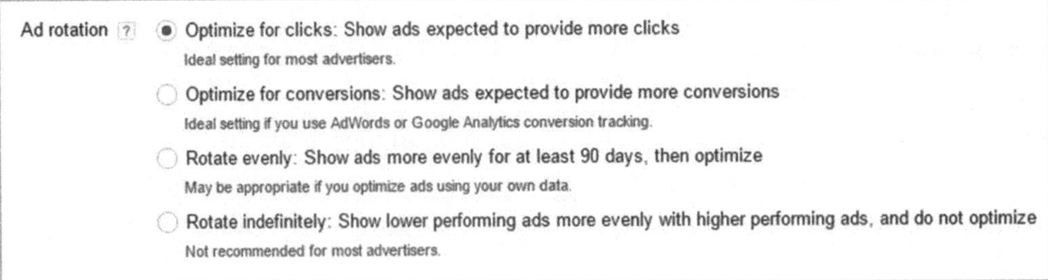

FIGURE 16–11. The Ad Rotation Menu Lets You Choose What to Optimize For. When First Setting Up a Local Ad Campaign, You Should Choose "Optimize for Clicks."

those ads (i.e., which ads get shown to searchers more often) is controlled in the Ad rotation section.

There are four options (as shown in Figure 16–11) and differing opinions about which is the best one to use. We will lay them all out, and you can decide which one is best for you.

Optimize for Clicks

This is the option we most frequently recommend to new advertisers. This option tells Google that you want them to favor the ad(s) in each ad group that their algorithm determines is going to get the most clicks. (Google will still show the other ads in the ad group some of the time, but the one it expects to get the highest clickthrough rate will get shown most of the time.)

If you do not plan on checking on your campaign regularly, this is the best option. This way, Google will automatically show your best performing ad much more frequently than your lower performing ads, which will lead to better results.

Optimize for Conversions

This option is only applicable if you are doing the call conversion tracking we recommend, in addition to tracking web form leads on your landing page.

As the name implies, this option tells Google to show the ad expected to get the most conversions more frequently than the others. This is a good option if your campaign is getting a lot of conversions each month (if there is not enough conversion data for Google to determine which ad is likely to get the most conversions, then it will just default back to optimizing for clicks).

Rotate Evenly

A lot of people recommend you choose this option for your ad rotation. This means if you have two ads in an ad group, each one will be displayed approximately 50 percent of the time.

If you are going to closely monitor your campaign and conduct frequent split-testing of your ads (more on split-testing in Chapter 20), then this is a great option. But you really need to keep a close eye on things.

The danger here is you may let underperforming ads keep running longer than they deserve, and they will steal impressions from your winning ad, which will hurt the results of your campaign.

Rotate Indefinitely

The previous option will rotate your ads evenly for 90 days and then automatically go back to optimizing for clicks.

This option to "rotate indefinitely" will rotate your ads evenly—forever! If you have a campaign with low-traffic volume, 90 days may not be adequate to get enough data for split-testing purposes. In that situation, the rotate indefinitely option can be used. However, there is no safety net here, so you must stay on top of things, or the long-term results of your campaign will suffer!

That covers it for your initial campaign settings. At the bottom of the Settings page, click the "save and continue" button, and you'll be taken to the next step of your campaign: placing ads and keywords into ad groups.

CREATING YOUR AD GROUPS

In Chapter 15, we broke the keywords for our imaginary personal injury attorney into four groups of highly related keywords and wrote one ad for each. Now we are going to take those groups of keywords and ads and turn them into four ad groups in our campaign.

If you took our advice and created a text document with your words and ads in them already, then setting up your ad groups in AdWords will just be a matter of copying and pasting everything into the right spot.

The first group of keywords are those related to "Accident Attorney," which is what we will name the group. (As with campaign names, you want to give your ad groups meaningful names so you know, just by looking at the name, what kinds of keywords are in the ad group. We recommend avoiding generic names like "Ad Group #1" and "Ad Group #2." Instead, call it "Injury Lawyer Ad Group" and "Accident Attorney Ad Group.")

Next, Google wants us to enter some ad copy. We are going to cover the components of winning ad copy in Chapter 18. For now, we are just going to set up one ad using the ad copy we used in the previous chapter which ends up looking like Figure 16–12 on page 98.

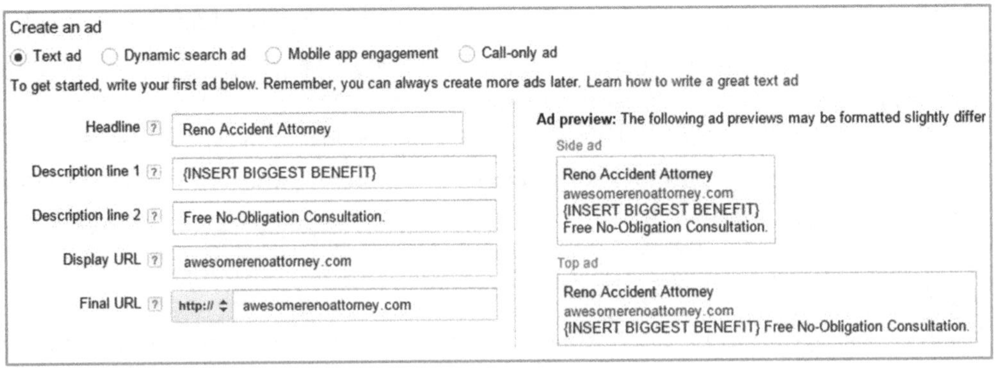

Create an ad

(•) Text ad ( ) Dynamic search ad ( ) Mobile app engagement ( ) Call-only ad

To get started, write your first ad below. Remember, you can always create more ads later. Learn how to write a great text ad

Headline: Reno Accident Attorney

Description line 1: {INSERT BIGGEST BENEFIT}

Description line 2: Free No-Obligation Consultation.

Display URL: awesomerenoattorney.com

Final URL: http:// awesomerenoattorney.com

Ad preview: The following ad previews may be formatted slightly differ

Side ad

Reno Accident Attorney
awesomerenoattorney.com
{INSERT BIGGEST BENEFIT}
Free No-Obligation Consultation.

Top ad

Reno Accident Attorney
awesomerenoattorney.com
{INSERT BIGGEST BENEFIT} Free No-Obligation Consultation.

FIGURE 16–12. When You Create an Ad, You Can Choose Among Several Ad Types

Scroll down the page a little, and there will be a box where you can enter all the keywords you want in this ad group. Simply copy the list from the Accident Attorney group in your text document and paste it into this box (make sure you include the appropriate symbols around all your keywords to set the match types for each), like we've done in Figure 16–13.

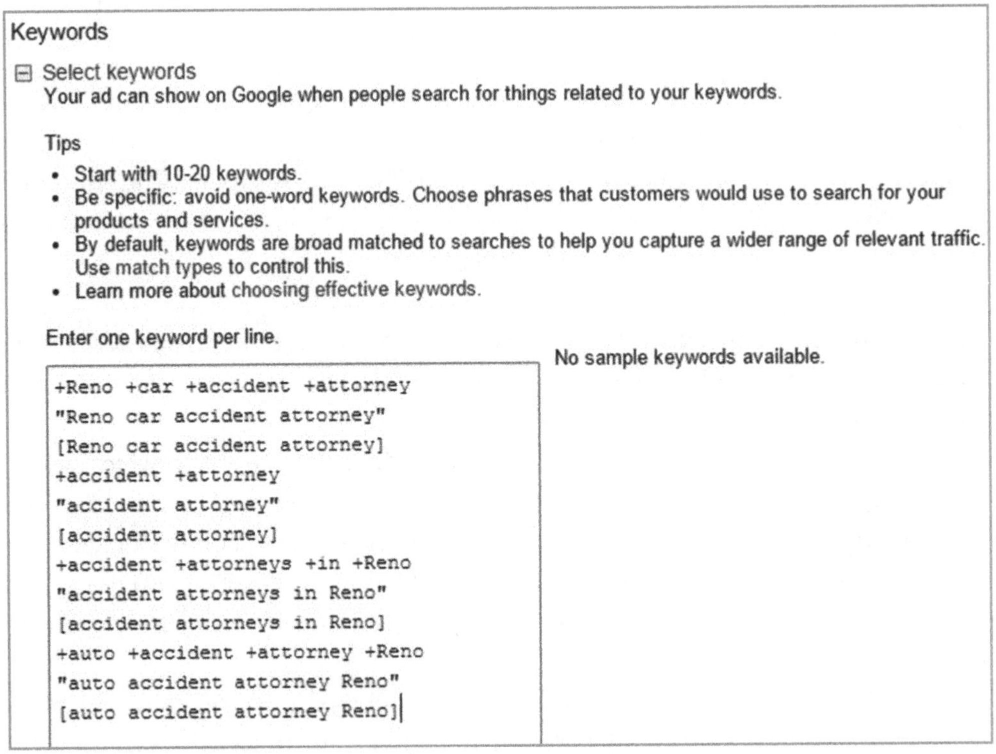

Keywords

Select keywords

Your ad can show on Google when people search for things related to your keywords.

Tips

- Start with 10-20 keywords.
- Be specific: avoid one-word keywords. Choose phrases that customers would use to search for your products and services.
- By default, keywords are broad matched to searches to help you capture a wider range of relevant traffic. Use match types to control this.
- Learn more about choosing effective keywords.

Enter one keyword per line.

No sample keywords available.

```
+Reno +car +accident +attorney
"Reno car accident attorney"
[Reno car accident attorney]
+accident +attorney
"accident attorney"
[accident attorney]
+accident +attorneys +in +Reno
"accident attorneys in Reno"
[accident attorneys in Reno]
+auto +accident +attorney +Reno
"auto accident attorney Reno"
[auto accident attorney Reno]
```

FIGURE 16–13. This Menu Lets You Enter Keywords. Your List in Any One Ad Group Should Always Be Narrow Clusters of Very Similar Keywords

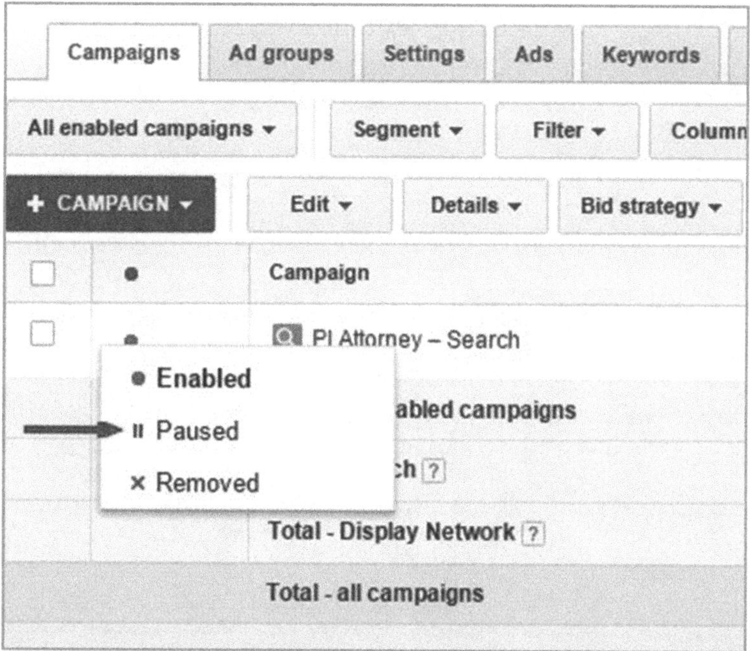

FIGURE 16–14. You Can Enable, Pause, or Remove Entire Campaigns in this Column Near the Left Side

Once you get all the information pasted into the right spots on this page, scroll to the bottom and click the "Save ad group" button.

You now have a live campaign with one ad group in it. Because we still have more to cover, we recommend you pause your campaign at this point. This will prevent your ads from running until you have everything set up the way you want it. To pause your campaign, click on the "Campaign" tab, click on the "Enabled" button under your campaign name, and change it to "Paused," as shown in Figure 16–14.

Adding Additional Ad Groups

With your campaign paused, you can now add the rest of your ad groups. In your campaign, go to the "Ad groups" tab and click on the big red "+ AD GROUP" button, as shown in Figure 16–15 on page 100.

That will take you to a page that is exactly like the one we went through previously. And just like you did before, simply copy and paste the information from your text document into the appropriate place.

Rinse and repeat for each ad group—and you are done!

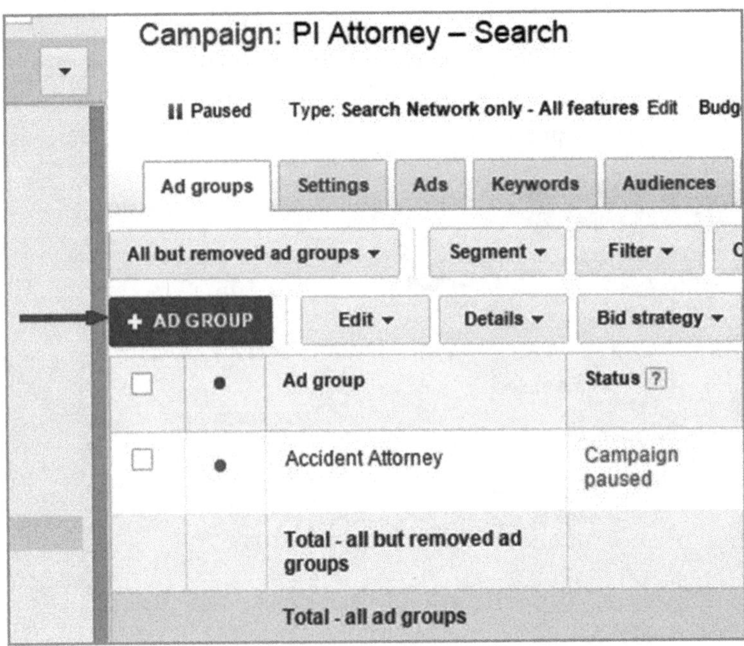

FIGURE 16–15. Inside Each Campaign Is the Opportunity to Create a New Ad Group

Chapter 17

Bidding Strategies Make or Break You

by Talor Zamir

My good friend John Paul Mendocha once beat the California state chess champion in a game of chess. John wasn't some sort of chess master either.

The guy was stunned. He demanded to know how he'd managed to beat him.

John wouldn't tell him. The guy hounded John for about a month, begging him to reveal his secret. Back and forth they went. Eventually, he's trying to bribe John to tell the secret. They strike an agreement. John says, "I played checkers not chess. Zero strategy."

What he did was so simple his opponent would never anticipate it.

Sometimes the way to win in Google AdWords is to play a different game than the rest of your competitors are playing. Google, for example, would like you to use AdWords Express so you're bidding the way *they* want you to bid.

And many times the keyword tools will fool you into thinking you have to pay more than necessary for a click.

Some of the most common questions we get from new AdWords advertisers are about bidding. And a lot of them come down to this: How much should I bid for clicks in my campaign?

Unfortunately, there are no easy answers. There are keyword research tools out there (like the Google Keyword Planner) that will give you bidding estimates for your keywords. However, you will often find those estimates to be highly inaccurate.

Much of what you end up paying for clicks depends on many factors very specific to your campaign, including:

- Whether you are targeting a big city or smaller town
- How many competitors you are going up against (and how many have entered or left the auction on any given day)
- The CTR (clickthrough rate) of your ads (more on this soon)
- What Google thinks about the relevancy of your keywords, ads, and website/landing page (your Quality Scores)

This variability is good, though. Because it really means that smart advertisers literally get ten times more bang for their buck than average advertisers do.

With all the factors that influence bid prices, it is difficult for even the keyword research tools to estimate how much you will need to bid for a keyword. You could have two new competitors start advertising in your city for the same keywords that you are bidding on (which would likely send your cost per click higher). Or you could have two competitors pause a campaign tomorrow (which would likely bring your cost per click down).

You can certainly use those tools as a rough guide to set your initial bids. Just understand that is only a starting point, and you will want to keep a close eye on your campaign when you start it and adjust your bids based on results.

BIDDING FOR THE TOP THREE POSITIONS

Heat maps that track the eye movements of people who conduct Google searches show that searchers focus on the results at the top left of the page—by far—more than any other part of the page. And that is exactly where Google puts the top three ads from AdWords.

So our advice is to bid on the high side to ensure your ads make it into those top three spots. We have seen those ads get clickthrough rates that are ten times higher (or more!) than the ads that appear in the right sidebar.

> The top three is where you want to be! (And for mobile, you need to be in the top two! More on this soon.)

SETTING YOUR INITIAL BIDS

Set your initial bids high enough, to where you think your ads will appear in the top three spots. Then, after the first two days or so, look at your results. If you see you are always in the first position, you can lower your bid to make sure you are not overpaying for clicks just to be in the top spot.

However, if you are in the first position after the first few days, and you are getting tons of leads and are happy with the results, then just leave it! (About half our clients are happy being in the first position because they are getting a great ROI and want to get as many leads as possible.) On the other hand, if you find that your ads are showing up lower on the page (below position three), then you will probably want to increase your bid prices.

What we have found is that aiming for an average position around 2.5 gives you the best bang for your buck. That gives you a nice balance. You are not always in position one, where you may be overpaying to always show up there. And you are not lower than position three, in danger of falling off onto the right side of the page where not nearly as many eyeballs will find your ads.

CHANGING YOUR BIDS

Keep in mind when you look at your results that bids can vary widely by keyword. So you do not want to just look at your overall campaign metrics, see that your ads are showing up in an average position of 4.0, and raise the bids for all your keywords.

Ideally, you will keep track of rankings and bids on a keyword-level basis. Look at where each keyword is ranking and adjust accordingly. To adjust the bid, go to the specific keyword in AdWords, and click on its "Max. CPC" as shown in Figure 17-1.

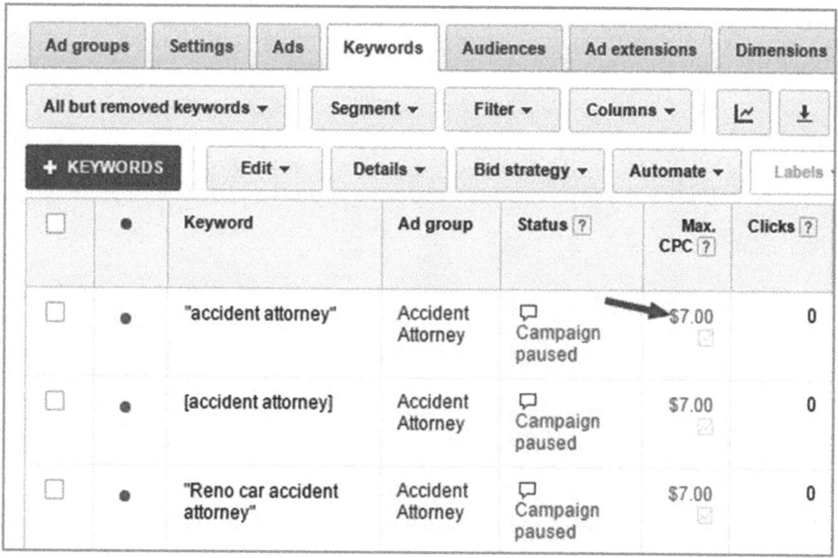

FIGURE 17-1. The Max. CPC Column Shows You Your Default Bid Price for Each Keyword

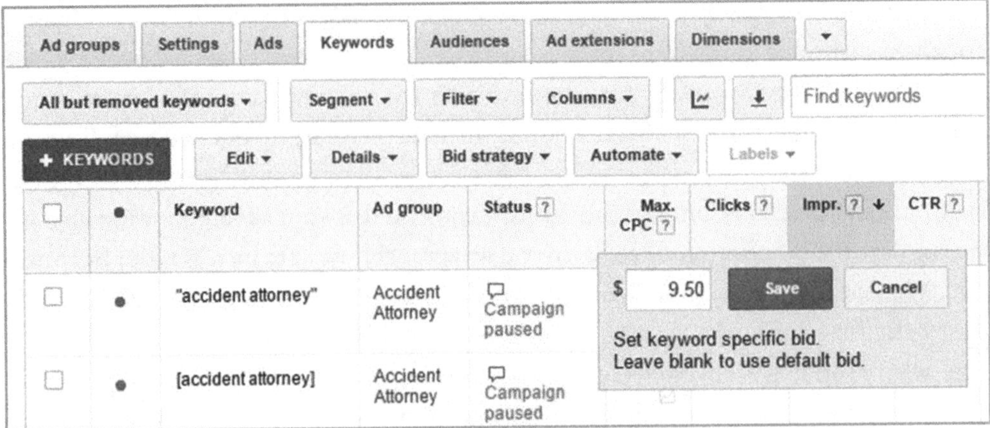

FIGURE 17-2. You Can Set a Keyword Specific Bid Unique to Each Match Type. No Other Form of Advertising Gives You Such Precise Control of Who Sees Your Ads and When.

That will open a box where you can enter your new bid and save it. (See Figure 17-2.)

You can also look at the average position of your ads at an ad group level. If you have grouped your keywords well, the keywords in each ad group will likely have fairly similar rankings.

If you want to adjust bids at the ad group level, click the "Ad groups" tab. Then next to the name of the ad group you want to adjust bids for, click on the bid in the "Default Max. CPC" column and type in your updated bid, as shown in Figure 17-3. This will adjust the bids for every keyword in the ad group.

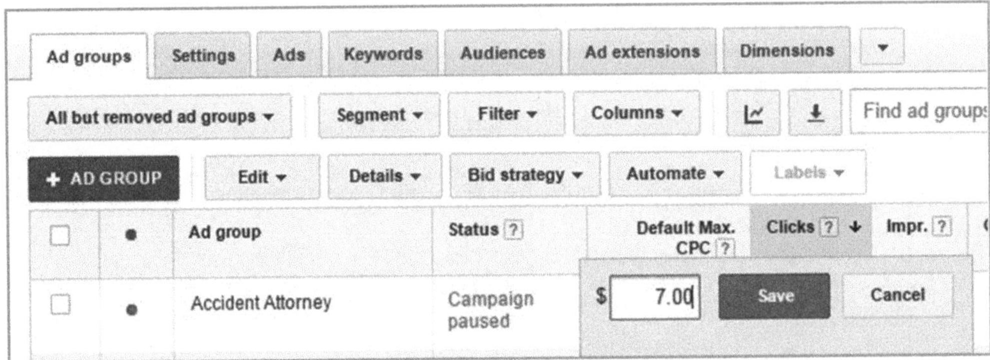

FIGURE 17-3. You Can Set Bids at the Group Level Instead of the Keyword Level if You Wish

As we have been saying with pretty much every part of your AdWords campaign, the bottom line is you can always make changes. So start high, see what that gets you, and adjust as needed.

Chapter 18

The Ultimate Local Google Ad

by Perry Marshall and Talor Zamir

Perry Marshall here. While I was in college, I did a stint selling vacuum cleaners door to door. Man was that hard work. Tons of rejection, and I made a sale only once every few weeks.

So years later when I suddenly found myself with thousands of tiny ads appearing all over the internet, knocking on doors *for* me and selling without me even being there, I thought I was in heaven.

Think of your Google ads as an army of tiny salesmen whose job is to attract the eyeballs of, and get clicks from, your prospects. *Your little ad salesmen do not have an easy task!*

They have to compete with the armies of other tiny salesmen that your competitors have, fighting for the attention of those same eyeballs and clicks. So you must arm your salespeople more thoroughly than the competition's so you win the battle for the eyes and clicks of your ideal prospects. The focus of this chapter is to help you do just that by creating The Ultimate Local Google Ad.

The components of the Ultimate Local Google Ad fall into two broad categories: Ad Copy and Ad Extensions.

AD COPY

The ad copy is the heart of your ad. You get a headline (with a maximum of 25 characters), two lines of additional ad copy (maximum of 35 characters each), and a display URL (maximum of 35 characters). That is not a lot of space! (It's 130 characters, not much different than the size of a tweet on Twitter.) It's just enough. You have to choose your words carefully and make the most of the space.

AD EXTENSIONS

Ad extensions provide extra space for ad copy that you can't fit in the headline and additional lines of copy. They also allow your ad to take up much more space on the search results page and stand out from your competitors that do not take advantage of them.

There are a variety of ad extensions you can use to display additional information next to your ads on Google. The Ultimate Local Google Ad harnesses all extensions possible: Sitelink, Location, Call, Callout, and Review. These are so important that we are giving them their own chapter. For now, just know that you need to use these in your ads, and we will dig into them more in the next chapter.

A GOOD AD VS. A BAD AD

Before we examine the components of the Ultimate Local Google Ad in more detail, let's take a look at an example of an ad that contains all the components needed for success.

The ad in Figure 18–1 is one we found when doing a search for "DUI attorney Los Angeles."

DUI Attorney Los Angeles - Unmatched DUI Dismissal Rate
Ad www.dui1guy.com/Call-Me-Direct-24-7 (888) 684-7553
Save Your License, Save Your Life
Free Consultation - 24/7 · 100% DUI Defense Only · 2013 Client Choice Award
Great DUI Dismissal Rate - Recent DUI Victories - Why Hire a DUI Lawyer?
Howard Hughes Center,, 6080 Center Drive, 6th Floor, Los Angeles, CA

FIGURE 18–1. Example of a Well-Constructed Ad

While we do not know how well this ad has performed for this law firm (this is not a client of ours), it stands out as being a well-constructed ad running for one of the most competitive and expensive keywords around. Notice the engaging, benefit-oriented copy, the call-to-action, and how much extra space it occupies by using ad extensions.

Now compare that to the ad for a different law firm in Figure 18–2 on page 107. Notice how much more compelling the ad copy is for the first ad and how much more space it takes up with its ad extensions.

There is nothing compelling about the second ad. If you saw these two ads in the same search, which one would you click on? (We hope you said the first one because

California DUI Attorney
www.ca-dui-attorney.com
California DUI Attorney.
Contact Us Today.

FIGURE 18–2. Example of a Lame Ad that Uses Minimal Real Estate

we would bet good money that's the one that will get the lion's share of the clicks here.)

YOUR AD COPY

Now that you have a picture of what a good ad looks like, let's break down the components of a good ad and, in particular, look at the ad copy an Ultimate Local Google Ad should contain.

When talking about ad copy, we want to start off by mentioning that copywriting is one of the most vital and valuable skills in marketing. There are many copywriters who employ all sorts of very advanced copywriting tactics. However, for the purpose of this book, we are going to assume that you are not an advanced copywriter, and, therefore, we are going to provide you with simple and proven ad-writing strategies that work great even if you are not a copywriter.

The good news is that based on our experience conducting our own tests and being behind the scenes of a number of AdWords accounts, copywriting for local business ads is pretty straightforward. You do not need to be a copywriting genius to succeed. Simply stick with the guidelines below, and you will be in good shape.

Following are are the main components of your ad copy and tips on how to make the most of each.

Your Ad Headline

The headline is arguably the most important piece of copy in your ad. It is the first part of your ad that most prospects will notice, and it will determine whether they pay attention to the rest of your ad.

After testing a lot of headline variations, the headline is also the easiest part of your ad to write. What we have found and what we recommend you do is to use your city and keyword in the headline. It cannot get more straightforward than that, right?! In the example of the "good" ad from the DUI attorney in L.A., the headline is "DUI Attorney Los Angeles."

If someone is searching for a DUI lawyer on Google, they already know they want a DUI lawyer. You do not have to try to convince them that is what they need.

Using a headline that tries to grab people's attention with an emotional hook or something more compelling like that may work well for other types of non-locally focused businesses. But for local businesses, we have found that *local is very important.* And you want to highlight the local angle in your ad, preferably in the headline.

Let's look at an example where you are in New York, but your office is in Queens. It's OK to use New York, but it would be much better to mention Queens specifically.

To take that even further, if you are a chiropractor in Flushing, Queens, and you only want to target a few-mile radius around your office, it would probably make sense to put "Flushing Chiropractor" in the headline. If someone is in Flushing looking for a chiropractor, and they see an ad that says "Flushing Chiropractor," it is more likely they will click on your ad than if it did not mention any city or even if it just mentions New York.

Generally, the more specific you are, the better. That said, you do not need to go too crazy. You want to focus on the 80/20 here and create ads for the biggest areas/cities you are targeting. We do not recommend you create ten different campaigns in ten different suburbs just to have the name of a local town in every ad. That is usually overkill.

Everyone's Favorite Radio Station: WIIFM

For the rest of your ad, there are a few key elements you want to try to get into the ad copy.

One is a call to action. For a local business, that typically will be something like "Call Now for Your Free Consultation" or "Call Now for Your Free Quote." Basically let your prospects know what action you want them to take and what their next step should be.

The Ultimate Local Google Ad will also contain some of the *benefits* a prospect will gain from using your service. Answer the questions "What makes you different from your competitors? Why should someone choose you?"

Everyone's favorite radio station is WIIFM: What's In It for Me! That is what you always have to be thinking. Put yourself in your prospect's shoes and think what benefit(s) they need to see in your ads to earn their click.

We've seen lawyers say things like: "State Bar of Nevada Certified." Don't you have to be State Bar of Nevada Certified to be a lawyer in Nevada?! That is not a very good benefit!

A good example of a benefit-focused ad copy would be a personal injury lawyer using "Free Consultation and No Fee Unless We Win." Now you are letting people know that there is a free consultation, and they do not even have to pay unless they win their case. That is a solid benefit. That is what's in it for them.

The "good" ad we shared at the beginning of this chapter also has a good benefit in it: "Unmatched DUI Dismissal Rate." We do not know if it is true or not, but it sounds like a strong benefit you would like if you'd just had a DUI.

Here are a few more examples of good benefits for ad copy:

- 100 Percent Guarantee
- We've Saved Our Clients Over $20 MILLION!
- Settle Your Debt for Pennies on the Dollar!

Even if other advertisers are using the same ad copy, if you find something that is working for you, keep using it! Just try to use it more effectively than your competitors by surrounding it with all your ad extensions and other strong copy.

If more competitors keep copying your ads, test some new ads to find something that works better. (We'll talk about split-testing more soon.) But do not worry about other people copying your ads—just focus on what you see is working for you.

Don't Forget the Display URL (Most of Your Competitors Do)

Did you notice the URL line in the DUI lawyer ad we shared at the beginning of this chapter?

It is: *www.dui1guy.com/Call-Me-Direct-24-7*

This line of copy is called the display URL in AdWords. A key rule to understand about the display URL is that it must be the same one used on the website you are sending your traffic to. What that means is you can't make your URL *greatduilawyer.com,* but send your traffic to your firm's actual site at *smithlawfirm.com.*

However, you can put anything you want *before* or *after* your URL, as in the example of the DUI attorney in Los Angeles. After his URL, *dui1guy.com*, he added a call to action: */Call-Me-Direct-24-7.*

Put together, it looks like this: www.dui1guy.com/Call-Me-Direct-24-7. This URL is not an actual page on his website (though it would be even better if it was). He just took advantage of the 35 characters available to add a call to action.

Alternatively, if he wanted to highlight the fact that he is local even more in his ad, he could add a subdomain to his display URL, such as ***SoCal**.dui1guy.com* or ***LosAngeles.**duiguy1.com.*

Again, you have 35 characters to play around with in your display URL. After you put your URL in there, take advantage of the characters you have left to enhance your ad's messaging.

Ad messaging and copy are also important for some of the ad extensions you can use to enhance your ads as you will see in the next chapter.

Chapter 19

Ad Extensions: Twice the Real Estate for No Extra Money

by Talor Zamir

From a distance, the Frilled Lizard looks like just an ordinary lizard. But if you get close to one and frighten it, it undergoes a stunning transformation.

It gets up on its hind legs, opens its mouth, and unfurls a skin flap (usually folded down against its head) that surrounds its head to reveal huge fans of red and orange scales. These frills take up much more space than a normal lizard's head, and whether you are a predator or not, they are extremely effective at getting your attention.

Ad extensions are like that. They are frills you can add to your ad to help it take up more space and stand out from the "normal" ads. (Though, obviously, your goal with ad extensions is to attract prospects to your ad instead of scaring away potential predators!)

Ad extensions are extra bits of copy and information that surround your ad's usual headline, two lines of body copy, and display URL. The more extensions you use, the more space your ad will take up and the more eyeballs and clicks your ads will get.

Ad extensions are very strategic in AdWords, and we recommend every local business use as many as possible in their campaigns. There are five types of extensions for local business owners to take advantage of. In this chapter, we are going to cover all five and share tips on making the most of each.

LOCATION EXTENSIONS

A location extension adds your company's address, phone number (sometimes), and a map marker to your ad. On mobile devices, having a location extension will include a link a user can click on to get directions to your office. You have probably noticed them under ads such as in the screenshot in Figure 19-1.

Atlanta dentists
www.dentistinsandysprings.com/
Visit Top Sandy Springs Dentist.
Discounts for First Time Patients.
6667 Vernon Woods Drive, Suite A-19

FIGURE 19-1. The Address Ad Extension Gives You 25 Percent More Real Estate for No Extra Money

One of the nice things about the location extensions is they can appear under your ad whether it is in one of the top three AdWords positions or in one of the ad positions on the right side of the screen. Some extensions, like sitelinks and callout extensions, can only appear if your ad is in one of the top three ad positions. That's another reason why it's so important to be in the top three.

To have location extensions, you need to have a Google My Business (formerly known as Google Places) account set up. Search for "Google My Business" to get started. For the purposes of integrating with Google AdWords, you do not need to go crazy here. You just need to fill in the basic information for your company. (*Note:* For local SEO purposes, you may want to consider hiring someone or filling out all the contents in more detail.) For now, just to get started, fill in the basic information necessary to set up your Google My Business account so you can integrate it with your location extension.

Once you have done that, head back to AdWords and click on the "Ad extensions" tab. Select "Location extensions" from the drop-down menu and click on the "+ Extension" link. (See Figure 19-2 on page 113.)

This will take you to the screen to link your AdWords account to your Google My Business account, as shown in Figure 19-3 on page 113. (If you have more than one business set up in Google My Business, you can set a filter to select the one you want to appear next to your AdWords ads.)

Other than that, it is pretty straightforward to set this up. Just link the account, click "done," and Google will display your local business info under your ads.

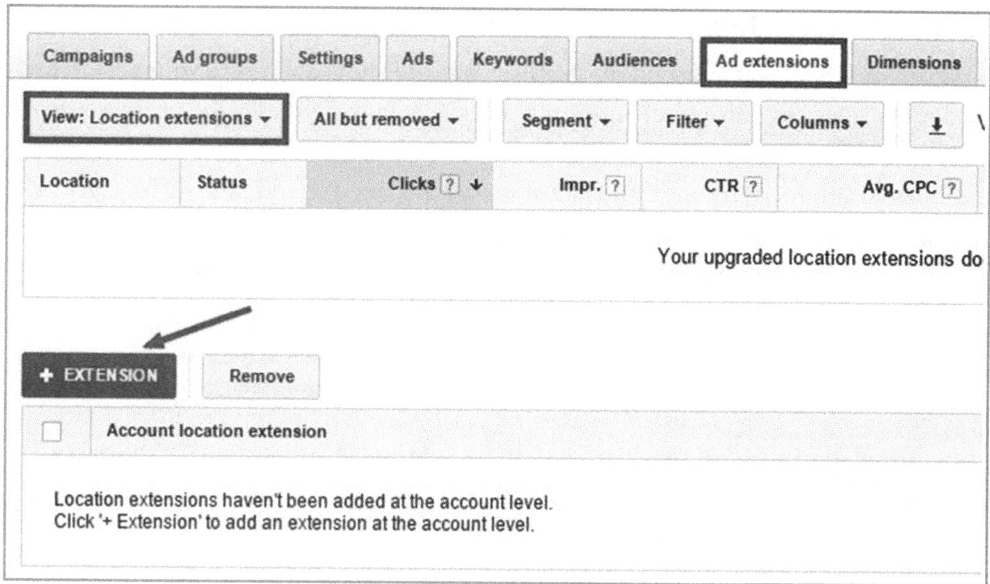

FIGURE 19–2. The Ad Extensions Menu Gives You All the Different Extension Types. Each Type Gets You More Clicks without Spending More Money.

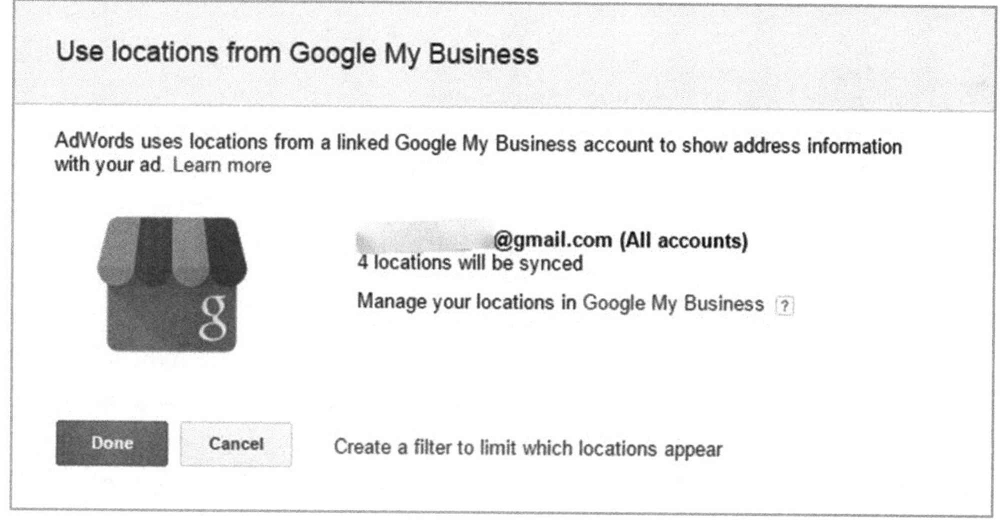

FIGURE 19–3. You Can Get Ad Extension locations from Google's "Google My Business" Feature

CALL EXTENSIONS

Call extensions let you add a phone number that will show up next to your ad. On high-end mobile devices, this phone number is clickable, making it easy for prospects to call you.

Like location extensions, call extensions are also simple and straightforward to set up. To add call extensions to your campaign, click on the "+ Extension" button on the "Call extensions" dropdown while on the "Ad extensions" tab. (See Figure 19-4.)

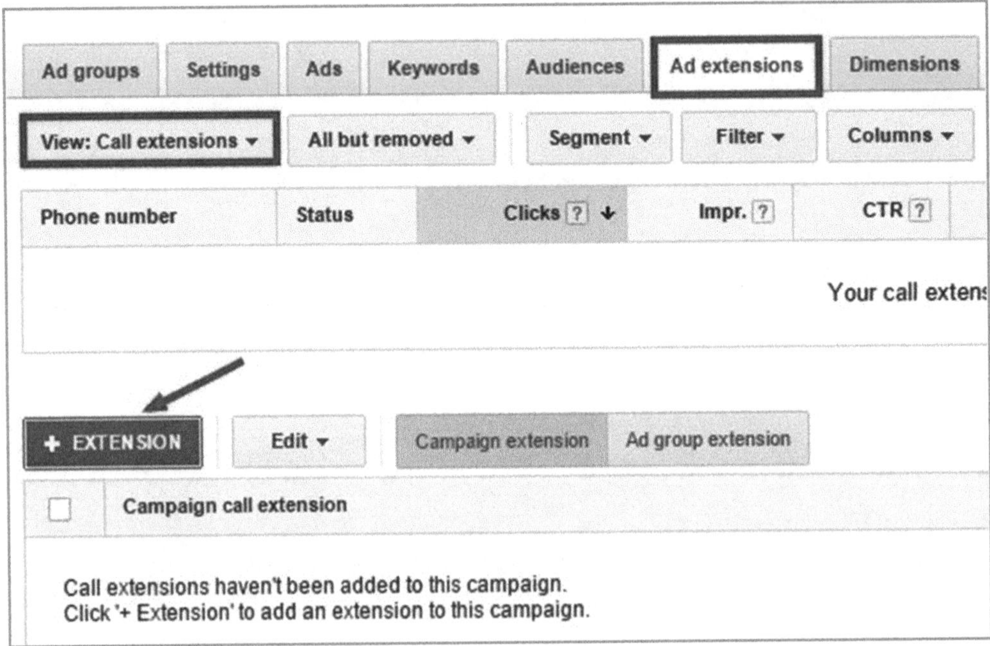

FIGURE 19-4. Call Extensions Let You Add a Google Tracking Phone Number to Your Ad. This Number Forwards to Your Telephone and Google Tracks Each Call to the Triggering Keyword So You Can Calculate ROI on Your Bids.

There are several decisions you need to make here as you can see from the screenshot in Figure 19-5 on page 115. The main one is whether to display your phone number or use a Google forwarding number. We recommend using the Google forwarding number, because that will let you track calls from call extensions (and by now you should understand how important tracking all your leads is!).

If you follow our advice and use the Google forwarding number (which is the default option), you can leave all the other options on the screen as they are, click "Save," and move on to the next ad extension.

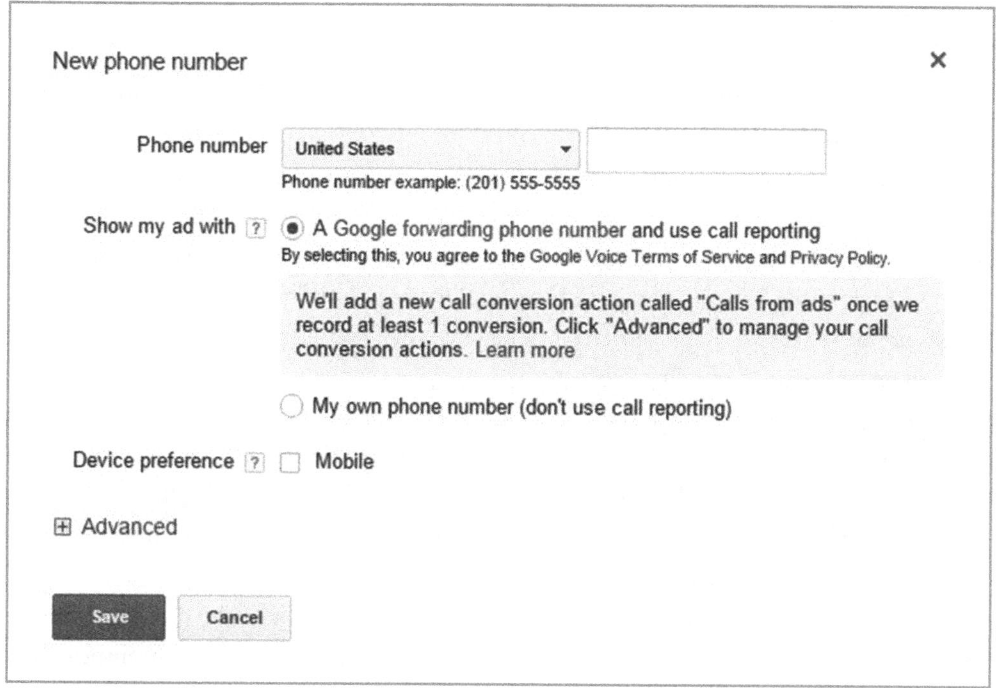

FIGURE 19-5. You Can Choose Between Displaying a Google Forwarding Number vs. Your Own Phone Number

SITELINK EXTENSIONS

Sitelink extensions are the most important ad extension because they really stand out. They make your ad bigger on the page (as you can see from the screenshot in Figure 19-6 where the sitelinks are in the box) and give you 25 extra characters to add some additional selling points—a huge bonus in our book.

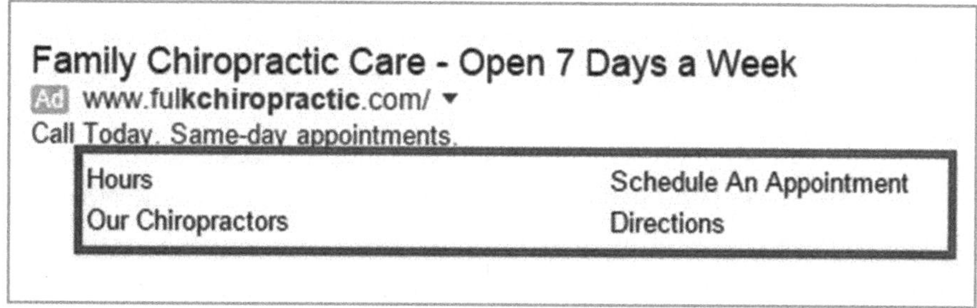

FIGURE 19-6. Sitelink Extensions Add Considerable Creative Ability to the Way You Describe Your Business

In the main part of your ad you list your best benefit(s). If you have lots of benefits, use sitelinks for additional benefits that you could not fit into your ad. (And if you have one or two benefits you really want to emphasize, you might consider repeating them in your sitelinks.)

For example, consider a cosmetic dentist who offers no money down or zero percent interest financing. Whether or not you included those benefits in your main ad, you could create a few sitelinks that say "No Money Down" and "0% Interest Financing."

Other possible benefits you could include in sitelinks might include "We do house calls" or "5 Year Free Replacement." A benefit that some, but not most customers appreciate can make a good sitelink.

Another use for sitelinks is for businesses that offer a few different types of services. So for the cosmetic dentist, if someone searches the keyword "cosmetic dentist," they might be looking for dental implants, veneers, teeth whitening, Invisalign, or something else. In that case, you might consider a sitelink extension called "Veneers," another called "Dental Implants," and another called "Invisalign."

Google's purpose with sitelinks is for you to be able to link to the different parts of your site that searchers may be interested in. And with sitelinks, they can pinpoint the exact information they are interested in as quickly as possible.

Keep in mind with sitelinks that each one has to lead to a *different* page on your website–you can't create two or more sitelinks that all link to the same page (or to the URL your main ad copy leads to). So in the case of a cosmetic dentist, you would need a unique landing page for veneers, dental implants, teeth whitening, etc.

That said, the landing pages can be very similar. If you start with the landing page you created based on the template we shared with you earlier in the book, you only need to change around 20 percent of it for your second landing page to satisfy Google's policy that each sitelink needs to go to a unique page.

Taking the "Veneers" sitelink as an example, you would copy your main cosmetic dentist landing page, tweak about 20 percent of the copy so it is focused specifically on veneers, and add that as a new landing page. Do the same for the other pages you set up for your sitelinks, and you will have four different landing pages that, in general, will convert very well.

You can also use sitelinks to include and/or reinforce your call to action. A few examples of these would be "Call for Free Consult" or "Get a Free Quote Now."

To add sitelinks to your campaign, click on "sitelinks extensions" from the drop-down menu on the "Ad extensions" tab and click the "+ Extension" button, as shown in Figure 19–7 on page 117.

On this screen click on the "+ New sitelink" button to create each new sitelink, as shown in Figure 19–8 on page 117. In the "New sitelink" window, enter the text you want

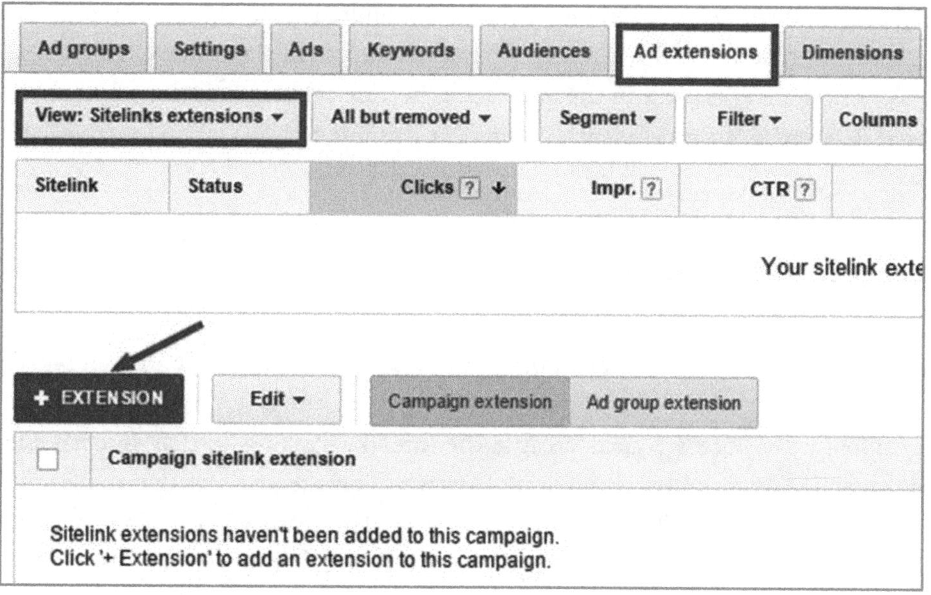

FIGURE 19-7. Add Sitelinks to Your Campaigns in the Ad Extensions Tab

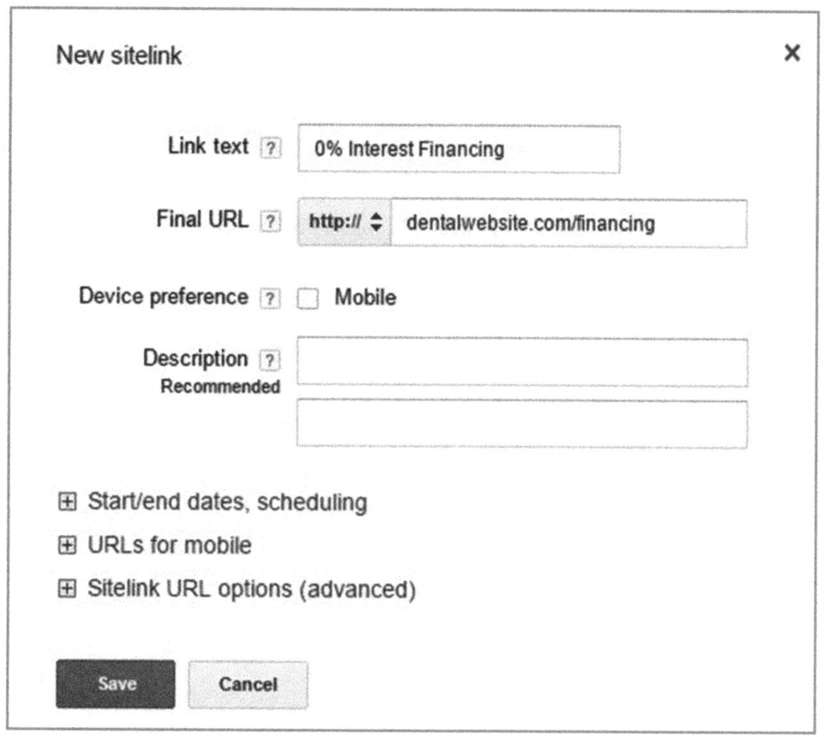

FIGURE 19-8. The Sitelink Menu Lets You Choose the Text and the Page Your Customer Lands on When They Click

to be displayed with your ad (remember, you are limited to 25 characters) in the "Link text" box. Next, add the URL the sitelink should point to in the "Final URL" box.

We recommend leaving all the other fields/settings alone, so at this point just click "Save." Repeat this process for each sitelink (we recommend you set up four), and you're done.

CALLOUT EXTENSIONS

Callout extensions are a feature that Google added in 2014. They give you additional room to add even more benefits and/or calls to action, making your ad even bigger on the page.

Callout extensions are great because they are like sitelinks in that you can add an additional line of copy around your ad. However, they are just text that make your ad bigger—you do not actually link them to any page. Therefore, you do not have to worry about creating a separate landing page for each callout extension like you do for the sitelinks.

If you put your best benefit(s) in your main ad, then your next most important benefits in your sitelink extensions, we recommend you take whatever is left over and put them in the callout extensions.

From what we have seen, sitelinks are still shown more than callout extensions, so you want to prioritize sitelinks over callouts. That is why we recommend focusing on putting your best benefits and messaging in your sitelink extensions first.

Something to keep in mind with callout extensions is that they are supposed to be different from your sitelink extensions. If you use "Open 24/7—Call Now" in your sitelink extension, you cannot use it in your callout extension. If you do, Google will, most likely, deny it.

To set up callout extensions, select "callout extensions" from the drop-down menu on the "Ad extensions" tab. Click the "+ Extension" button and then the "+ New callout" button, as shown in Figure 19-9 on page 119.

For each callout extension you create, simply enter the text in the "callout text" box and click "Save," as in Figure 19-10 on page 119.

As with sitelinks, we recommend setting up four callout extensions in your campaign.

REVIEW EXTENSIONS

If you or your company has been endorsed by a respected third-party source, you can highlight it next to your ad and link to it with a review extension.

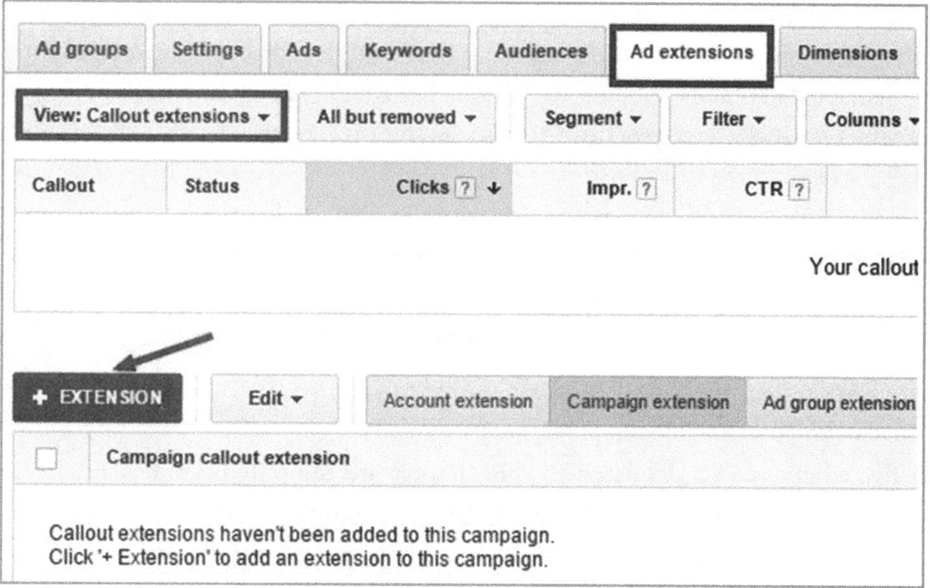

FIGURE 19-9. Callout Extensions from the Ad Extensions Tab

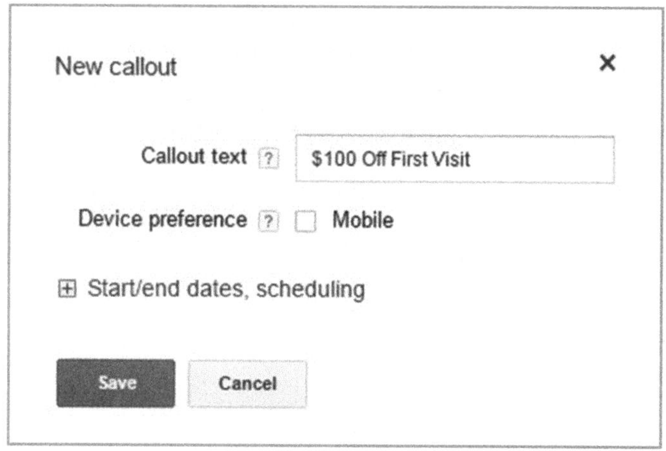

FIGURE 19-10. Callout Extensions Let You Add More Detailed Information about Features or Services

What is important to note, however, is that you cannot simply link to a review that a customer posted about your business online (or even link to customer review sites like Google or Yelp). The reviews have to be from a credible third-party source like the media or an industry organization. If you have gotten an award or some positive review from a third-party source that has been posted online, you can create a review extension.

Most local businesses don't use review extensions, and it's not a huge deal, so don't go crazy if you don't have something that qualifies for one. However, if you can use them, you definitely should! We do not use them that often because many local businesses have not received third-party recognition like this such that Google will accept for use in a review extension.

If you have received some review or honor you believe fits the bill, we recommend you enter it as a review extension. The worst Google can do is not allow it. If they accept it, however, your ad will take up even more space on the page, and you will have given prospects one more reason to click on your ad.

More Extensions to Come?

The five ad extensions discussed in this chapter are the only ones available to local businesses at the time we are writing this. However, Google is one of the most profitable companies in the world, and about 90 percent of their revenue comes from Google ads. Therefore, we believe that Google may continue to roll out features like callout extensions and other things that increase the size of the ads on the page to promote more clicks.

Remember:
More space = more copy = more eyeballs = more clicks!

Don't forget, they are a publicly traded company that needs to show growth to their shareholders quarter over quarter. And with most of their money coming from Google ads, it is pretty safe to say that they are going to protect this platform and only do things that are going to help it.

So keep your eye out for new ad extensions or other features that will let your AdWords ads spread their frills and take up more space. We will also post information about any future ad extensions on our website. If you haven't already, sign up for notifications at www.UltimateLocalBook.com.

Chapter 20

Split-Testing Your Ads: The Key to Continuous Improvement

by Talor Zamir

Have you ever heard of the book *Drug Testing for Fun and Profit?* No one has, because it was never published, at least not with that title.

The author (who had worked in the pharmaceutical industry) was told by his publisher that Wal-Mart would not sell the book with that title and he needed to change it. They gave him a list of alternative titles, but he did not like any of them. So he went a different route.

He set up an AdWords campaign and created 12 different ads, each one containing a different potential book title in the ad copy. Over the course of a week, he conducted a split test of the 12 ads to see which one his prospects responded to most favorably. One week and $150 later, there was a runaway winner and *The 4-Hour Workweek* title was chosen. As you probably know, this went on to become a best-seller for Tim Ferriss. He sold over a million copies.

You may not be looking to choose the title for a book you are working on, but split-testing ad copy is definitely a strategy you will want to employ in your AdWords campaign.

THE WORLD'S GREATEST MARKET RESEARCH ENGINE

We need to come clean and let you in on a little secret: In this book, we have been sharing some of our proven ideas for ad copy (and landing

> While experienced marketers are skillful in determining what has a good chance of working, and your common sense will also give you an idea of what "should" work, at the end of the day, it is your prospects who will tell you what actually does work.

pages). And as much as we would love to tell you all the ad copy we have ever written were huge successes because of our incredible copywriting genius, we would be lying if we said that.

The truth is, even experienced marketers never truly know which ads will perform the best and which ones will bomb. No matter who writes the ad and what you think of the ad copy, it is ultimately up to your prospects to determine which ads get their juices flowing.

While a lot of people fail to think of it this way, AdWords is a very powerful market research tool you can use to test different ad concepts (or potential billboards, TV and radio messages, book titles, headlines, etc.) quickly to see which ones your prospects respond to. AdWords is not a focus group . . . it is much more powerful than that.

The magic of AdWords is that no one sits and ponders an ad before clicking on it. A prospect sees your message, her brain runs an instant gut reaction, and she makes a decision—either she clicks or doesn't.

Sitting around debating ad copy for hours will not do you any good. Hiring a focus group to sit around and discuss their feelings and reactions to your ad copy is a waste of your time, and theirs.

SPLIT-TEST WITH EASE

Google makes it so easy to do real-time split-testing of different ads. Simply create two ads in each ad group of your campaign (you can split-test more than two ads at a time, but we recommend you stick with two or three to start), then let them battle it out for the hearts and minds of your prospects. Once the ads have collected enough clicks and conversions where you can judge which one is the better performer, delete the poor performing ad and create a new ad that will compete against the winning ad.

If you repeat this process over and over, after several weeks or months, you will find the performance of your ads will get better and better. Split-testing your ad copy is one of the surest ways to improve the performance of your AdWords account over time, so we recommend sticking with it for the long haul.

We can pretty much guarantee that most of your competitors are not savvy or patient enough to do this, so continual split-testing will put you light years ahead of them.

SPLIT-TESTING IS NOT JUST ABOUT CLICKTHROUGH RATES

Before we started using the call conversion tracking system that we mentioned earlier in the book, we used to optimize our ads for the highest clickthrough rates (CTRs).

However, you now know that you should be tracking conversion for all phone calls as well as contact form submissions on your landing page.

Because you will have that conversion data, CTRs are not the best way to judge the winning and losing ad in a split test. *The most important statistic that you are going to look at when split-testing your ad is your cost per conversion (i.e., your cost per lead).*

Let's say, for example, you write a really outrageous ad, and it gets a lot of clicks and a high CTR. You may find that people could just be clicking on your ad because it is so outrageous, but very few of them convert into a lead. In this case, the ad is not very profitable, and it would not make sense to declare that ad the winner of a split test based on its CTR.

Remember, it is not just about which ad is getting the highest CTR. It is more important to know which ads are getting the highest conversion rates and lowest cost per conversion. Focusing on cost per conversion in your split tests will let you make the most profitable decisions for your business's AdWords campaigns.

SIX THINGS YOU CAN TEST IN YOUR ADS

Not sure what to test in your ads? Here is a list of some simple things you can try to boost the performance of your ad copy.

Display URLs

In a previous chapter, we discussed the display URL and how you can put additional text around your URL. This is a great place for split-testing. Try variations like:

- yourdomain.com/Free-Consultation
- yourdomain.com/Houston
- Houston.yourdomain.com
- yourdomain.com/Call-Now

Switch the Second and Third Lines of Text

Surprisingly, simply switching the second and third lines of text in your ads can make a significant difference in ad performance.

For example, using ads we shared earlier in the book, if you had an ad that was:

Reno Accident Attorney
{INSERT BIGGEST BENEFIT}
Free Consult 24/7 * Call Now.
awesomerenoattorney.com

Change it to:

> **Reno Accident Attorney**
> Free Consult 24/7 * Call Now.
> {INSERT BIGGEST BENEFIT}
> awesomerenoattorney.com

Benefits

You may think a certain benefit is the greatest one in the world. But as we mentioned earlier, it is really not about what *you* think. It is about what your customers will tell you with their actions.

Maybe you put what you think is a relatively minor benefit in a sitelink extension. Or maybe you did not even mention it until your callout extensions. That could still be something you would want to switch and test in an ad.

For example, we had a client where we were split-testing one ad that featured their "100% Lifetime Warranty" and another ad that featured "0% Interest Financing Available." Those are two very different and compelling benefits. Without split-testing, we would not know which one more people would respond to.

Questions (and Pre-Qualifying Prospects)

Asking a question in your ad is a great thing to test. Here's an example:

> **Owe 20K+ to the IRS?**

The interesting thing about this example is that not only is there a question in the ad, but notice we are also pre-qualifying people. We make it clear our offer is geared toward people who owe more than $20,000 to the IRS.

While we may get a lower CTR on that ad, we are probably more likely to get a higher conversion because we are directly addressing the ad copy to our ideal customer. Mentioning this in your ads should, in theory, keep anyone who does not owe $20,000 or more from clicking on your it.

This pre-qualification is a great tactic and is another thing to test in your ad. (We don't recommend going too crazy with it! We don't want you to pre-qualify people so much that they never click on your ad.)

Dynamic Keyword Insertion (DKI)

Dynamic keyword insertion (DKI) is a feature in AdWords that lets you insert a searcher's actual query into your ad. You set it up by using the following format:

{KeyWord: Reno Chiropractor}

If you have the above as a headline in your ad and someone types in the search query "chiropractor in Reno NV," then the headline of your ad will become:

Chiropractor in Reno NV

If the search query typed in by the searcher is longer than 25 characters, then Google will use the copy you put after the "Keyword:" in DKI, which in the above example is "Reno Chiropractor."

Some people swear by DKI. In our experience for local businesses, we have found that a lot of times you get a higher CTR without it. However, it is definitely something you could test and see what works best for your campaign.

ALL CAPS

Another trick we really do not hear many people talking about at all is using caps in your ads. Google will only allow you to use caps, typically, for words that are no more than seven characters. (Also, note that you cannot use the word "free" in all caps.)

For example, we have used the word "ALERT" in all caps. That has been a very high-performing ad. We use "ALERT" and also use the date along with it. For one client, every month we will go in and switch the month from February to March, and March to April. So depending on the month, it will say, "ALERT Feb. 2016" or "ALERT March 2016"in the ad.

Also, you may have an ad with the headline:

Injury Lawyer Chicago

And in the next ad you are split-testing, the headline could be:

INJURY Lawyer Chicago

ADDING ADDITIONAL ADS TO YOUR AD GROUPS

In Chapter 16, when we set up our campaign, we added one ad to each ad group. Since we need at least two ads in each ad group for split testing, we have to place more ads in each of our ad groups. To do that, you first go to the ad group you want to place the ad in and click over to the "Ads" tab.

Next, click on the big "+ Ad" button and select "Text ad" from the drop-down menu. That will bring up a screen that looks like Figure 20-1 on page 126. Simply enter your ad copy into the appropriate boxes, click the "Save ad" button at the bottom, and you are done.

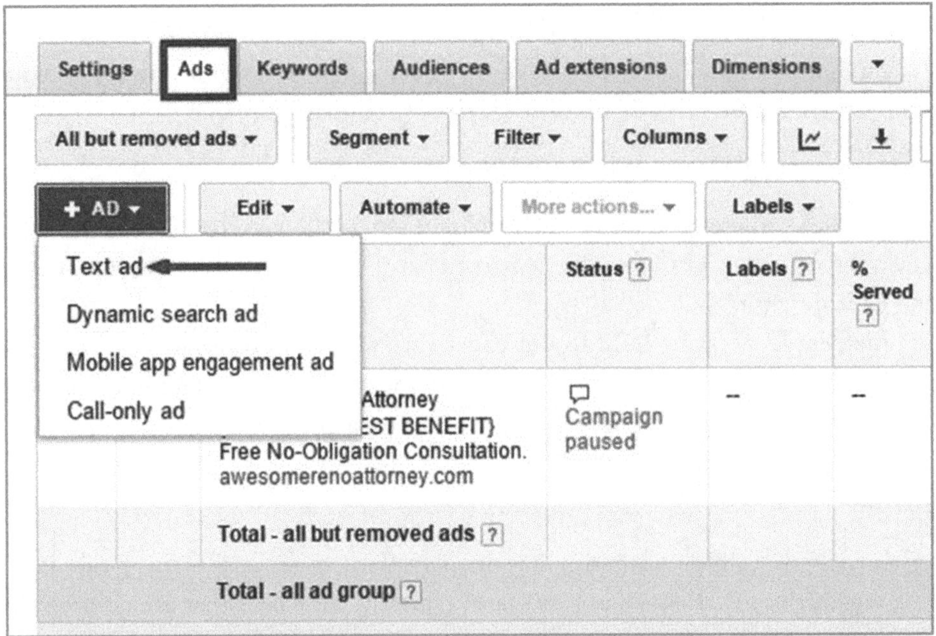

FIGURE 20–1. You Can Create Several Types of Ads in the New Ad Menu

UNLIMITED POSSIBILITIES

The six split-testing ideas in this chapter are just the tip of the iceberg. There are unlimited ad variations you can test in your campaign.

If you are stuck in an ad-writing rut and need help, we suggest looking at the Swiss Army Knife video series at https://perrymarshall.com/marketing/sak. The Swiss Army Knife is a systematic creativity method for crafting every kind of sales message. It asks you incredibly insightful questions about your customers and breaks you out of any ad-writing rut you are stuck in.

If we had to choose one thing that separates the very best AdWords campaigns from all others it would be split-testing.

Split-test your ads.

Split-test your landing pages.

Split-test consistently.

Doing that over time is the key to outperforming the competition in AdWords.

Chapter 21

Conversion Tracking

by Talor Zamir

On a recent mastermind call, we were discussing the results from an AdWords campaign run by another member of the group who we will call John. Please understand, this mastermind group is made up of some extremely savvy marketers. And John is no exception. He has a long track record of successfully helping clients and is a seasoned AdWords pro.

He was struggling with a campaign he was running for a local business he is a partner in. He wanted to get this campaign and website up and running quickly, so he hired a company to design the site (mainly for SEO purposes), hired a copywriter to write a landing page, and decided not to bother with setting up the conversion call tracking system because he just wanted to get things started really quick.

In the beginning, he was getting halfway decent results, so he kept on running things without tracking call conversions, but in the end, the results just were not there. He looked up one day and said, "Shoot, I've spent around $20,000 on ads and don't have the ROI I'm looking for."

Unfortunately, when he came to us for advice, other than sharing with him the proven landing page template to help improve his landing page conversions, we really could not give him much advice on his keywords or ads because he was not tracking conversions.

Remember, if you are not tracking conversions, then you are blindfolded.

In a situation like that, what can you say? You cannot give him advice like pause this keyword or that ad because you have no idea which keywords and ads produced the conversions!

If you are tracking conversions, you have a huge advantage over your competitors and will be able to outspend them and get more leads because you will be getting lower costs per lead and tracking everything. You will know exactly which parts of your campaign are profitable and which are not.

As you can see from John's story, even experienced marketers do not get this right all the time, and it will inevitably come back to bite them (and you, if conversion tracking is not in place in your campaigns). We would hate to see you follow all the other steps in this book, but then say, "You know what? Let me just give it a shot without conversion tracking." Then you spend a bunch of money and say, "Well, we pretty much just broke even the first month so it did not really work out for me." And then you pause your campaign.

Breaking even in your first month is actually not bad, because if you have identified that half your ad spend was for keywords that did not produce enough conversions, then the next month when you pause those keywords, you become profitable. Then, every month as you get more data and start optimizing your campaign more and more for conversions, you should be able to increase the ROI. Just keep getting lower and lower costs per conversion, thereby increasing the ROI on your campaign.

That is the path to long-term success with AdWords, and it is completely contingent on you tracking all the conversions each keyword and ad is producing.

THE MOST IMPORTANT METRIC: COST PER CONVERSION

Prospects and new clients always ask us what the cost per click will be in their AdWords campaigns. That is the wrong question to be asking. Because at the end of the day the cost per click is not really the most important metric. The most important metric, by far, is cost per conversion.

Every time I (Talor Zamir) mention that I work with personal injury lawyers, almost the first thing out of everyone's mouth is, "I heard they have such a high cost per click. How can Google AdWords work for them when the cost per click is so high?"

What people need to understand is that if a cost per click is high, it is only because those leads are hot, responsive, and valuable. It also means that if you have a high conversion rate on your landing page, and you are optimizing your campaign the way we are showing you, then you are going to be able to get great results in a very competitive niche where leads are extremely valuable.

For example, let's say we have a campaign for a personal injury lawyer. Even if they pay $50 a click, while many people think that is a lot, if the landing page converts at 25 percent, then they would be getting leads for $200 each. Most personal injury lawyers would be very happy to get good, high-quality leads for $200.

Cost per conversion is everything. It is the most important metric and the one that you really need to focus on.

It is really important to stay focused on what the cost per conversion is and optimize your campaign for that metric. Some keywords may have a higher cost per click, but also have a higher conversion rate. Other keywords have a much lower cost per click, but you may have a much lower conversion rate.

While you should be monitoring cost per click, it is not the be all and end all that many people think it is. The most important metric is cost per conversion, and that is what you need to keep your eye on when optimizing your campaign.

THREE THINGS TO WATCH WHEN OPTIMIZING YOUR CAMPAIGN

Keywords

When optimizing your campaign, the number-one thing you are going to be looking at closely is the keywords. On the "Keywords" tab, look at which keywords are giving you a good cost per conversion and which are not. As you can see from the screenshot in Figure 21-1 on page 130, even within the same campaign the cost per conversion can vary widely by keyword.

If you find a keyword with a high cost per conversion, it does not necessarily mean that you have to pause that keyword. You might find that a certain keyword is getting you an OK cost per conversion or one that is even a little high. In a situation like that maybe you see that your ad is always running in position 1.0, and you could be overpaying for that keyword. Instead of pausing the keyword, you could simply lower your bid. Therefore, you would be paying a lower cost per click, and, assuming you keep the same conversion rate, that keyword may end up working out for you.

If a keyword is really not converting well, even after you lower your bid for it, then you can outright pause it.

Ads

The second thing we recommend looking at is your ads. We talked about split-testing your ads, and that is what you are going to do here. When you see which ads are getting you a high cost per conversion, you are going to pause those and leave the ones that are getting you the lower cost per conversion.

Clicks ?	Impr. ?	Cost ?	CTR ?	Avg. CPC ?	Qual. score ?	Converted ↓ clicks ?	Cost / converted click ?
2,954	181,052	$19,205.62	1.63%	$6.50	--	218	$88.10
279	6,625	$2,626.67	4.21%	$9.41	8/10	25	$105.07
306	27,700	$2,333.00	1.10%	$7.62	7/10	23	$101.43
99	425	$389.90	23.29%	$3.94	8/10	20	$19.50
58	369	$217.51	15.72%	$3.75	8/10	15	$14.50
118	1,790	$1,562.61	6.59%	$13.24	10/10	8	$195.33
48	2,484	$357.15	1.93%	$7.44	6/10	6	$59.52
13	29	$104.74	44.83%	$8.06	8/10	6	$17.46
80	12,297	$468.23	0.65%	$5.85	7/10	5	$93.65
16	348	$182.99	4.60%	$11.44	10/10	5	$36.60
252	6,958	$1,701.13	3.62%	$6.75	7/10	4	$425.28
28	945	$296.98	2.96%	$10.61	8/10	4	$74.24

FIGURE 21-1. Notice the Widely Varying Cost Per Converted Click in this Ad Group

Here is a helpful tip to keep in mind when optimizing your ads: As we mentioned previously, we have found that if the ad copy in your ad matches the ad copy on your landing page, it tends to increase your conversion rates. And what you definitely want to avoid is creating any disconnect between your ad and your landing page.

For example, say you run an ad that mentions a "100% money-back guarantee" or "interest-free financing," but that benefit is not mentioned on your landing page. That disconnect can make a prospect think twice about contacting you because they may fear you are trying to pull one over on them with some sort of bait and switch.

If your ad mentions a benefit that is getting a lot of prospects to click on the ad, obviously that is an important benefit and needs to be backed up on your landing page. So, as much as possible, make sure your ad and landing page are consistent.

Mobile

The next thing we recommend looking at in your local campaign is the mobile conversions. In the next chapter we will examine the mobile landscape in a lot more detail, but for now, we will look at it from a conversion standpoint.

In some niches, we have found that we get mobile leads for less than *half* the cost per conversion of desktop traffic leads. An example is in a case like an injury lawyer where someone might get into a car accident and then do a search on their phone for a lawyer. That is generally a very high-quality lead, and you can have a very high conversion rate if they find you and click on your ad to call you.

If your cost per conversion is much higher on mobile, which in some niches it may be, you could consider adjusting your mobile bid down. Or you could turn mobile traffic off completely so your ads do not show on mobile at all (more on this in the next chapter).

You can see how your mobile traffic is performing compared to your desktop traffic at a campaign, ad group, keyword, and ad level.

If you want to view it at an ad group level, click on the "Ad groups" tab in your AdWords account and then click the "Segment" button. From the drop-down menu, click the "Device" option as in Figure 21-2.

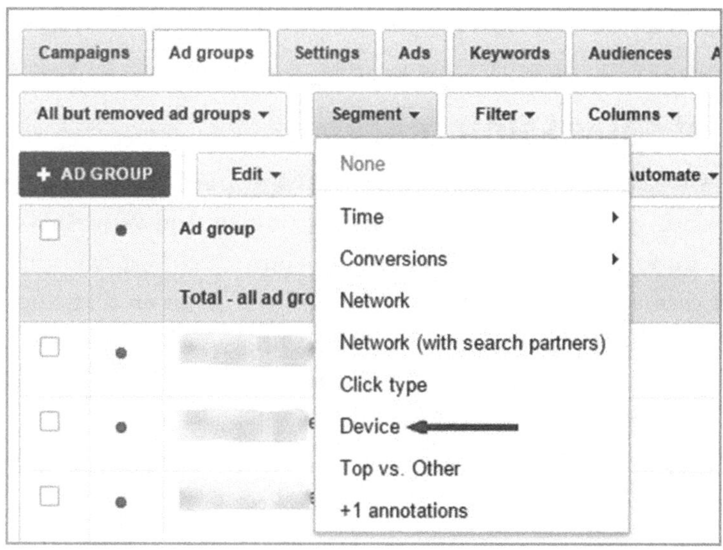

FIGURE 21-2. The "Segment" Menu Lets You View Conversion Data as a Function of Time, Device, and Several Other Factors

That will produce a screen like you see in Figure 21-3 where the data for "Computers," "Mobile devices with full browsers," and "Tablets with full browsers" are broken out so you can see how each source is performing. (*Note:* Google currently doesn't allow advertisers to adjust their bids for tablets the way you can for mobile.)

		Eligible	$1.30	499	16,148	3.09%	$4.78	$2,386.05
Computers ?				125	4,635	2.70%	$3.98	$497.61
Mobile devices with full browsers ?				302	9,845	3.07%	$5.19	$1,565.89
Tablets with full browsers ?				72	1,668	4.32%	$4.48	$322.55
		Eligible	$6.34	317	14,944	2.12%	$5.58	$1,769.65
Computers ?				140	6,120	2.29%	$5.49	$768.65
Mobile devices with full browsers ?				139	6,802	2.04%	$5.70	$791.99
Tablets with full browsers ?				38	2,022	1.88%	$5.50	$209.01
		Eligible	$1.00	221	13,976	1.58%	$4.61	$1,018.82
Computers ?				62	4,095	1.51%	$4.10	$254.21
Mobile devices with full browsers ?				136	8,669	1.57%	$4.85	$659.08
Tablets with full browsers ?				23	1,212	1.90%	$4.59	$105.53

FIGURE 21-3. Breaking Down Your AdWords Stats by Device Type

SETTING UP CONVERSION TRACKING

Google makes it easy to track your leads/conversions in AdWords. The first thing you will need to do is generate your conversion tracking code in your AdWords account. When logged into AdWords, at the very top of your screen, you will find the 'Tools" menu. Under that, one of the options is "Conversions." Click on that, and you will end up on a screen that looks like Figure 21-4 on page 133.

Click on the "+ Conversion" button, and you will have a few options to choose from as in Figure 21-5 on page 133.

In most situations for a local business, you will want to select the "Website" option. When you select that, there are a few choices to make.

- First, give your conversion a name like "Contact Form Completion" and click "Done."
- Under "Value," we recommend selecting the "Don't assign a value" option.

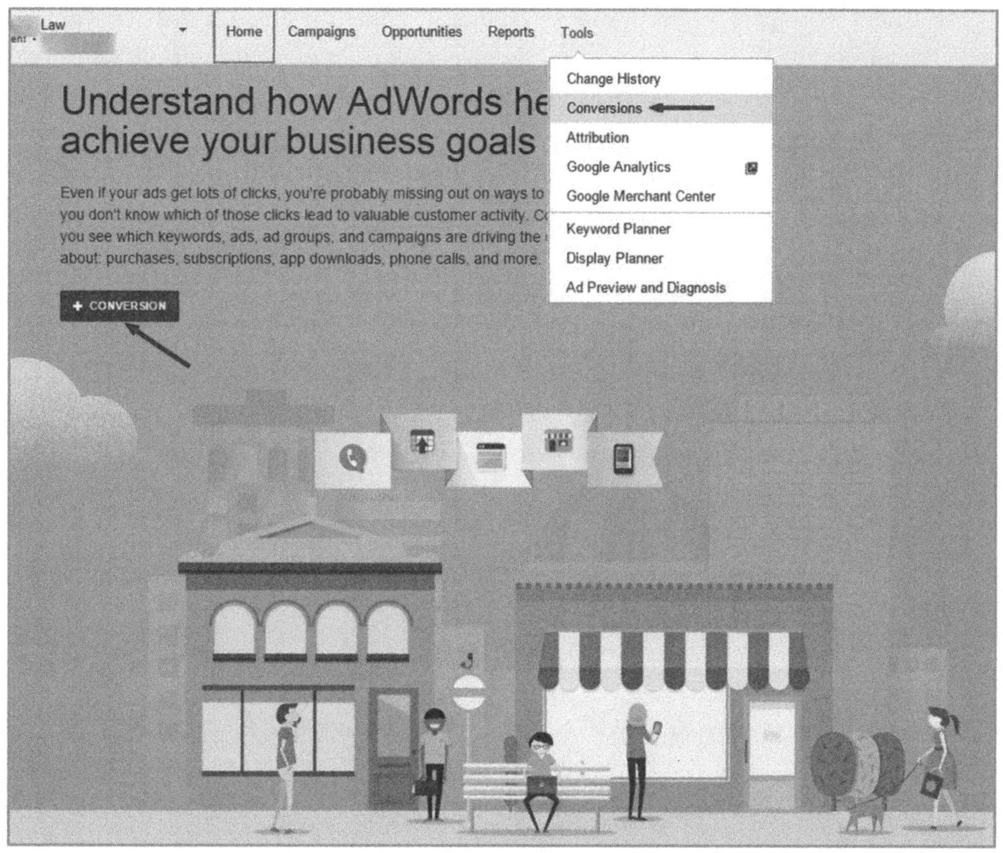

FIGURE 21-4. Google's Conversions Menu Is One of the Most Important Ingredients in the Whole AdWords System

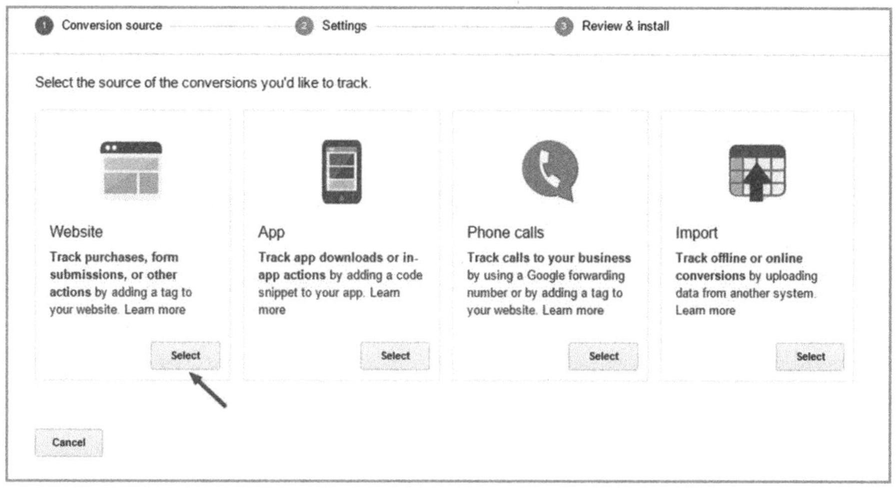

FIGURE 21-5. You Get to Define Exactly What Kind of Actions You Want to Track and Where

- Under "Count," we recommend changing from the default "All" option to "Unique." This simply means that if one person contacts you multiple times, you only count that as *one* conversion (which for most local businesses is how you want to count leads).
- And, finally, under "Category," you can select "Lead" from the drop-down box (though if you skip this step, it is not a big deal).

If you followed those instructions, your screen should now look like Figure 21-6.

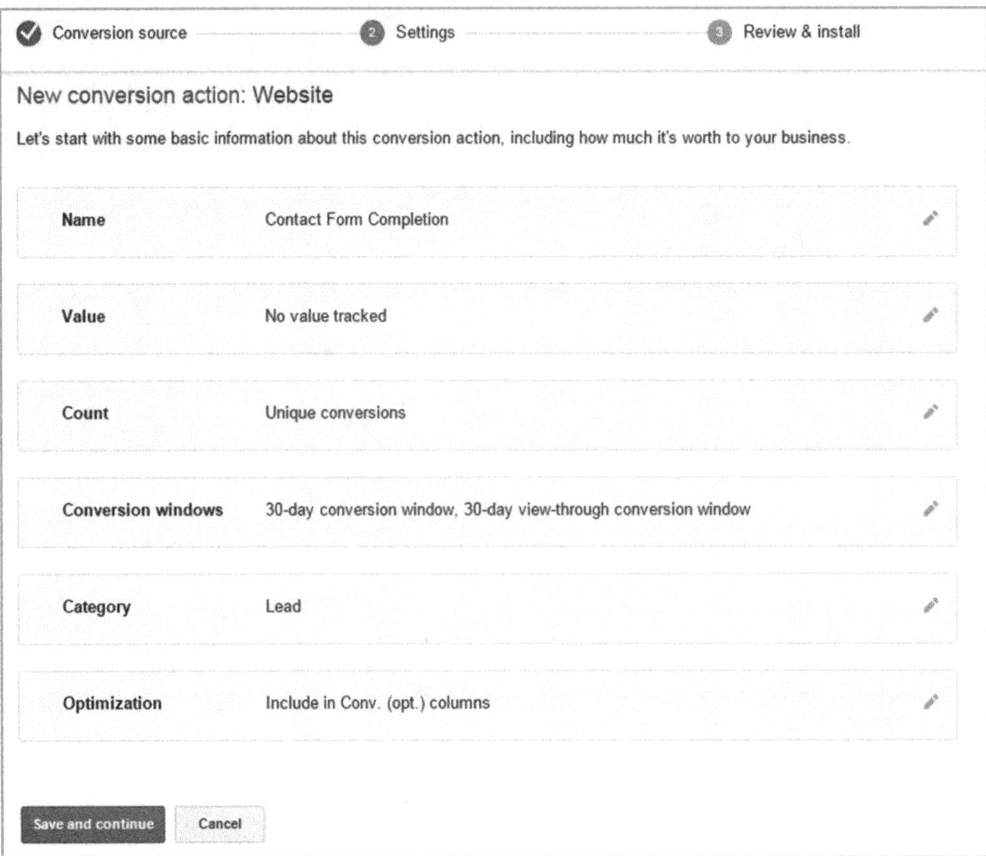

FIGURE 21-6. This Menu Confirms the Choices You've Made So You Can Create Your Conversion Code and Place It On Your Website

You can leave the "Conversion windows" and "Optimization" fields at their default options and then click "Save and continue."

At this point, Google will generate a conversion code for you. If you created this code to track when someone completes a contact form on your site, you or your webmaster should place the code on the "Thank you" page that visitors are redirected to after successfully submitting their information. Google provides instructions on exactly how to do this if you need them.

For call tracking using a third-party company (see our recommended list of providers at www.UltimateLocalBook.com), contact the call tracking company and they will help you get call conversion tracking set up properly.

Yes, this all requires a little technical know-how, but remember, if you do not have conversion tracking installed, you are flying a jet airplane blindfolded with no radar. So deal with any minor technical issues to get it set up correctly (or hire someone more technically inclined than you for a few bucks) because the long-term ROI of your campaign depends on it.

Chapter 22

Mobile Search Advertising: The Future of Local Business Marketing

by Talor Zamir

It's now impossible to go outdoors without seeing people with their heads buried in their mobile devices. At the store, at our kids' soccer games, at a restaurant, and even in our cars we are addicted to our smartphones. And your prospects are no different (in fact, many of those people you see buried in their phones *are* your prospects)!

So it should come as no surprise to hear that mobile search has been skyrocketing year after year. Mobile search has become one of the biggest areas of profitability for Google and it is only going to continue to grow.

Here are just a few statistics that underscore the huge importance of mobile search in local markets:

- According to a 2015 poll by BrightLocal, almost 40 percent of U.S. adult mobile phone users had searched for a local business on their phone at least once a month over the previous year.
- Research from BIA/Kelsey estimated there would be 81.8 *billion* U.S. local search queries done via mobile in 2015. They estimate that by 2019 that number will be 141.9 *billion*!
- As of mid-2015, the number of mobile searches now exceeds desktop searches.

Our experience certainly backs up the news reports. We have many clients who have more than half their leads coming from mobile.

There are two key factors that make mobile so powerful for local businesses. One is that local businesses have an especially high percentage of prospects searching for them on mobile devices. The other is that, for most local businesses, you are trying to generate a phone call, so having a prospect already on their smartphone makes placing a call even easier. All it takes is one click and they can instantly call you!

This makes it critical to make sure you have "click to call" enabled on the phone numbers on your landing pages. You also want to make sure your landing page is mobile responsive, so when prospects look at your landing page it is mobile friendly and they can easily read the copy and see all the benefits. Then they just need to tap your phone number to place a call to you. Having this in place will lead to higher conversion rates.

Mobile leads can also be higher-quality leads, depending on the niche. One prime example is someone who was just in an accident and does a Google search on their phone for a car accident lawyer. That is someone who is going to be a very hot, very motivated lead.

That is true in a number of niches, and we often find that high-quality leads come from mobile. If someone is searching specifically for a local business from their mobile device, they are probably not just browsing. People tend to browse a lot more from their computer than from a mobile device.

MOBILE AD POSITIONING

Earlier in the book we shared our finding that typically the best "bang for your buck" for ad positioning is around 2.5. In that position you are usually showing up in one of the top three spots, yet you are not overpaying for your clicks just to be number one.

However, things are a bit different for mobile. Whereas with desktop searches there will usually be three ads above the organic search results, in mobile there will only be one or two. Because of this, it is very important to watch your mobile stats and make sure that your average position for mobile is two or preferably higher.

You do not want to be at position number three on mobile, because it means that you are probably dropping to the very bottom of the page or possibly page two. And that means you are going to get a lot fewer impressions, a lower clickthrough rate, and miss out on a bunch of potential leads.

Mobile conversions are something you want to keep a close eye on, especially in the first week or two after launching your campaign. If you notice you are getting really good leads from mobile, then you may even want to consider raising your bid higher to be number one and maximize things to capture even more leads from mobile.

ADJUSTING YOUR MOBILE BIDS

Google used to give you the option of running mobile-only search campaigns in AdWords. Unfortunately, that is not the case anymore. Instead, advertisers now have the option of adjusting their bids for mobile devices in their campaigns.

If you go to the "Settings" tab of your AdWords campaign there are a few buttons toward the top of the page, one of which is "Devices." (See Figure 22-1.)

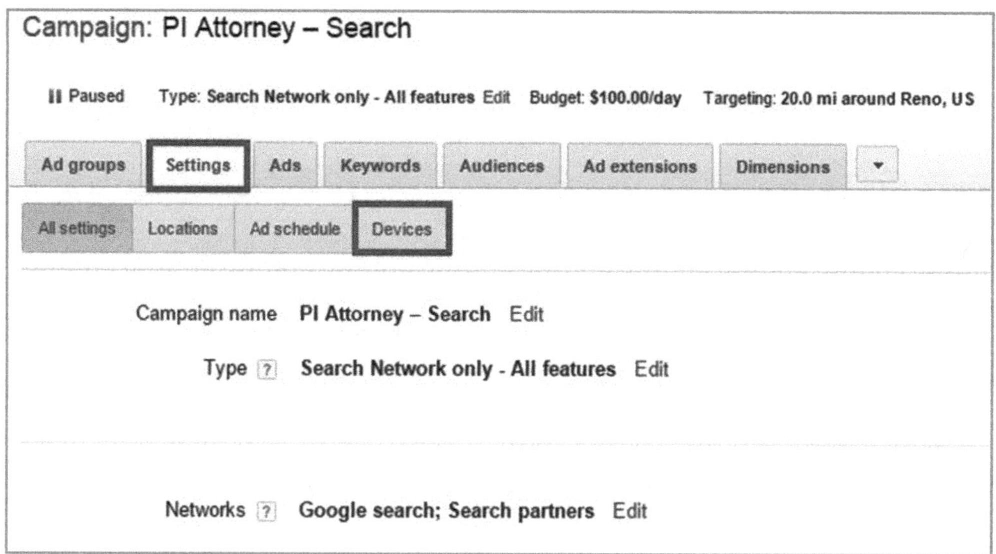

FIGURE 22-1. The "Devices" Menu in Campaign Settings Lets You Adjust the Mobile Device Bid

By clicking in the "Bid adj." column in the row titled "Mobile devices with full browsers" you will get a little window to appear where you can set the bid adjustments for your mobile traffic as in Figure 22-2 on page 140.

If you find mobile traffic is not converting well for you, it is possible to decrease your mobile bids by 100 percent, which will effectively stop your ads from showing up in mobile searches. Or if mobile traffic is converting at a little higher cost per conversion than you would like, decrease your mobile bids by 10 percent or 25 percent or whatever percentage you think makes sense based on the data.

If mobile traffic is converting well, you can increase your bids for mobile anywhere from 1 percent to 300 percent to improve your mobile ad positioning.

Unfortunately, it is no longer possible to set a bid adjustment for desktop/tablet traffic in AdWords. However, if you want to limit the amount of desktop traffic you get in your campaign and have it serve ads primarily on mobile devices, here is a trick you can use: First decide what you want your bids to be for mobile traffic. For example, let's

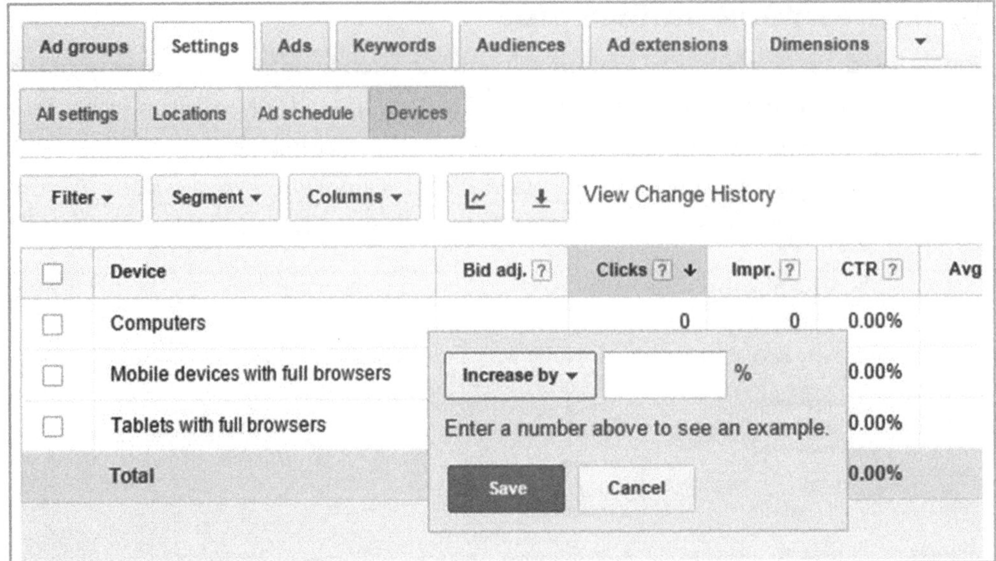

FIGURE 22–2. To Change Your Mobile Bid, Click on the "Mobile Devices" Menu in Device Settings

say you ultimately want to bid $10 per click for mobile traffic. In your campaign, set the bids for your keywords at $2.50. Next, go to the "Settings" page where you can adjust your mobile bids (as described above) and increase your mobile bids by 300 percent.

By doing this, you will end up bidding very low on desktop traffic so you will not get many impression and clicks. However, by increasing your mobile bid adjustment by 300 percent, the $2.50 bids you set for your keywords will turn into $10 bids for mobile traffic. While this is not a perfect solution to prevent your ads from running on desktops, it is the best option in AdWords at the moment.

CREATING MOBILE OPTIMIZED ADS

In AdWords, you have the ability to create mobile-optimized ads. This is very easy to do. When you are creating a new ad (as we showed you how to do in Chapter 18), there is a checkbox for "Device preference" where your only option is "Mobile." Checking this box does not guarantee the ad will only run on mobile devices, but they are given "preference" on mobile devices. (See Figure 22–3 on page 141.)

It is not mandatory to do this and set up separate ads for desktop vs. mobile traffic. However, there are a few benefits to doing this.

First, it can help you better split-test your ads because, in each ad group, you can create two mobile ads that you can split-test against each other and two desktop ads that you can split-test against each other.

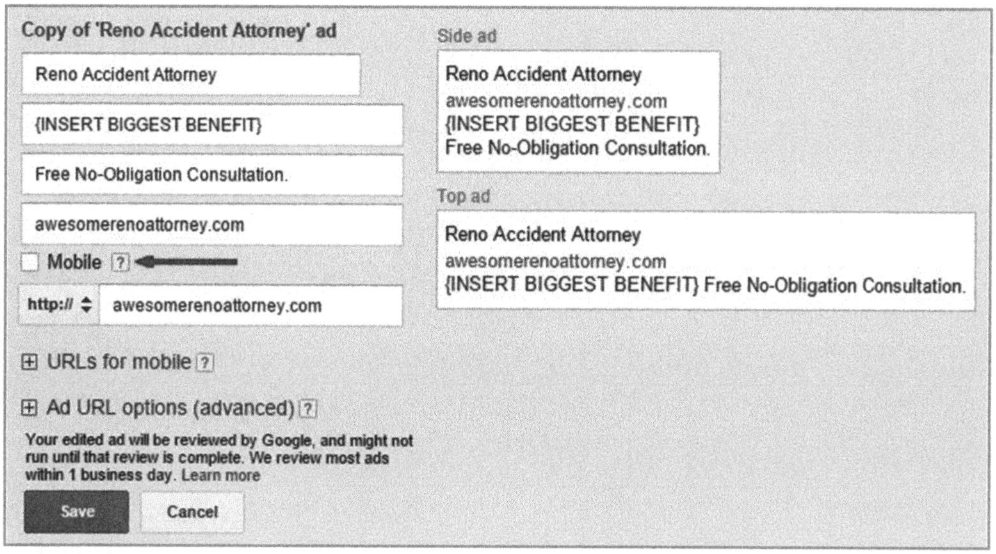

Copy of 'Reno Accident Attorney' ad
Reno Accident Attorney
{INSERT BIGGEST BENEFIT}
Free No-Obligation Consultation.
awesomerenoattorney.com
Mobile [?]
http:// awesomerenoattorney.com
URLs for mobile [?]
Ad URL options (advanced) [?]
Your edited ad will be reviewed by Google, and might not run until that review is complete. We review most ads within 1 business day. Learn more
Save Cancel

Side ad
Reno Accident Attorney
awesomerenoattorney.com
{INSERT BIGGEST BENEFIT}
Free No-Obligation Consultation.

Top ad
Reno Accident Attorney
awesomerenoattorney.com
{INSERT BIGGEST BENEFIT} Free No-Obligation Consultation.

FIGURE 22–3. You Can Designate a Particular Ad as Mobile Specific. This Ensures that Mobile Users See Exactly What You Want Them to See.

Even more important is that you can better customize your ad copy for mobile devices. For instance, it is good practice to emphasize the words "Call Now" in your mobile ads because you really want people to call you rather than click through to your website.

Call-Only Campaigns

In 2015 Google announced a new type of campaign dubbed "Call-Only" campaigns. This allows you to create campaigns where you are just trying to generate a phone call to your business. The ads prominently display your phone number, a description of your business, and a button to call you.

At this time, we do not recommend doing the new Google call-only campaigns. So far we have not had great success with them. The ones we have tried have had low conversions and, surprisingly, more than half the impressions were somehow showing up on desktops!

Hopefully, Google will improve this type of campaign over time, but when you're just starting, we suggest you simply set up a normal campaign and monitor mobile traffic.

That aside, make sure you give mobile traffic the proper amount of attention it deserves in your campaigns. It may just turn out to be the most profitable source of traffic you can get!

Chapter 23

Scale Up Your Lead Flow Once You Have a Winner

by Talor Zamir

Now you have been running your campaign for a few weeks or months and things are going great. You are really happy with the results and the cost per lead, but you want more leads! Maybe you spent $500 and got five or ten leads, which is awesome, but now that you have a taste of what's possible, you want more!

Once you have increased your AdWords budget and are maxing out what you can spend on your initial campaign, how do you scale up? How can you get more clicks and leads and take your campaign to the next level where you are really bringing in lots of leads on a daily basis and are maxing out your full potential of what you can get from PPC? That is exactly the question we are going to answer in this chapter.

BING ADS

When you are ready to scale, the first place we suggest looking is Bing Ads. Bing Ads is Microsoft's version of AdWords, except the ads will run on both the Bing and Yahoo! search engines.

While they are not Google, the concept is still the same. It is still someone doing a specific search for your service. Going to Yahoo! and Bing is the next closest thing to Google AdWords, and that is why it is the first step we recommend when scaling up.

Because Bing and Yahoo! get about 30 percent of search traffic, we typically find that you can get 30 percent more traffic by adding Bing Ads to your marketing mix. While there is substantially less traffic compared to Google, there is also less competition, so click costs tend to be lower on Bing Ads. Between the lower click costs and solid conversion rates, we have had clients get a cost per conversion in Bing Ads that is one-half to one-third what it is on AdWords. That said, because of the traffic levels and total number of conversions available, we prefer to always start with Google and then expand to Bing Ads later on.

Microsoft knows that Google AdWords is the 800-pound gorilla in the space and have made Bing Ads very similar to using AdWords. And they have made it extremely easy to copy your AdWords campaign over to Bing Ads.

In fact, once you create a Bing Ads account, there is a place where you can log into your AdWords account and directly import it into Bing Ads (see Figure 23–1). This makes replicating your account quick and easy, so we recommend you take advantage of this option.

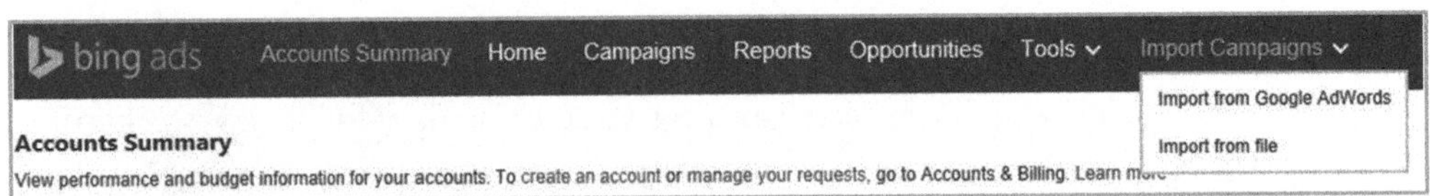

FIGURE 23–1. Bing Makes It Very Easy to Import Campaigns from Google, Minimizing the Effort Necessary for You

We do have a few tips/words of caution when importing your AdWords campaigns into Bing, however. First, double-check the geo-targeting settings in your campaign before you import it into Bing. Depending on how you are targeting the geographic areas your ads run in, those settings may not copy over to Bing Ads correctly. And if Bing Ads does not recognize the geo-targeting settings, they will be reset to the default, which shows ads in the *entire* U.S. and Canada.

Second, Bing Ads defaults to showing ads on its "Search network," including Bing and Yahoo! as well as "syndicated search partners." We have found Bing's "syndicated search partners" traffic to be of very low quality and do not recommend you have your ads running there. So we always change this from the default option to the "Bing and Yahoo! search (owned and operated) only" option, which means our ads will only show up on Bing and Yahoo!

The unfortunate thing here is that this setting is controlled at the ad group level, so you have to go into every ad group in your campaign to change it. You have to click on an ad group, go to the "Settings tab," and under "Advanced settings," select the Bing and Yahoo! only option as shown in Figure 23–2 on page 145.

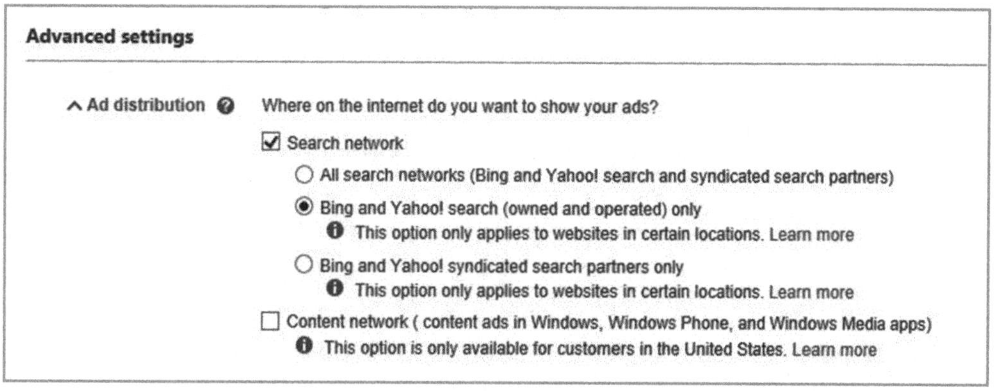

Advanced settings

^ Ad distribution ? Where on the internet do you want to show your ads?

☑ Search network

○ All search networks (Bing and Yahoo! search and syndicated search partners)

◉ Bing and Yahoo! search (owned and operated) only

ⓘ This option only applies to websites in certain locations. Learn more

○ Bing and Yahoo! syndicated search partners only

ⓘ This option only applies to websites in certain locations. Learn more

☐ Content network (content ads in Windows, Windows Phone, and Windows Media apps)

ⓘ This option is only available for customers in the United States. Learn more

FIGURE 23-2. Just Like Google, Bing Allows You to Choose Which Networks to Advertise On

ADDING MORE KEYWORDS

The next thing we recommend considering to expand your campaign and get more leads is to add more keywords. If you started with a very targeted list of keywords as we recommended and are happy with the results, this would be the time to start expanding and adding some new keywords that may be a little broader than your original choices.

This applies to match types where if you just started with exact match and phrase match keywords, you could now expand to broad match modifier keywords.

It also applies to the actual keywords in your campaign. An example is a chiropractor who started their campaign with keywords that specifically mention "chiropractor" and "chiropractic" in them. That is smart because you know people who are typing in keywords that contain "chiropractor" or "chiropractic" in them are specifically looking for a chiropractor. You do not have to convince those people they need a chiropractor. But if things are going really well in your campaign, you could start testing some new, broader words like "back pain treatment Reno" or "spinal decompression" and see if you get conversions from them.

Another example would be for a plumber who started their campaign focusing on keywords that contained phrases like "plumber" or "plumbing contractor." Once things are going well, they could consider expanding to keywords like "leaky toilet" and "water heater replacement."

Once you have your core keywords working and are getting a good cost per conversion on them, it is time to start experimenting with additional keyword variations in your campaign. Some may not convert well, but keep testing and you should be able to find additional keywords that will help you expand your campaign profitably!

ADVERTISING 24/7

As we stated previously, we only recommend running your AdWords campaign when you have someone available to answer the phone. If, like most businesses, you only have someone available to answer the phone during normal business hours, then you should have your ad schedule set to only run your campaign during that time.

However, if things are going well and you want to scale up and get more leads, one of the best ways to do that is to run your ads 24/7. If you do this, we would encourage you to get an after-hours answering service so a live person always answers your phone no matter when a call comes in. We will have more on answering the phone in an upcoming chapter because it is a critical piece of the puzzle.

EXPAND YOUR GEO-TARGETING

Another option for scaling your campaign is to expand the geographic radius by an additional five or ten miles and see if it is profitable. Or if you had only selected a few specific cities and zip codes, add more to your campaign and see if you can attract prospects that live further away.

In fact, depending on your business and how far away you can work with clients, you could potentially target the entire metro area where your business is located or even your entire state. A plumbing company who has to physically go to a client's home should only advertise in the areas they serve. However, a law firm that is licensed statewide and can work with clients largely over the phone could potentially advertise statewide.

We have a client who is an attorney in an extremely competitive market in the U.S. With the relatively small budget he had set aside for AdWords, the clicks were so expensive in his area that he was not generating enough leads to justify continuing with AdWords. Instead of giving up, however, we recommended focusing on a couple of counties outside his metro area, but still relatively close by. Click costs were less expensive in these counties and there was less competition, so he was able to generate enough leads with his campaign and has been consistently generating a three times ROI. In fact, things have gone so well that he opened a satellite office in the area to better serve his clients there.

This leads to another important lesson regarding AdWords: Once you have the keywords, ads, and landing pages in place and are generating a good ROI on your campaign, you can use what you have built to expand your business. If it works in Tampa, chances are good you can replicate things in Orlando, Miami, etc., and do really well in those other cities, too.

That is the true power of the model you are acquiring in this book. Knowing how to profitably buy leads from AdWords is an extremely powerful skill and one you can use to grow your business in your current location and, if you have the drive to do it, expand and open other locations. It's great when you have confidence you can turn on AdWords and get a consistent stream of clients coming your way.

Chapter 24

Remarketing: A Powerful Strategy Every Local Business Should Use

by Talor Zamir

My friend Jessica was shopping for lavender window blinds.

The very next day she was reading an article in *The New York Times* online, and what do you know . . . a banner ad with a picture of lavender window blinds.

"Whaaaaat? How did *that* get there?"

Remarketing ads. That's how it got there. Someone put a pixel on the lavender window blind site and those ads were following her around all over the web.

Remarketing, also known as retargeting, is one of the best ROIs you will get from any type of advertising or marketing. It is always a great strategy to put remarketing in place. In fact, we cannot think of an online marketing campaign that you would not want to use remarketing for.

The reason for this is simple. Even with a good landing page, typically 80 percent or more of the people who hit that landing page will not convert into a lead. However, those people did do a search related to your product/service and clicked on your ad. So they obviously showed a lot of interest in your company and what you offer.

Imagine this: One of your prospects hits your landing page. They are genuinely interested in what you offer, but maybe they are just thinking, "Ah, you know what, I am not ready to call right now. Let me think about it a little bit more and maybe I will get back to them. I'll probably make a decision in a couple of days and call them back then if I'm still interested."

We know that if you do *not* retarget, the chances of that prospect remembering exactly who you are and coming back to your site to contact you are slim to none. You obviously would want to follow up with those people and try to stay in front of them again. And that is exactly what remarketing allows you to do.

With remarketing, you add some code to your site, and everyone who hits your landing page will get a cookie dropped onto their device. This will allow you to remarket to them. With remarketing, the day after visiting your site a prospect will see your ads while searching around the web or in their news feed if you use Facebook retargeting.

GETTING STARTED WITH GOOGLE REMARKETING

Setting up a remarketing campaign is quite simple, and we are going to walk you through the process here.

The first step is to get the remarketing tag installed on your site. You want this tag to go on every page on your site. One of the great things about remarketing is it does not just work with PPC traffic. You can use remarketing to reach every visitor to your site whether they got there from PPC, organic, social, or directly typing in your URL.

To get your remarketing tag, log into your AdWords account and find the "Shared library" link down the left side of the page. The first option you will see there is "Audiences," which is what you want to select. Clicking on "Audiences" will take you to a screen that looks like Figure 24-1.

Click on the blue "Set up remarketing" button and it will open up this window as in Figure 24-2 on page 151.

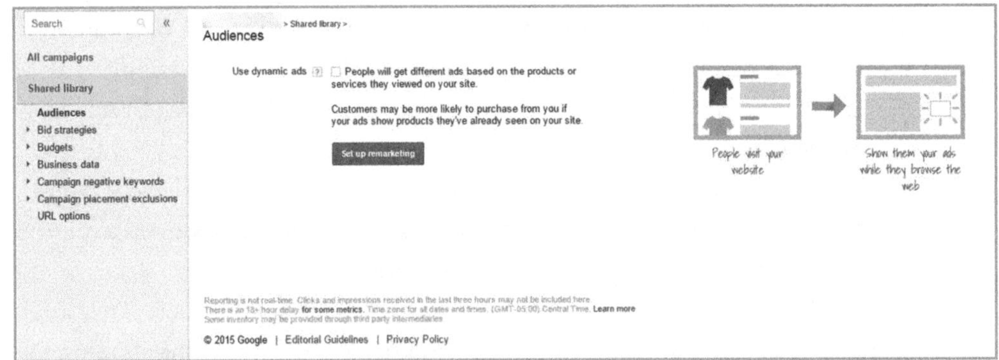

FIGURE 24-1. The Audiences Menu Lets You Define Individual Groups of People You Want to Retarget

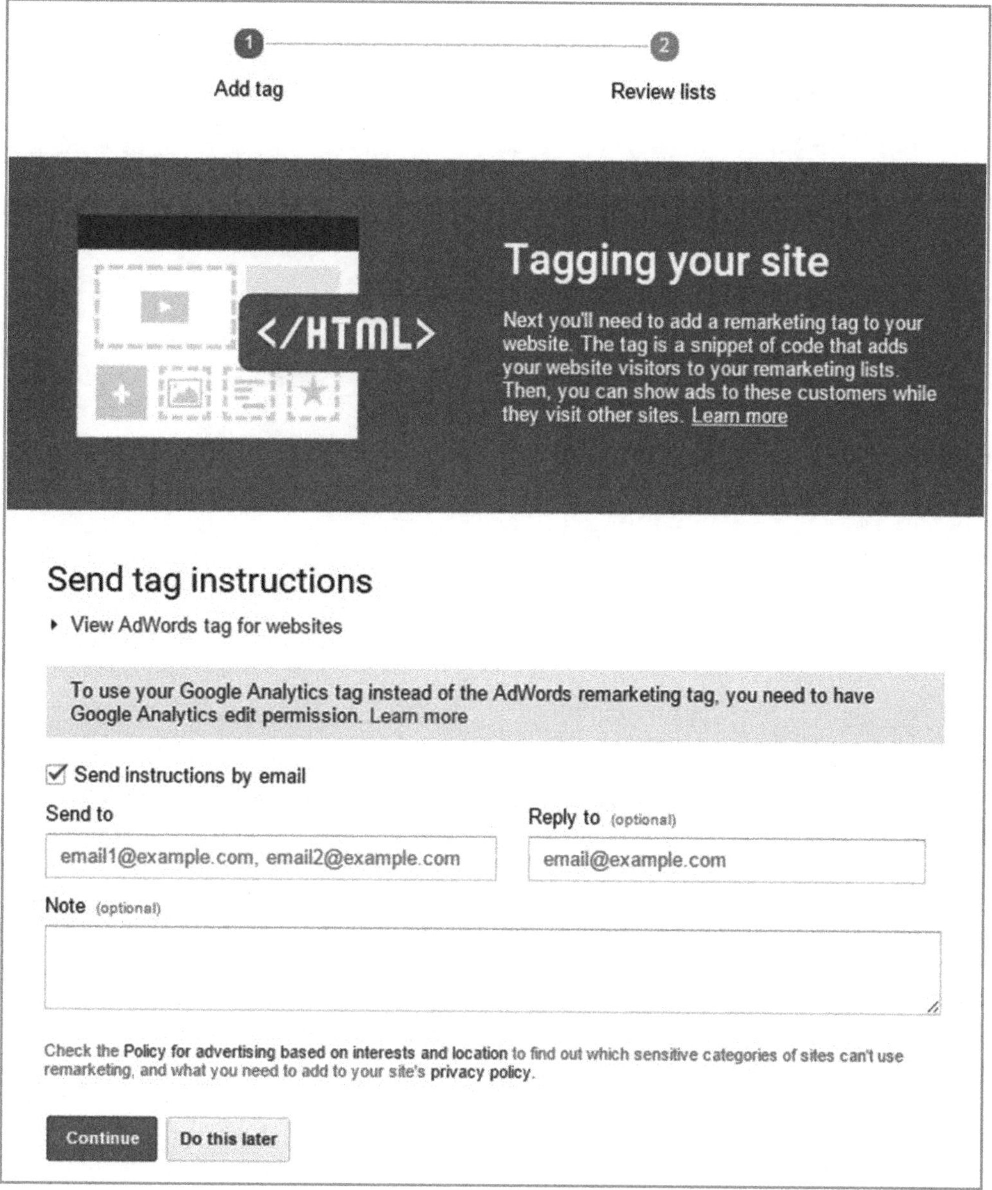

FIGURE 24–2. The Tagging Menu Generates Retargeting Code for Your Site

If you have a webmaster that manages your website for you, simply enter their email address in the "Send to" box. This will automatically email them the code and instructions needed to get the remarketing tag on your site.

If you are going to add the code yourself, just click the "View AdWords tag for websites" link in the window, and that will display your remarketing tag, which you can copy and paste into the code of your website.

With the code installed on your website, it is time to create your remarketing campaign. Under the "Campaigns" tab in your AdWords account, click the "+ Campaign" button, and select the "Display Network only" option from the drop-down menu, as in Figure 24-3.

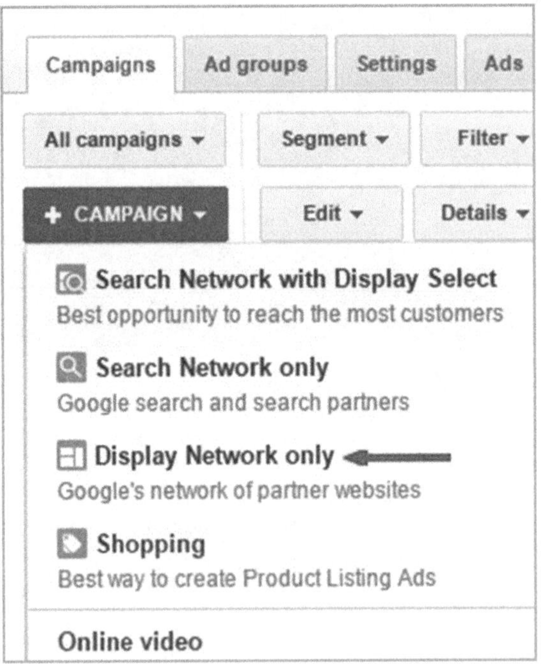

FIGURE 24-3. Retargeting Is Done on the Display Network Only

Name your campaign "'Remarketing" and select the "No marketing objective" option. Next, select the locations, bid strategy, budget, etc., just as you did when setting up your Search campaign.

There is one little tweak we suggest you make here. It is to "Frequency capping," which you will find under the "Ad delivery: Ad rotation, frequency capping" in the "Advanced settings" section. If you leave this at the default option, your remarketing ads could appear an unlimited number of times to prospects who visit your site. That could be overkill. Sometimes it can feel downright creepy. We don't want that. Our goal here is to remind prospects about your business, not to annoy them!

There are a number of different options for limiting the number of times a prospect sees your ad. In the screenshot in Figure 24-4 on page 153, we have set things so that no one will see more than four ads from this campaign each day. But there is no ideal setting here. Look at the options and decide what makes sense for your business. Typically you don't want to go above 10 to 15 impressions per day.

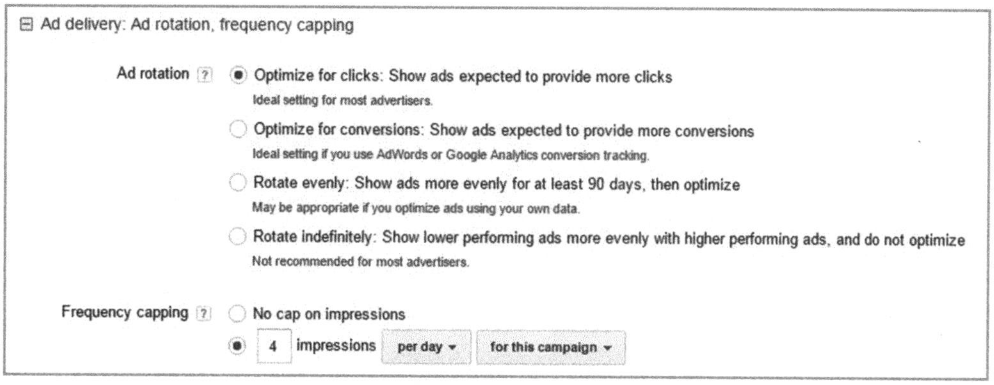

⊟ Ad delivery: Ad rotation, frequency capping

Ad rotation [?]
- (●) Optimize for clicks: Show ads expected to provide more clicks
  Ideal setting for most advertisers.
- ( ) Optimize for conversions: Show ads expected to provide more conversions
  Ideal setting if you use AdWords or Google Analytics conversion tracking.
- ( ) Rotate evenly: Show ads more evenly for at least 90 days, then optimize
  May be appropriate if you optimize ads using your own data.
- ( ) Rotate indefinitely: Show lower performing ads more evenly with higher performing ads, and do not optimize
  Not recommended for most advertisers.

Frequency capping [?]
- ( ) No cap on impressions
- (●) 4 impressions per day ▾ for this campaign ▾

FIGURE 24–4. You Can Set the Maximum Number of Times a Customer Sees Your Ad Each Day

After selecting your settings, click "Save and continue," and it is time to set up your first ad group.

Give the ad group a name in the "Ad group name" box and enter a default bid. Remarketing clicks are generally much cheaper than Search clicks, so we would recommend starting with a bid around $2.

Under the "Choose how to target your ads" header, select the "Interests & remarketing" option and click "Remarketing lists" from the drop-down menu as in Figure 24-5.

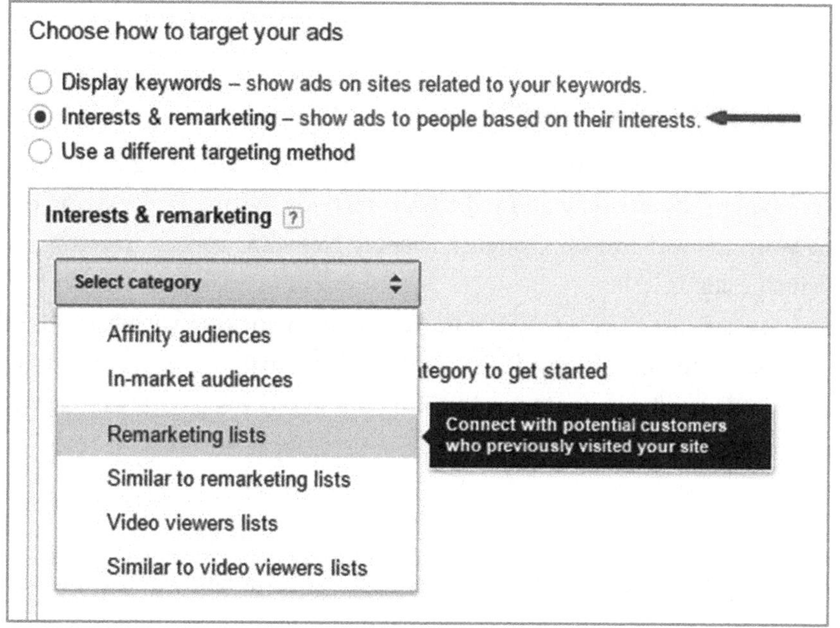

FIGURE 24–5. You Can Match Specific Ads to Your Remarketing Efforts

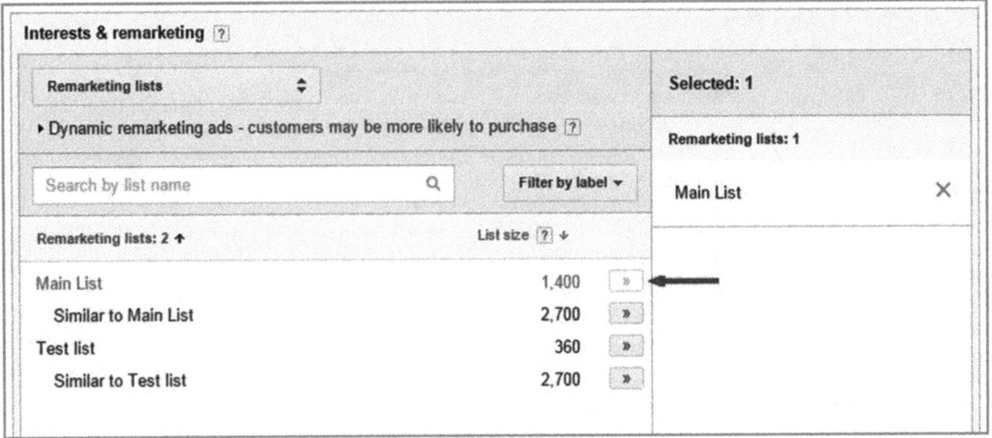

FIGURE 24–6. Once Remarketing Groups Are Defined, You Can Check their Status and Watch them Accumulate

After making that selection, you will see all your remarketing lists below. We will talk about segmenting and creating additional remarketing audiences later in this chapter, but for now, you will probably just have one remarketing list created called "Main List." Select this list by clicking the arrow button next to it (and make sure you select "Main List" and *not* the "Similar to Main List" option), as in Figure 24–6.

At the bottom of the screen, there is an option "Let AdWords automatically find new customers." Uncheck that box, then click "Save and continue."

CREATING REMARKETING ADS

At this point, it will be time to write some ads for your remarketing campaign. With a Search campaign, you are only allowed to run text ads. With a remarketing campaign, however, your ads will run on Google's Display Network, so you have the option of running image ads as well.

When you are just starting, we would recommend sticking with text ads. You can simply copy some (or all) of the ads in your Search campaign over to your remarketing campaign and that will give you a good starting point. Once you enter and save your ads, your remarketing campaign will be live!

Image Ads

After your remarketing campaign has been running for a while and things are going well, you can experiment with adding some image ads to the campaign and see how they perform.

Google has a number of different image ad sizes you can create. However, what we have found is that 300 x 250 is the most common image ad size, with 728 x 90 the second most common. To keep things simple, we recommend just creating ads of those sizes.

You can have a designer create these ads for you. Just tell them you want banner ads that are 300 x 250 and 728 x 90, and the file size must be less than 50Kb.

If you want to create the image ads yourself, Google gives you a few easy options to do this right within AdWords. You can find them on the "Ads" tab by clicking the "+ AD" button. Selecting the "Image ad" button will bring up an interface where Google will scan your landing page/website and grab whatever images and ad copy snippets it finds to create an ad for you (after it does this, you can alter things manually).

The other option is the "Ad gallery," where you can select from ad templates Google has created and customize them for your business.

Any or all of the above options are worth trying. Just make sure you are split-testing and keeping an eye on which ads are performing well and pausing the ones that are not. One of our favorite image ad design firms is www.BannerAdQueen.com, and our customers like them because they understand Google AdWords, split-testing, and retargeting.

SEGMENTING FOR SUCCESS

Google creates a default "Main List" for remarketing that targets everyone who lands on your website. However, you may not want to target every person who comes to your site. Or you may want to target different messages to different visitors (in fact, it is a good idea to tailor your messaging this way).

Segmenting your site traffic into different audiences can help you significantly improve the results you get from your remarketing campaign. Following are a few examples of how you could use it.

People who have already contacted you (and have hopefully become clients) probably do not need to see your remarketing ads over and over again. So one audience you can create in AdWords is a list of every site visitor with the exception of those who have triggered a conversion during their visit.

If you have a lot of existing clients visiting your site (i.e., maybe you have an online portal they use to log in to access information), then you do not want them to see your remarketing ads aimed at your prospects. In this case, you can create an audience that excludes any visitor to your site who visits the login page for existing clients.

For a business that has multiple practice areas/offers multiple services, you will want to create separate audiences for each. For example, if your law firm practices DUI, family law, and tax law, you should target each group separately. In this case, you tag all the

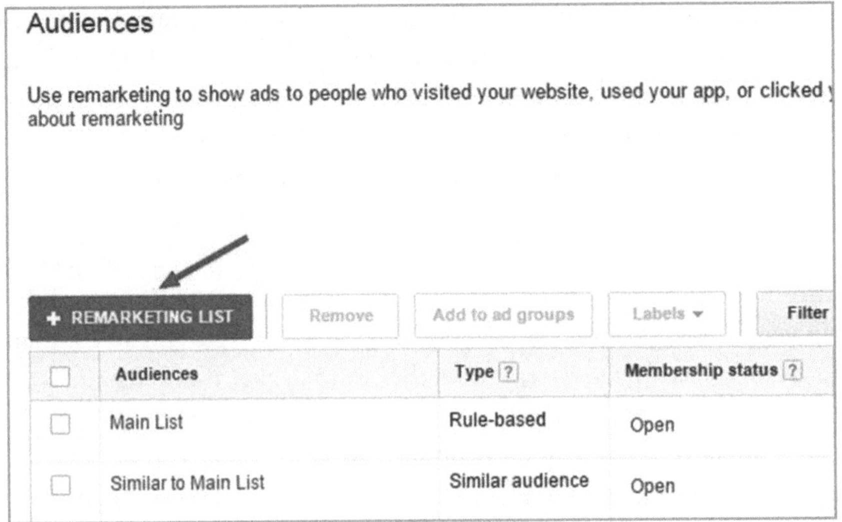

FIGURE 24–7. You Can Retarget Unique Audiences for Different Groups of Customers or Product Lines

people who visit a DUI-related page on your site and then create an ad group in your remarketing campaign for that audience, and create ads that specifically mention DUI and lead to your DUI landing page. Then do the same for all the visitors to the family law and tax law pages.

To create these audiences, go back to the "Audiences" page under the "Shared Library" in your campaign. Once there, click on the "+ Remarketing List" button, as in Figure 24–7.

When creating a new remarketing list, you will give your list a name and then decide who to add to it. Here you can create lists of people who have visited specific pages of your site, people who did not visit a specific page on your site, and/or create custom combinations. There are plenty of options, and Google has good examples and instructions on how to set this up, so we are not going to cover all the options here.

After you select who to add to your list, select a membership duration (more on this in a minute) and click "Save." You can then create a new ad group in your remarketing campaign that targets specific ads to this audience.

Membership Duration

While the default is 30 days, you can set your remarketing list to target people anywhere from 1 to 540 days after they visit your site. Different experts will give you different opinions on how long you should set the membership duration for.

How long is your sales cycle? A fertility clinic would likely want to set a longer duration of at least 180 days. On the other hand, for a company that specializes in cleaning up flood damage, even 30 days may be too long (though a good strategy for them may be to run water damage cleanup ads for a few days and then target those same people with mold remediation ads after that). A plumber might target people very heavily for a few days (with a high impression cap instead of a low one), then after that assume the overflowing toilet has been solved and stop showing ads.

The bottom line here is you know your business better than anyone and you understand how long people are going to likely be in the market for your services. So choose the membership duration of your remarketing lists accordingly.

EXPANDING YOUR REMARKETING BEYOND ADWORDS

Google is not the only game in town when it comes to remarketing. The other options we recommend are Facebook and even YouTube.

What we will say is, right now, we believe Facebook retargeting is actually the most important option out there. While Facebook advertising may not always be right for every local business, we think that Facebook *retargeting* is great for local businesses (and every business in general) to have in place.

Chapter 25

Convert Those Leads into Paying Clients and Profits

by Perry Marshall and Talor Zamir

Perry Marshall here. I have a friend who runs dental practice management seminars. This guy chose to exercise his considerable chutzpah at one of his bootcamps.

Some states allow phone calls to be recorded without notifying the other party, and my friend hired a telephone mystery shopper to call the practices in those states.

They recorded the calls . . . *and played them live at a seminar with hundreds of dentists in attendance.*

"We called Dr. Martin's office in Birmingham, Alabama, and here's how the call went." Then everyone hears the phone call over the speakers.

"Martin Dental, can I help you?"

"Yes, I would like to talk to someone about implants."

"Just a moment, ma'am."

The hold music begins, and . . .

. . . Drags on for 2 ½ eternal minutes.

Dr. Martin is sitting there cringing the whole time, being humiliated in front of his peers.

Do you think he's going to let *that* happen again?

As embarrassing as it was for Dr. Martin to sit through that, the case he lost cost a lot more than his plane fare for the practice management seminar.

Incompetent handling of inbound phone calls is a *huge* source of loss.

Your AdWords campaign is humming along and you are getting lots of high-quality visitors to your landing page. And the landing page is doing a good job of converting those visitors into leads. All the numbers are looking good, but you are frustrated because you do not seem to be generating more clients and revenue.

What is the problem here?

While AdWords can make the phone ring, it is up to you to convert those leads into clients. Unlike in ecommerce where the entire transaction takes place on the website, for local businesses, human interaction is required to close the deal.

THE X-FACTOR

When we work with clients, we can set up the best landing pages and Google AdWords campaigns on the planet, but at the end of the day if they do not know the right way to answer the phone, those leads will largely go to waste. When people are calling and a business cannot convert those calls into customers, that is an X-factor that cannot be controlled by AdWords and needs to be monitored and worked on internally by you and your staff.

Whenever someone's getting lots of leads, the online marketing piece seems to be good, and they're not closing sales, there's a disconnect. And it's usually in our clients' office.

Think about it. Just like how when you double conversion of a landing page, you will get twice as many leads, the same goes for when you answer the phone and handle those incoming leads. You can double your ROI by having a really good sales system for handling incoming calls.

If you have someone who is untrained in sales and is not doing a good job of getting people into the office or following up with them, you may convert only 1 out of every 4 leads into a customer, or maybe one out of every 40.

We have heard recordings of calls that were completely botched by the person answering the phone. One Cosmetic Dentist had his 19-year-old niece answering the phone. A prospect called asking if they do dental implants—one of the *main* things this cosmetic dentist does (in fact, he charges around $12K for dental implants!). His niece told the caller she had to go find out and put the prospect on hold for over three minutes! By the time she got back on the line, the prospect had hung up and was likely calling the next ad on the page.

> If you have someone answering your phone who is well trained and instead of converting one out of every four leads into a client, they are able to convert two out of four, then you have literally just doubled your business!

How much is a cosmetic surgery case worth? OUCH!

This is important not only with Google AdWords but for all aspects of your business, no matter where the leads come from. It is a key factor that you should spend some time focusing on and making sure that it is being handled correctly.

You may even want to start recording your inbound calls by implementing a call-tracking system that also records the phone calls. This will let you hear how good of a job your team is doing and what needs to be improved.

SIX TIPS FOR CONVERTING LEADS INTO CLIENTS

1. Do Not Let Calls Go to Voicemail!

This is a cardinal rule if you are spending any money on advertising and marketing. You must not let calls go to voicemail! This is one of the biggest problems we see where calls come in and nobody answers, the call goes to voicemail, or the caller is put on hold for two or three minutes.

You do not have an existing relationship with most people who click on your ads. This is cold traffic, and if they call and get your voicemail, most people will not leave a voicemail. They will just hang up and call the advertiser in the next ad.

Same thing if you put them on hold for three minutes. They are still sitting in front of their computer or on their mobile phone, and the temptation is overwhelming to just hang up and call the next person. Make sure you are equipped to handle the calls and you have a system in place to do it well.

One of our clients, a dentist, has a call center that she uses so that she has a live person answering the phone 24/7. The call center is even able to schedule appointments.

Earlier in the book we recommended you only have your ads turned on when people are around to answer the phone. Using a call center will let you run ads all day with the confidence that any call will be answered by a live person, which will lead to higher conversion rates.

2. Mystery Shopping

The acid test for your phone crew is mystery shopping. Like my friend who runs dental seminars, have someone call your business and play prospect. Make sure the mystery shopper knows how to act like your customer. Record every call. **Many entrepreneurs are appalled when they find out what is actually going on when a customer calls their business.**

You founded your business, you poured your blood, sweat, and tears into it. You know it costs 90 bucks just to make that phone ring, and you've spent months building advertising systems and making mistakes. You can't imagine someone screwing all that up and letting a customer go down the drain.

But your employees are not you. It's not their 90 bucks, it's yours. It's not their blood, sweat, and tears, it's yours. They have no skin in the game. So they're lackadaisical.

Quality control is crucial. Hire that mystery shopper and monitor what goes on. Make it known that at all times, the calls are being recorded and any call may be monitored. Performance and raises should be judged by how well customers get treated on the phone.

3. Invest in Sales Training

Even if it may not be in their official job description, *everyone* who answers the phone in your office is a salesperson! They should have a basic understanding of sales and how to properly handle incoming calls professionally.

At the very least, buy the people who answer the phone in your office a book or two on sales. Even better is to invest in a course or even hire a sales trainer to come in and work with them. This investment can pay huge dividends down the road.

4. Use Systems and Scripts

Whether those answering your phones have sales training or not, it is a good idea to have systems in place so calls are consistently handled the way you want—no matter who answers the phone.

In most cases, you do not want your employees winging it too much on the phone, so giving everyone a script can be helpful. Richard Jacobs owns Speakeasy Marketing, a firm that specializes in marketing for attorneys. He understands the importance of handling incoming phone calls and works with his clients to develop scripts for their employees.

One of the effective scripts he has his clients use is along the lines of this:

> *"Oh, Mr. Jacobs isn't at the phone right now, but he wants to make sure he talks to you, so let me get his calendar. I see he's available this Thursday at 11 A.M. or 2:30 P.M. and Friday between 9 A.M. and 10:30 A.M. If you get your calendar out right now, let's schedule a time when it's good for you."*

This script makes the person calling feel important, which will give them a good feeling about your company and doing business with you. Even more important, it sets an appointment on the spot and gets that initial commitment from your prospect right then and there.

5. Always *Get Contact Information*

Whoever answers your phone should take down every caller's contact information, including their email address. If you do not have their contact information, you have no way to follow up with them and the lead will go to waste.

6. Use Email Marketing

When you get the email addresses from clients and prospects, you should have some sort of system where you can send out emails at least on a monthly (though preferably on a weekly) basis to your email database.

We always ask clients if they have ever sent out emails to their contacts. If not, we will have them gather all the email addresses they have and put it into a system like MailChimp, iContact, or any other email service provider, and then send out at least an email or two to their list.

There are no shortage of things you can send. Maybe you have some sort of sale or special promotion going on that you could share. Or maybe it is just a great story about one of your customers. You could send them a video, which will help develop a closer bond between you and your potential customers. You could also send a good article you have written or a helpful tip. Basically send things that will keep you in front of them regularly and continue to build a relationship with them, which can help generate more business and referrals in the future. If you are not using email marketing and email follow up, you are leaving a ton of money on the table.

One of the great things about email is you can completely automate it. Once a prospect gets on your email list, you can have a series of emails automatically sent to them without you ever having to click send. This form of email marketing is called an autoresponder. A good autoresponder strategy can easily double your sales conversion.

We have an in-depth strategy for those who want a proven formula for using autoresponders to grow their business, which you can find at www.UltimateLocalBook.com.

WHAT TWO OF OUR MOST SUCCESSFUL CLIENTS HAVE IN COMMON

Two of our most successful clients are lawyers who are spending tens of thousands each month on AdWords. It is not a coincidence that both have trained salespeople answering their phones. It is one of the reasons they are getting such a great ROI on their campaigns and, therefore, they want to keep spending more and more on marketing to get more leads. How your leads are handled is one of the most important factors to the success of any marketing you do.

Chapter 26

What to Look for When Hiring a PPC Agency

by Adam Kreitman, CEO of Words That Click

Note from Perry Marshall: *There are many things you can outsource—janitorial services, payroll, painting the office, cooking, cleaning, mowing, snow shoveling, bookkeeping, and taxes. The majority of those things are simple, straightforward, and inexpensive to outsource.*

Marketing is very hard to outsource successfully. Pay-per-click marketing is doubly hard, because 95 percent of "pay-per-click experts" do not know what they are doing because ***they did not learn AdWords on their own dime.***

This chapter is about outsourcing PPC from Adam Kreitman, a man who is well qualified to speak on the subject. Warning: Outsource your online advertising with great care. And if you are in a time crunch, get a cook, maid, or lawn service FIRST. And whatever you do, don't abdicate your number-one job, which is marketing yourself to the world.

In this book, Talor and Perry have given you a complete blueprint on how to create a highly effective pay-per-click (PPC) campaign for your local business. But even with all this information in hand, there may be some of you who have no interest setting up and managing things yourself. You have a business to run, family obligations, hobbies, etc., and already feel like there are not enough hours in the day and would be perfectly happy turning things over to a PPC expert to handle it all for you.

For those of you who are interested in outsourcing the management of your PPC campaigns, I've been asked to help you become an educated consumer so you know what to ask and look for before making a hiring decision.

I understand it may seem a bit self-serving to have someone who runs a PPC agency giving you this advice. And that may be. However, I've been behind the scenes of hundreds of AdWords campaigns, talked to many local business owners over the years about their experiences with agencies, and have talked with those who own and/or work for various online marketing companies. So it is drawing upon that background, knowledge, and experience that I offer the following advice to help you make a smart decision about hiring someone to handle your PPC campaigns.

SIX QUESTIONS TO ASK BEFORE HIRING A PPC AGENCY AND WHY

1. Will I Keep Ownership of My AdWords Account?

This is a biggie. Your AdWords campaign should be set up and managed in a Google account that you own and will always and forever have access to.

Some agencies, particularly bigger national/international ones, will not use an AdWords account directly owned by their clients. Instead they use an internal agency account that your campaign is managed through that you cannot get direct access to. You will just get monthly reports that cover the metrics they choose to share with you.

There are a few big drawbacks to this scenario. First, you don't truly know what is going on in your account. You cannot see which keywords/search terms your ads are being triggered by, how the campaign is structured, how often someone is logging in and optimizing the campaign, etc.

You also have no idea how much you are actually paying for clicks vs. paying the company in management fees. I heard from one employee at a company like this that the company would mark up click costs around 100 percent. So if your report shows you are paying $10 per click, the reality is that your Google clicks only cost $5 and the other $5 goes to the management company.

Is that worth it? Well, because you don't have direct access to your account and there is no transparency, it's difficult to tell.

Lastly, account history is important in AdWords. So if you decide at some point you want to switch to another company or handle PPC management internally, you don't have access to that history. Even if the account was not managed well and you would want to start from scratch anyway, it is still beneficial to be able to log in and mine the historical data to help create your new campaigns.

So make sure there is transparency. *Have your campaign running in an AdWords account you own and control.* Any agency you hire can simply link to your account (you do not even need to give them your Google username/password), so you are still in control of your account and data.

2. How Are Results/ROI Tracked and Reported?

I know that Talor and Perry have hammered home the importance of tracking your ROI. You have to be tracking conversions. You have to use dynamic call tracking. You have to know your cost per conversion.

So when hiring an agency, it is important to understand if and how they are going to track conversions in your campaign. Do they use dynamic call tracking to link calls back to the ads and keywords that are making your phone ring? Are they tracking submissions from any contact forms on your landing pages?

One frustration I commonly hear from business owners is that they get confusing reports from agencies. The reports give basic information about the campaign: the top keywords, how many clicks their campaigns got, what the clickthrough rates of the ads are, etc.

However, they often do not get clear reporting on what matters most: leads. Ultimately, you want to know if AdWords is generating an ROI for you or not, so make sure the reporting you get from an agency makes that very clear to you.

3. Will the Agency Create Dedicated Landing Pages for My Campaign?

By now you understand that your AdWords account is only part of the picture in generating leads from AdWords. A good chunk of the heavy lifting is done by the landing page(s) you send your traffic to. Because of the importance a landing page has on the performance of your campaign, one of the first questions you should ask an agency is whether they will create landing pages for you.

A few years back it was difficult to find an agency that even mentioned landing pages when talking with clients. That is starting to get better as more PPC professionals are catching on to the importance of having dedicated landing pages for their campaigns. But a lot of them still do not do this, and many that do don't do it well. Unless you are going to create the landing pages yourself based on what you have learned in this book, you should hire an agency that is highly skilled in landing page creation/optimization.

You also want to know who is going to be writing and creating the landing page, which ties in to the next question.

4. Who Will Create and Manage My Campaign?

One thing I have learned over the years is that it is extremely hard to scale high-level PPC management. Offering a high-quality service at reasonable prices to the masses is extremely difficult, and I have not come across a company who has cracked the code on how to do this.

In talking to local business owners and PPC professionals, what tends to be the case is the big agencies hire low-salary employees that are cost-effective for the company. However, lower-level employees usually do not have the experience and skill set required to create and/or manage a PPC campaign and are probably not who you want working on your campaigns.

Usually the most talented PPC marketers are the ones who are marketing experts themselves (usually with a strong background in direct response marketing and copywriting). They are the ones you want to have reviewing your campaign, writing your ads/landing pages, and focusing on your conversions.

Also, find out if your regular contact at the company is going to be the individual who is managing your campaigns. Having that direct line of communication is critical so you can work with them to discuss strategy, ad and landing page copy ideas, new services/products that your business is offering, etc. Being in regular contact with the actual people managing your campaign (especially when they are marketing experts) can make a significant impact in the results of your marketing.

I hope I am being clear that you **cannot** just "throw this over the wall." If you don't keep a close eye on it, it won't be done right.

5. Do They Work With My Competitors?

Take a look at the three ads in Figure 26-1 on page 169, from three different house painters in Albuquerque. And see also those from two different chiropractors in St. Louis (Figure 26-2 on page 169).

These ads appeared right next to one another in the AdWords auction exactly as shown in the screenshots. Aside from the fact the ad copy is weak, how can anyone differentiate among these businesses? This is a risk you take if you hire a firm that works with competing businesses. (It's also a risk if the firm doesn't have good copywriters so they just steal other people's ads.)

Even if the PPC agency creates unique copy and landing pages for you and your competitors, how do they decide who gets the ad copy and landing page they've developed that perform the best? It's better to avoid situations like this completely and work with a firm that is exclusive and will not work with your competitors.

Albuquerque House Painters
www.octaviospainting.com/
Painting experts in **Albuquerque**.
Call us today at (505) 225-3576 !

Painters
www.markspaintingmaintenance.com/
Painting experts in **Albuquerque**.
Call us today at (505)-225-1274 !

Painters
www.ziapaintingdecoratinginc.com/
Painting experts in **Albuquerque**.
Call us today at (505)-206-5767 !

FIGURE 26–1. Different Companies with the Same Ad!

"Top Rated" **Chiropractor**
www.thestlouischiropractor.com/
St. Louis Chiropractic Clinic.
Back Pain, Neck Pain & More - Call!
1076 Old Des Peres Road, Saint Louis
(314) 227-9427

"Top Rated" **Chiropractor**
www.saintlouismochiropractic.com/
Saint Louis Chiropractic Clinic.
Back Pain, Neck Pain & More - Call!
916 Olive Street, Suite 301, St. Louis
(314) 667-4433

FIGURE 26–2. Another Example of Different Companies with the Same Ad

That said, it can be beneficial to hire a firm that has experience in your specific vertical. If they have proven ad copy and landing pages that have gotten results for similar businesses, that gives you a great starting point. However, it is much better that the experience comes from working with businesses similar to yours that serve different parts of the country than yours.

6. Do I Have to Sign a Long-Term Contract?

This one is pretty straightforward. It can take a few months for a new PPC campaign to really get traction. Because of this, some firms require a three- to four-month commitment so they are given an honest shot at optimizing a new campaign for a client and getting good results for them.

Any more than that, however, is unnecessary. There is no good reason to lock yourself into a six-month or yearlong contract for PPC management, so be very wary of situations where that is a requirement.

HIRING AN AGENCY DOES NOT MEAN YOU ARE OFF THE HOOK!

Outsourcing the management of your campaign *might* make a lot of sense. However, doing so does not mean you can simply hand the reins over to an agency and forget about it. While PPC experts at an agency should know more about PPC and marketing than you do, you know more about your industry and business than they do.

And it is by marrying your knowledge about what's going on in your business and their knowledge about your campaign and what's going on in the world of PPC that will produce the best results.

So be an active participant in the process. Stay in touch with the agency and let them know about any new developments, events, promotions, etc., going on in your business. Log into your AdWords account every now and then and take a look around and see what is going on in there. Check to see that ads are constantly being split-tested and losers are being deleted and replaced with new winners. Get on the phone with them every so often to brainstorm marketing strategies and ideas that can help generate more leads for your business.

That is the key to having a successful, long-term relationship with the PPC agency you hire.

■ ■ ■

Adam Kreitman owns Words That Click, LLC (http://wordsthatclick.com), an award-winning marketing firm in St. Louis that specializes in PPC for local service businesses. You can reach him via email: adam@wordsthatclick.com.

Chapter 27

Local SEO Techniques

by Richard Jacobs, founder of SpeakEasy Marketing

Note from Perry Marshall: *The strategies you're about to learn are much different from the pay-per-click [PPC] and landing page strategies we discussed earlier in this book. They are almost completely unrelated and should be looked at as two separate investments.*

This chapter is guest-written by Rich Jacobs, founder of SpeakEasy Marketing, which specializes in marketing for attorneys.

Before I get into any tactic or trick on how to do local SEO, you've got to understand the landscape of Google's search results, because it is very different from what you might think. First, I'll talk about website structure. Then I'll go into details about what constitutes real results in SEO and a few other concepts before we even get into *how* to do the SEO to get more organic traffic to your website.

Everyone's obsessed with keyword rankings and Google maps rankings. Those things *are* very important—in fact, I used to check my old website's rankings every hour, like some people check their stock prices!

I'm not saying that ranking your website on page one of Google for local searches isn't important—it is. It's also critical to get at least five reviews in Google maps (so you get the gold stars next to your listing). However, there is more to local SEO success than getting reviews and being on page one of Google for a few keywords. You've got to learn how to see things in a different way.

Here's what I mean: Imagine a tree with many branches up top, many roots below the ground, and one tree trunk in the middle. This is what your website looks like in the eyes of Google's spiders. Your website is not just a homepage (a trunk). Your website is not just one or two dimensions—it's three-dimensional. And just like the sun illuminates every branch and leaf of a tree, every single page of your website is exposed to Google search, at all times (same with Yahoo! and Bing).

Designed properly, every page of your website will be exposed and indexed by Google. If you think about your website using this analogy, rather than a website as a single page (i.e., a tree with no branches, just a stump), you realize that every page of your website is important. Taking this analogy further, to give people the shortest path to what they're searching for, Google allows people to enter your website from *any page* thus providing a better user experience.

Knowing this, you don't want to have a site with just a homepage and maybe a few additional pages; to do SEO the right way, you want to build a website with *hundreds of different pages*. Why? Because just like the root of a tree, each page can burrow into a unique area of the soil and absorb its nutrients, as each page of your website can contain a unique article that describes a specific aspect of what your business does.

If you compare two trees, one with a very small root system and one with a deep, expansive root system, the one with the more expansive root system will be resistant to floods and falling over and dying. The one with the small root system (i.e., the fewer number of pages) will not thrive nearly as well. It won't get nearly as much business.

Let me be more specific: If your website has hundreds of pages and you cover every possible aspect of what you do, people with specific problems in your niche are much more likely to see a particular article on your website that *exactly matches what their problem or question is.* Google will then show them that specific article, and they'll click through and land on that specific page.

And as Perry Marshall teaches, we know from Google PPC and from marketing in general the more specific you can answer someone's questions, the more likely you are to get them as a customer.

Don't worry, I'm also going to tell you *how* to get on page one for hundreds of keywords and build your website to hundreds of pages of content.

MEASURING SUCCESS IN LOCAL SEO

How do you know if your local SEO efforts are working? What most folks do is they'll run a rank checker to see, for example, if they're number four for Dallas personal injury lawyer or number three for New York dentists, but your ranking for one keyword is not important.

A better way is to use Google Analytics and webmaster tools to see how much traffic your website is getting from the search engines and for what keywords—this is called your "organic traffic." If your website is getting two to five visits today, it doesn't matter what it looks like or what its keyword rankings are. (Even if you have first-page rankings and a visually stunning website, you can still get little traffic and zero business.)

How can this be? The reason is, you must have a critical mass of people coming to your website on a regular basis in order for them to take action. Not sure if you knew this, but most websites have a 1 percent conversion rate, many far less. That means if you don't get at least 100 visitors to your site in a month, there's pretty much no chance of getting a phone call or email asking for help (i.e., a "lead"). You've got to build your website's traffic to a minimum of 500 visits a month, often a lot more. (*Note:* SEO results are much different from Google AdWords and high-converting landing pages like Talor and Perry teach about in this book, which can convert at 10 percent to 20 percent.)

Today, I care nothing about keyword rankings for my attorney clients. Instead, I worry about their website's organic traffic because if I can ramp it up to 30 visits a day, then 50, then 100 visits, *now* they have enough critical mass to get regular leads from valid potential clients, and then to work on conversion optimization.

You want a flow of qualified prospects calling, emailing, or filling in a request form *every single day*, right? This is how you more accurately measure success: Is the number of visitors from search engines to your website growing each month? Or is that number stagnant or declining? What level of organic traffic do you have? If your SEO efforts increase the traffic, then you're headed in a profitable direction.

DIAGNOSING SEO PROBLEMS USING YOUR WEBSITE'S STRUCTURE

Before we move on to specific SEO tactics, let's talk about website structure and how to diagnose why your website is having SEO problems vs. conversion problems.

Situation 1: Google Analytics shows that you're getting one, two, maybe even five visitors a day. In this situation, no matter how the website looks, it's not going to help you; no matter how the website ranks, it's not going to help you—*you must get more traffic!*

Situation 2: You're getting 20, 30, even 50 or 100 visitors a day, but you're getting very few leads (calls, emails, form submissions). In this case, *you've got a conversion problem.*

In Situation 2, it looks like you're getting adequate traffic from the search engines, but if you're getting little to no business, it means: 1) Your website's design elements are not keeping searchers' attention, 2) not answering their questions, 3) not solving their problems, or 4) distracting visitors to the point of inaction and frustration. This situation is much harder to address because it seems like things should be working, and on the surface, there's no reason why they're not working.

It's important to talk about conversion, because it ties in to the right way to do local SEO. Every website, if you think about it, is only composed of a few different types of pages. Let's say you're a dentist. Most dentist websites have five different types of pages: 1) homepage, 2) contact us page, 3) about us page, 4) maybe a dentist profile page, and 5) article pages that provide information on various aspects of dentistry, prices, hours, availability, insurance, etc.

If you look at the pages themselves, an effective SEO dentist's website will be composed of 95 percent or more dentistry content/articles. In a 100-page website, the homepage, about us, contact us, and profile page comprise a mere 4 percent of all the website's pages.

What I've noticed on every single website I've looked at (having seen over 1,000 websites) is that the 80/20 rule holds. There will be four to five pages on your site that get the lion's share of traffic, typically 80 percent to 90 percent. When focusing on conversion, those top trafficked pages are the ones you should focus on, in descending order of traffic, to improve on and make most compelling, informative, and useful to visitors. Why? Because the top five pages of your website are the most heavily trafficked and will have the most influence on getting you more business.

The homepage is almost always one of the top five most trafficked pages of any website, but most likely the other busiest are article pages. I've found this 80/20 analysis to be a very important and useful shortcut to help you improve your website's conversion rate.

SEO TACTICS TO BUILD YOUR WEBSITE'S TRAFFIC

There's no mystery here: SEO is relatively simple and has just a couple core elements.

Core Element 1: Create Unique, Valuable Content on a Regular Basis

We've already talked about *why* this will help you. One of the best ways I've found to create content is to interview yourself or have someone interview you once a month, on a one-hour recorded phone call. Once transcribed, a one-hour phone interview will become approximately 12 to 15 articles (about 8,000 words). If you commit to this process once a month and you answer frequently asked questions, misconceptions, mistakes, how to select a person in your industry, and other valuable questions, you'll have created a useful, engaging, and SEO-effective amount of content that Google, Yahoo!, and Bing will reward with more website visitors.

You'll be adding substantial amounts of unique (in website industry vernacular), easily understood, conversational content to your site each month. This will help you tremendously in the search engines. Over time, it will build your website to hundreds of pages of content, and you will start getting a heck of a lot more organic traffic that you can convert to revenue.

Core Element 2: Obtain Backlinks from Relevant, Third-Party Websites

I once had a consultation with a top SEO guru named Mike Marshall (an amazing man who tragically passed away last year). He was the SEO guy for 1-800-Flowers and the U.S. Patent Office—aka a heavy hitter. I paid Mike for a whole day consultation on SEO. The most important thing I got out of the consultation came when I asked him, "What's better SEO-wise: a single, relevant, high-quality backlink from an authoritative website in my niche, or a thousand mediocre links from nonrelevant sites?" **Mike said, without missing a beat: "a single, relevant, high-quality backlink will beat 1,000, maybe even 10,000 mediocre links."** *I knew then just what to do.*

When my team does link building (which still works, and is critical to my clients' websites' success), we target and accept links only from relevant, authoritative websites. If you're in a legal industry, that means legal-related sites. If you're a dentist, that means dental or health-related sites. If you're in the financial industry, that means finance- and money-related sites.

Don't go after sites where the links are not relevant. Don't try to get hundreds of thousands of links; you don't need them, and they'll actually hurt you. You only need three to five relevant, high-quality links to get significant traffic growth to your website over time.

LOCAL SEO IS VERY SIMILAR TO NATIONAL SEO

You now know the two core elements of SEO. Local SEO works in much the same way. In the old days, you used to be able to "fool Google" and build out specific pages for the keywords you wanted to rank for, especially if your chosen keywords were different cities in your area. Websites would have dozens of pages, each titled and stuffed with keywords like: "Los Angeles DUI Lawyer," "Beverly Hills DUI Lawyer," "Hollywood DUI attorney," and "Santa Monica DUI attorney."

Now, instead (and more reliably), Google bases its search results and your rankings on your company's physical location. Make sure all your location addresses are displayed on your website and you have created a Google maps listing for each location. Because Google wants to show local results to searchers who are looking for *local* help, and because Google knows your smartphone, tablet, or laptop's location (where you're searching from), it will show you local results (not a dentist 50 miles away).

Google reads the address(es) on your website, and if a searcher is within a 15-mile radius of your business's address, you have a better likelihood of not only showing up on page one, but higher up on the page—if your website has been optimized properly and is mobile-friendly.

Conversely, if a person is 20, 30, or 50 miles away, no matter what you do, it's almost impossible to force Google to show your website preferentially to that searcher. So a critical strategy is to *make sure* that you have a Google maps listing for each of your locations and you also have your address(es) displayed on your site and linked back and forth to your Google Maps listings. Google will then naturally show people that are close to you.

But what if you want customers from a nearby city that's "too far away"? The best way to do that without trying to force Google (which doesn't work anyway) is to get a second location. I'm not talking about a UPS store or P.O. box, but to negotiate with a local business owner in that town to allow you to use their address and receive the occasional mail piece there. Maybe they'll rent you a conference room if you're a professional, or just let you receive mail at that location.

If you can get a second location, an executive suite, conference room, or mail drop, you can now add a second Google maps listing and put that address on your website, and now Google will associate your business with that second address as well and start showing you to searchers in that area. Beyond that, I have found it nearly impossible to force Google to show you where you want to be shown, not where it thinks you are.

GETTING "ENOUGH" FAVORABLE REVIEWS IN GOOGLE MAPS

Why are reviews important for your business and where should they go? Reviews are extremely important today. I've seen many studies that say the majority of searchers read and depend on them to make their decision and to judge which business they should call.

Imagine you and your significant other are hungry and you're looking for a Chinese restaurant for dinner tonight. You Google "Chinese restaurants," or you use Yelp, and see that one restaurant has 50 reviews that are all four stars, but another one has 450 reviews that are all four stars. General Tso's chicken notwithstanding, which one would you go to? You'd go to the one with 450 reviews. Why? Because you think in your mind *"that many people can't be wrong."* The same thing applies in your industry.

Thankfully, for some industries, very few reviews are needed, and most businesses have zero reviews, so if you have five or more, that's all you need to stand out. In other industries, the baseline may be 100-plus reviews, so you may need 300 or more.

Either way, reviews are critical, and you need to have them in more than one place to be most effective, such as Google Maps, Yelp, Thumbtack, Judy's Book, or other websites. One benefit of Google Maps is that once you get at least five reviews, gold stars appear in your listing, which helps draw the searcher's eye and gets you more business.

Other local review sites are Thumbtack, Judy's Book, etc. You have to know which local sites are used most often by people in your industry and then you must obtain good reviews on all of them. You also need 10-plus reviews on your website itself.

The more reviews you have, the more often you'll win the battle for a customer's wallet. If you notice the various websites in your industry and you see sites with tons of testimonials/reviews, you'll literally feel yourself being compelled to buy, especially if you read 10 or more reviews. It's happened to me, it's happened to people I know, and I know it has happened to you too. You might not have thought about it, but those reviews have power.

There you have it—the few, core methods that underpin successful local SEO (and national SEO as well). There's no magic, no voodoo, and no mystery.

If you adhere to these core elements and max them out, you'll do fantastically well with local SEO, you'll never fear Google's next algorithm update, and build a solid business on the back of organic traffic.

A FINAL WORD OF CAUTION

Because SEO is so competitive, and even local SEO can be very competitive, you cannot expect results fast. It takes, on average, six months to really start to do well SEO-wise, and honestly, a year of solid work is often needed. But if you commit to this process for one year, it's like getting in shape—your business will be healthy financially, the health benefits won't disappear overnight, and you'll be in a great position to get lots of new business. Don't fear the process: Get started today and you'll see tremendous results and a very positive ROI for many years to come, especially after a year of good work.

■ ■ ■

Through SpeakEasy Marketing Inc., over the past six years Richard Jacobs has helped over 557 law firms nationwide attract more leads and clients. He's spoken at several legal conferences and is author of *Secrets of Attorney Marketing Law School Dares Not Teach* (available on Amazon). Richard has also created over 100 authors through his Speak-a-Book process (while reusing the content for SEO purposes) in a range of industries, including CPAs, lawyers, doctors, and more. You can contact Richard via email at RJ@SpeakEasyMarketingInc.com.

Chapter 28

Facebook and Facebook Ads for Local Businesses

by Keith Krance, founder of Dominate Web Media and co-author of *Ultimate Guide to Facebook Advertising* with Perry Marshall

Close your eyes for a second and think back to the last time you reconnected with an old friend or colleague by using Facebook. Maybe it was someone you went to high school or college with, someone you used to work with, or a friend from kindergarten.

Have you ever used Facebook to message someone and you didn't have their phone number or email address? Like a schoolteacher, a distant relative, or friend of a friend?

Facebook has become the fastest way to find almost anybody, anywhere. Most people use Facebook instead of Google when they're looking for specific people.

I recently attended my 20-year high school reunion. Everyone was amazed how great of an event it was: how many people showed up and how many people kept in touch immediately *after* the reunion. We've actually already planned another minireunion six months from now at a local venue.

Why was this reunion so much better than some of the recent 20-year reunions four to five years ago with different classes at my same high school? One reason: The reunion organizer created a "Class of '95" Facebook group.

The Facebook group kept everyone eagerly anticipating the event. And because so many people had so much fun and so many people who were not able to attend the reunion still got to see all the shared photos, one person suggested that we do another meetup in six months. And now the next event is on the calendar.

FACEBOOK DOESN'T WANT TO BE COOL

Some critics say that Facebook is doomed because it's not "cool" anymore. But Facebook isn't out to be the next teenager's hot social network or app. It doesn't care about being cool—it wants to be a "utility."

You may or may not spend much time on Facebook, but you can be certain that the majority of your potential customers are spending at least some time on Facebook every day.

As of March 31, 2015, there are now over 1.4 billion active users on Facebook. And if you consider the fact that there are 3 billion people on planet Earth that currently have internet access, this means that almost half the connected planet has an active Facebook account. And over 800 million of those users log on to Facebook every day, *an average of 14 times a day!*

Facebook Is Your Mobile Channel

Facebook and Instagram account for over 23 percent of the total time spent on mobile devices. That's more than Twitter, Snapchat, and all the rest combined, according to the internet analytics firm comScore.

Also according to comScore, people are watching six times the amount of video via Facebook on their mobile devices than they are on YouTube. The average monthly minutes spent on YouTube via a mobile device is 31 minutes. The average monthly minutes watching video on Facebook via mobile is 182 minutes! (Monthly minutes on desktop are about the same: YouTube is 54 minutes per month, and Facebook is 53 minutes.)

This makes perfect sense if you think about it: People typically go to YouTube looking for a solution to a problem. Yet people will scroll through their Facebook newsfeed whenever they're bored, waiting in the dentist's office, trying to connect with someone, etc., which is much more frequent.

How Do You Put Your Message in Front of this Massive Audience?

Now that you know the majority of your customers are on Facebook, the question is how do you put your message in front of your ideal target audience in a way that gets them to take action and buy your stuff?

If Google is now the online version of the Yellow Pages, Facebook is the online version of the party, coffee shop, or social event. Have you ever been to a party or any social gathering and met "that guy"? You know, the one who 30 seconds after he shakes your hand is already pitching you his financial planning services, insurance plans, or "business opportunity that will help you enjoy a residual income for the rest of your life."

The conversation goes something like this:

"Hi, I'm Joe. How are you?" he says.

"Hi, I'm ______. I'm doing great, how about you?" you reply.

"Oh that's great!" he says half yelling, with his face about ten inches from yours. "You know, I've had a great week too. Busy! I've been helping people get one step closer to becoming financially free all week long. Are you financially free yet? I'd love to help you put the right pieces in place to create a residual income for the rest of your life. I have a couple openings next week.–I'd love to get together and see if I can help you out. Would Tuesday at 1 P.M. work, or is Wednesday at 10 A.M. better?"

After quietly listening and nodding your head, what do you want to do?

If you're anything like me, you want to seize him by his shoulders, twist him around, and kick him in his rear end out the front door! And you want to go to the bathroom and wash your hands after shaking his.

Nobody likes "that guy" or "that girl" who is always selling something at a party or social gathering. However, some of the biggest deals and sales ever made have been born from two people meeting at a party or a coffee shop.

Of course, any savvy business owner or entrepreneur understands that it might take three, four, and possibly five or six connections with the same person before you have built a *real* relationship that may lead to an appointment or a meeting.

Let's go back to the party and start over. Imagine meeting that same person at a party and the conversation goes a little different this time. Maybe something like this:

"Hi, I'm Joe. How are you?" he says.

"Hi ,I'm Keith. I'm doing great—how 'bout you?" you reply.

"I'm doing great, too, now that the week is over," he says with a sigh of relief.

"Long week, huh? What do you do?" you reply.

"Yep, it was a pretty long week–but a good one, though. I'm a financial advisor," he says. "I specialize mostly in helping 30- to 50-year-old folks raise the money they will need for

college tuition, and still have enough left over to actually retire. What about you? What do you do?" he asks.

"I'm a business consultant. I help entrepreneurs and small businesses put in systems to scale their business with fewer hours of work per week. I have a 5- and 7-year-old, and I keep thinking college is gonna sneak up on me a little too fast."

Joe replies, "There's a tax loophole 90 percent of parents don't know exists. Works best when children are under ten. Google '529 plan' sometime. If you're intentional about it, you can sock away an extra $20K or so while your kids are growing up. Anyway, are your kids playing sports this year?"

The conversation moves on. Maybe you ask more about his financial advising, maybe you don't. But when you leave the party you don't feel like you have to wash your hands after meeting Joe. Maybe you mention the college fund loophole to your spouse while driving home.

The next day, as you are driving to work, you drive past a billboard on the right side of the road and you see a photo of Joe and the name of his company on the billboard! That billboard has probably been there for a month, but you never noticed it until now. The message on the billboard says: *"Give Your Child a Head Start for College. Start Small and Save Big. Visit www.SaveForCollege.com to take the quiz and find out how much money you will need when your child turns 18."*

You think to yourself, "Oh, wow, that's Joe, the guy I met last night who gave me that college funding tip!" Do you think you would go visit his website and fill out a survey, or even possibly schedule a call or appointment with him? Maybe. Maybe not.

But my guess is that you'll have a much higher likelihood of visiting his site and taking action after he provided some value and tipped off his authority by giving you that insightful nugget of information, *without* trying to sell you something. He gave you an "aha moment" at the party. He whetted your appetite just enough to leave you wanting more—and luckily he had some good systems in place to make it easy for you to find him later (a billboard on your way to work).

Facebook advertising is no different. However, the great thing about Facebook is you can automatically be building relationships and providing value with potential customers or clients simultaneously all over the world, with strategic systems in place to transition some of those new relationships into subscribers and customers.

Just imagine if you could clone yourself (or your best salesperson) and start attending parties, conferences, networking events, and coffee shops all over the world, building relationships along the way. You're planting seeds along the way with all these new friends and peers to eventually move a percentage of them into your database as clients or customers.

Clone Yourself . . . and Crash Any Party in the World

Would you like to mingle with high rollers with a net worth over $1 million at the Metropolitan Museum of Art in New York City? See Figure 28-1.

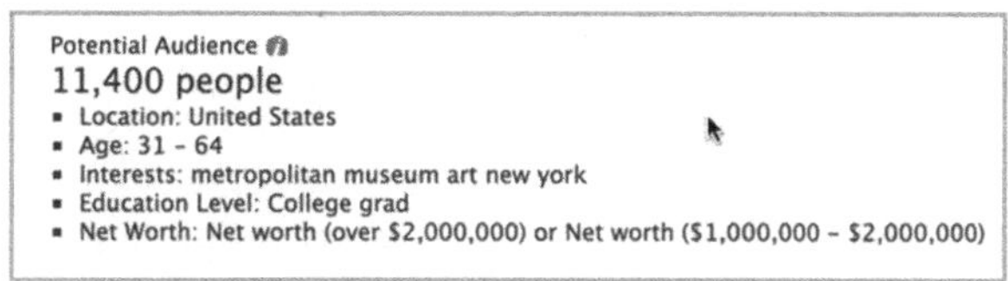

FIGURE 28-1. Facebook Fans of the New York Metropolitan Art Museum

How about simultaneously attending all the best BNI chapter meetings around the world? Or chamber of commerce? Or Rotary International? (See Figure 28-2.)

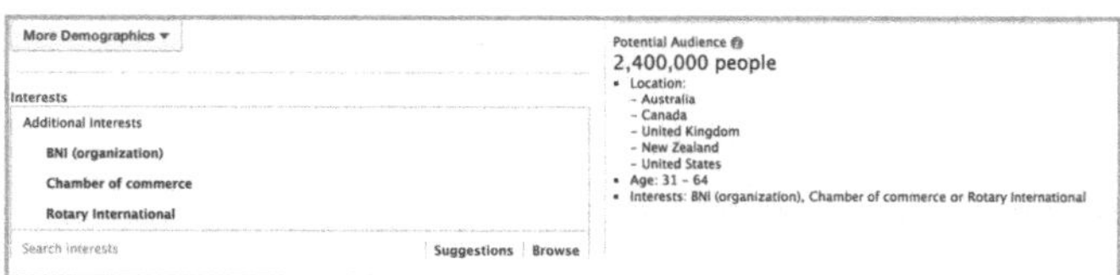

FIGURE 28-2. Chamber of Commerce, BNI, Rotary Targeting

These are just two examples of some basic targeting inside the Facebook Ads platform. The possibilities are endless. More on the different targeting options later in this chapter.

THE FIVE-STEP FACEBOOK FAST START FORMULA

After spending over $5 million on Facebook ads over the last five years in over 28 different industries, and currently averaging between $150,000 to $250,000 per week in Facebook ad spend, we have figured out a few things along the way (see Figure 28-3 on page 184). We've made lots of mistakes but have also had lots of big wins. My goal is to only give you advice on what really works now so you can save your hard-earned money and precious time, and do things right from the start.

This is why I developed a simple, easy-to-implement five-step process that will work in any industry, especially a local business or someone brand-new at Facebook Ads.

STEP 1: PUBLISH "FACEBOOK-FRIENDLY" GOODWILL CONTENT

The first step to success on Facebook is to create a piece of high-value content that Facebook users can consume without paying for it or exchanging their contact info for it. We call this "ungated content," and it serves three main purposes.

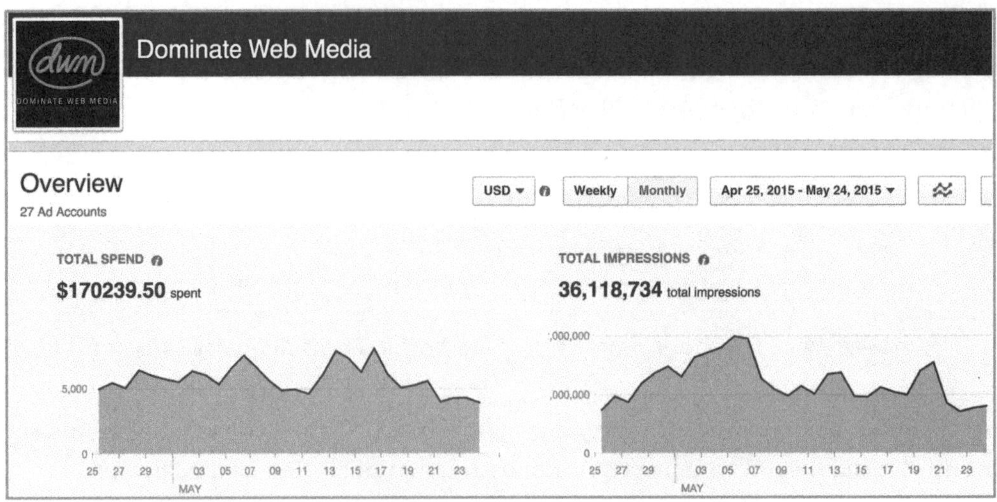

FIGURE 28-3. A Snapshot of an Average Monthly Spend Inside My Facebook Ads Business Manager

1. It Builds Trust and Goodwill, and Helps Indoctrinate People into Your Business or Brand

Think about the good guy at the party—Joe. Just imagine if Joe would've said something like this 30 seconds after meeting you: "Hey, there's this great tax loophole that 90 percent of parents don't know exists that can help you pay for your kids' tuition, and if you just give me your phone number and email address, I'll tell you what it is."

I would've been like, "What? Are you kidding me? Get lost, dude!"

This initial piece of content is equivalent to you shaking hands and meeting somebody at a party, or you showing up at a networking event and starting to make friends with people.

2. It Builds Your Facebook Ads Account with High Relevance Scores and Low Negative Feedback

This is something you won't hear many "Facebook experts" talk about, but it may be the most important takeaway from this chapter. Facebook gives you a "relevance score" of 1 to 10 on every ad you create. This is similar to a Google Quality Score. The higher the relevance score, the lower your cost per click (CPC) will be, and the more impressions Facebook will serve you.

According to Facebook, this is how relevance scores work:

> *Relevance score is calculated based on the positive and negative feedback we expect an ad to receive from its target audience. The more positive interactions we expect an ad to receive,*

the higher the ad's relevance score will be. (Positive indicators vary depending on the ad's objective but may include video views, conversions, etc.) The more times we expect people to hide or report an ad, the lower its score will be.

However, the most interesting thing is that past ad account history can affect future campaign pricing and decisions. What this means is that if all you do is run lead-generation and sales promotions every day, you will be building up a stack of low-relevance, high-negative feedback campaigns in your account, and Facebook will start to price future campaigns higher in terms of CPC and cost per lead.

Think about it as making deposits into the bank of goodwill. Every time you run a campaign that is highly engaging, with low negative feedback, lots of likes, comments, and shares, you are making goodwill deposits. And whenever you run a conversion-focused campaign, you are making withdrawals of goodwill.

Facebook is totally fine with you running conversion-focused campaigns, like driving traffic to opt-in pages, sales pages, etc. However, if those are the *only* campaigns you are running, then you will eventually pay the price, in either click costs, conversion costs, or—worse—getting your ad account banned from Facebook.

3. It Builds Your Website Custom Audience Lists (Retargeting Lists)

One of the most powerful aspects of the Facebook Ads platform is the ability to create and segment different custom audiences based on user behavior. This feature is also cross-device capable, which means if someone lands on one of your pages or watches a Facebook video ad on their mobile device, you can retarget that same user at a later date on their desktop device. This is huge.

For example, you may find that you can generate leads at a better ROI targeting mobile devices, but your sales conversions are horrible on mobile. No worries, you can run your content amplification and lead generation campaigns targeting mobile and your sales page campaigns on a desktop computer.

Another game-changing Facebook feature is you can create a "lookalike audience" based on any of your website custom audiences. A lookalike audience is a new audience that you can have Facebook create based on similar interests, demographics, and behaviors. According to our contact at Facebook corporate, Facebook uses over 2,000 data points to create lookalike audiences.

For example, this means you can create a lookalike audience based on your subscribers or customers. You simply create the lookalike audience based on the visitors who land on the opt-in or sales confirmation page visitors land on after opting in or buying your product.

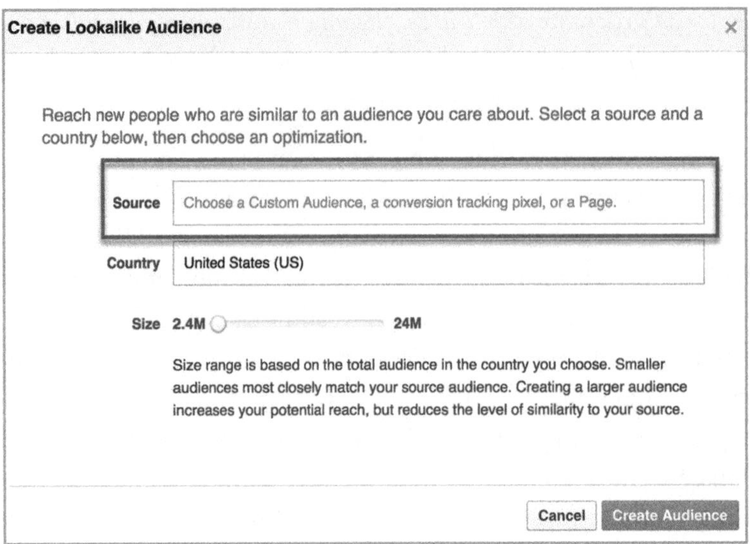

FIGURE 28-4. You Can Drive Traffic to a Custom-Built Audience, to Traffic that Visited a Specific Page, or Saw a Specific Pixel.

In Figure 28-4 you can see how easy it is to create a lookalike audience based on one of your custom audiences, conversion tracking pixels, or Facebook pages you have admin access to.

In Figure 28-5 on page 187 I have created a lookalike audience that will be 2.4 million people in the United States, all with similar interests, behaviors, demographics, etc., as my existing customers.

Examples of Goodwill Content

The most common type of goodwill content is a blog post or article. We also call this "epic content" or "anchor content."

Why epic content? Because the purpose of this piece of content is to indoctrinate, educate, and smoothly transition users into taking the next action. It needs to be something good—not just a 500-word blog post. We have epic content blog posts that are sometimes 3,000-plus words that we amplify with Facebook ads.

But the good news about this epic content strategy is that the goal should not be to go out and create a bunch of new articles every single week. The goal is to create one to two pieces of really good anchor content and use Facebook's amazing targeting capabilities to amplify that content to your ideal target audience.

The article in Figure 28-6 on my site is 3,457 words; it's basically a step-by-step guide to running Facebook ads with maximum ROI and keeping your account from getting banned by Facebook. We could easily charge money for this article, but we don't. We

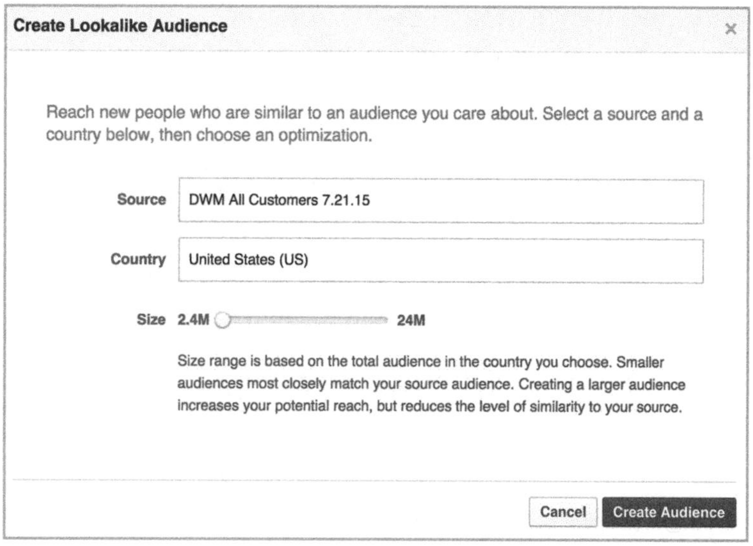

Create Lookalike Audience

Reach new people who are similar to an audience you care about. Select a source and a country below, then choose an optimization.

Source: DWM All Customers 7.21.15

Country: United States (US)

Size: 2.4M – 24M

Size range is based on the total audience in the country you choose. Smaller audiences most closely match your source audience. Creating a larger audience increases your potential reach, but reduces the level of similarity to your source.

Cancel | Create Audience

FIGURE 28-5. Lookalike Audiences Are Groups of People Facebook Generates Who Are Similar to Existing Customers or Fans, Built by Matching 2,000+ Types of Data that Facebook Tracks. This Is a Very Powerful, Effective Way to Greatly Expand Your Reach.

FIGURE 28-6. This 3,457-Word Article Serves as "Epic Content" for Attracting and Building Trust with Ideal Customers Over Time

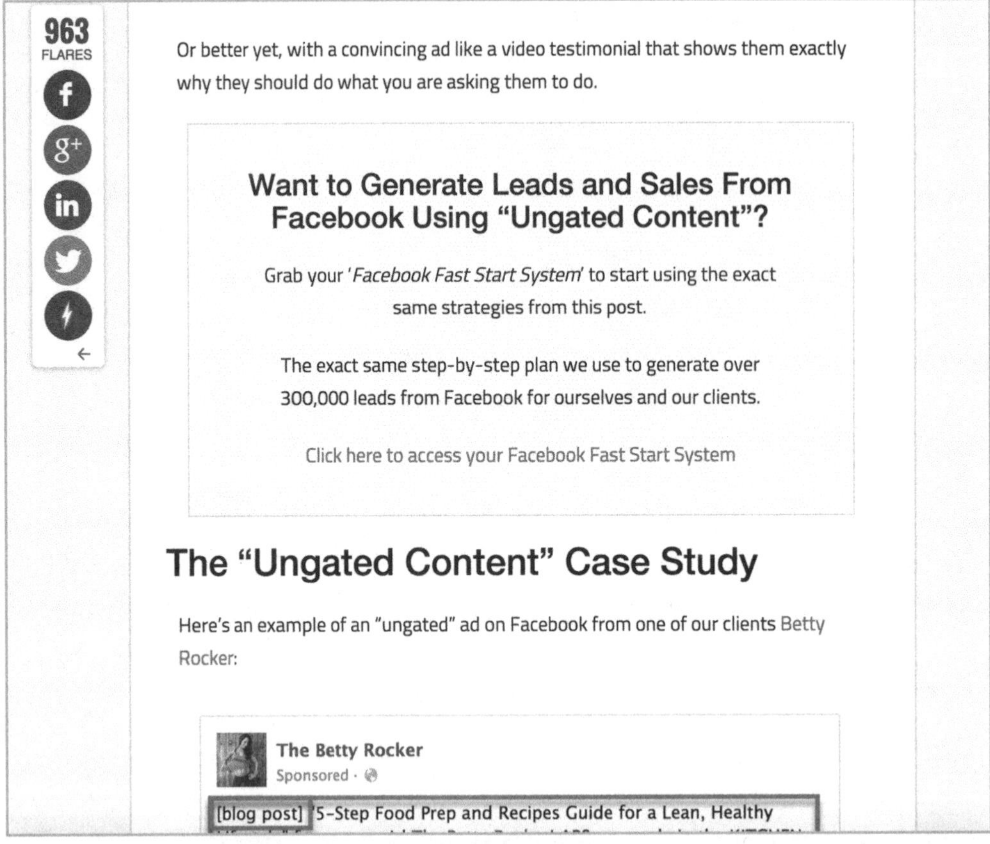

963
FLARES
Or better yet, with a convincing ad like a video testimonial that shows them exactly why they should do what you are asking them to do.
Want to Generate Leads and Sales From Facebook Using "Ungated Content"?
Grab your 'Facebook Fast Start System' to start using the exact same strategies from this post.
The exact same step-by-step plan we use to generate over 300,000 leads from Facebook for ourselves and our clients.
Click here to access your Facebook Fast Start System
The "Ungated Content" Case Study
Here's an example of an "ungated" ad on Facebook from one of our clients Betty Rocker:
The Betty Rocker
Sponsored
[blog post] 5-Step Food Prep and Recipes Guide for a Lean, Healthy

FIGURE 28–7. This Article Contains a Call to Action Form Repeated Several Times to Engage Readers and Get Them Deeper in Our Funnel.

know there is plenty more to learn about Facebook Ads, and there are also many people out there who want more "hand-holding" or full account management, of which we offer both services.

One of the keys to getting the best ROI from your content amplification is the strategic placement of calls to action (CTA) throughout your site and inside the post itself. The CTA box in Figure 28–7 (with the gray background) is placed throughout this article several times to incentivize readers to take action.

However, even if the user does not take action the first time reading an article or watching a video on your site, it's no big deal, because you will be tracking every visitor and automatically adding them to your custom audience inside your Facebook Ads account! This is essentially an "invisible list" that you can now target at a later date with a more promotional, conversion-focused ad campaign.

You will not have access to the contact information on these visitors, and you do not "own" this audience like you would own an email subscriber in your email management

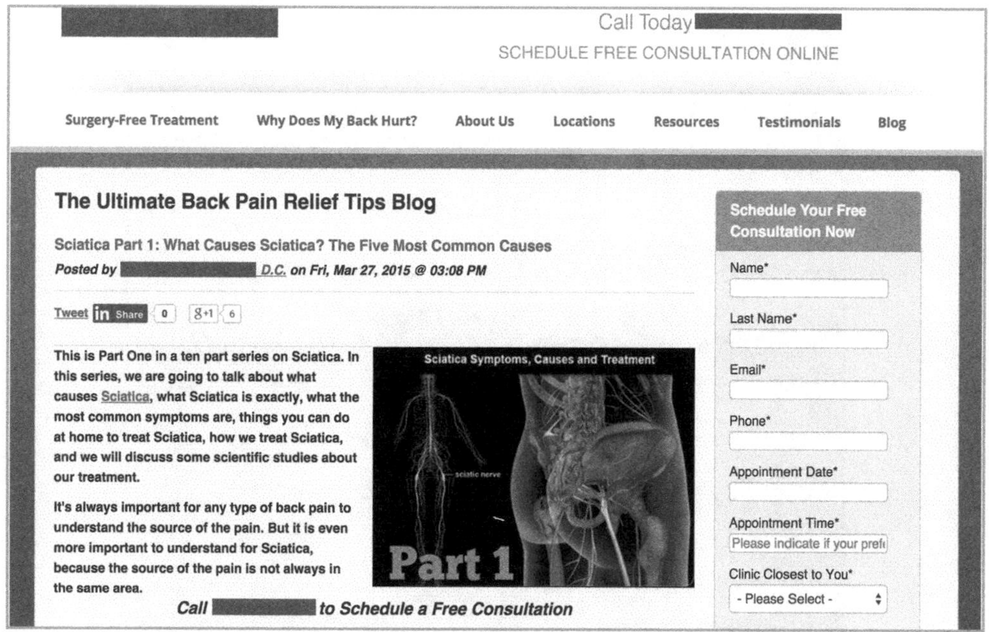

FIGURE 28–8. Example of Epic Content by a Back Pain Specialist.

software. Facebook owns the data and keeps it private. But it is still a very valuable asset that you will be able to use in several ways down the road.

Figure 28–8 is another example of an article that a local back therapy clinic amplifies with Facebook Ads on a continual basis. This is not the only page they are promoting with Facebook Ads; this is just one of the first cogs in the overall machine.

What if You Don't Have a Blog?

If you don't have a blog and you still want to capitalize on this strategy, then you can create a content-rich Facebook Video Ad. The main purpose of this video is to create goodwill. This would normally be a longer video than one focused on conversions. Around three to ten minutes is fine, depending on the content.

You can still have a soft CTA in this video, but the core objective is to build goodwill and brand awareness, knowing that you will be following up this ad with a more direct marketing ad focused on conversions. Think about it as a one-two punch.

Figure 28–9 on page 190 is a nine-minute video, in which I walk viewers through the entire Nine-Step Perpetual Traffic Blueprint, while adding soft CTAs throughout the video to register for an upcoming webinar. I call this a "content with CTA" video. Notice how I also list out the entire nine steps of the process in the post itself. (If you click "see more," you would be able to see the entire post.)

FIGURE 28–9. This Video Delivers Rich Content Along with a Definite Call to Action for Viewers Who Want More.

One of the great features of Facebook Video Ads is you can create custom audience (retargeting audience) lists out of your viewers. If you are using the Video Views Objective, Facebook will automatically create two new audiences in your account: a "viewed" audience and a "completed" audience.

In Figure 28–10 you can see the audience Facebook created from a recent video ad. The "viewed" audience is all users who watched ten seconds or more of your video. The "completed" audience is all viewers who watched at least 95 percent of your video.

☐	Video Engagement - "9-Step Social Campaign Blueprint" - 867056236663374 - Viewed	Custom Audience	14,100
☐	Video Engagement - "9-Step Social Campaign Blueprint" - 867056236663374 - Completed	Custom Audience	200

FIGURE 28–10. Example of a Large, Less Focused Audience (14,100 Members) and a Much Smaller Audience that Viewed the Entire Ten-Minute Video (200 Members).

The "completed" audience in this example is a little smaller than normal, because this was a 9:41-long video. Remember, this was a "Content with CTA" video, so the main objective was to build trust and goodwill, not to just get webinar registrations. And you will start to build trust, goodwill, and branding after the first ten seconds of your videos.

As you begin working on creating your first piece of goodwill content, you will also want to set aside some time to research your potential target audiences, which is the next step in the Five-Step Fast Start System.

STEP 2: TARGET AUDIENCE RESEARCH

You can create the best piece of content in the world, but if your ads are placed in front of the wrong target audience, you will be flushing money down the toilet. However, the good news is that Facebook has the best tools on the planet (which are all free!) when it comes to discovering insights about your customers' likes, interests, and behaviors.

It is a fairly simple process: You can get 80 percent to 90 percent of your target audience research done by using Facebook's three main tools: Facebook Audience Insights, Facebook Search, and Suggested Interests.

Audience Insights

Audience Insights is a research tool in your Ads Manager. Once in Audience Insights, you can enter your Facebook page, your main competitor's page, an industry leader's page, an interest, or a topic associated with your business, and Facebook will return an enormous amount of related data.

In Figure 28–11 on page 192, for example, I entered "Tony Robbins" into the Interests section on the left side. To the right it will spit out tons of data about Tony's specific audience: demographics, page likes, location information, activity, household data, and purchase data.

I have "Page Likes" selected and you can see that it shows the "Top Categories" that Tony Robbins fans are most interested in the upper half of the page and Page Likes data on the lower half.

In Figure 28–12 on page 192, you can see the Page Likes data that Facebook reveals about Tony Robbins. This is my favorite section of Audience Insights, as these results can be great potential interests for targeting your ad campaigns.

In Figure 28–13 on page 193, I have a "Custom Audience" selected on the left and "Household" data selected on the right. As you can see, Facebook not only helps you find new target audiences, but it can also give you incredible insight on your existing subscribers or customers. Note the additional ideas Facebook is giving me based on my custom audience.

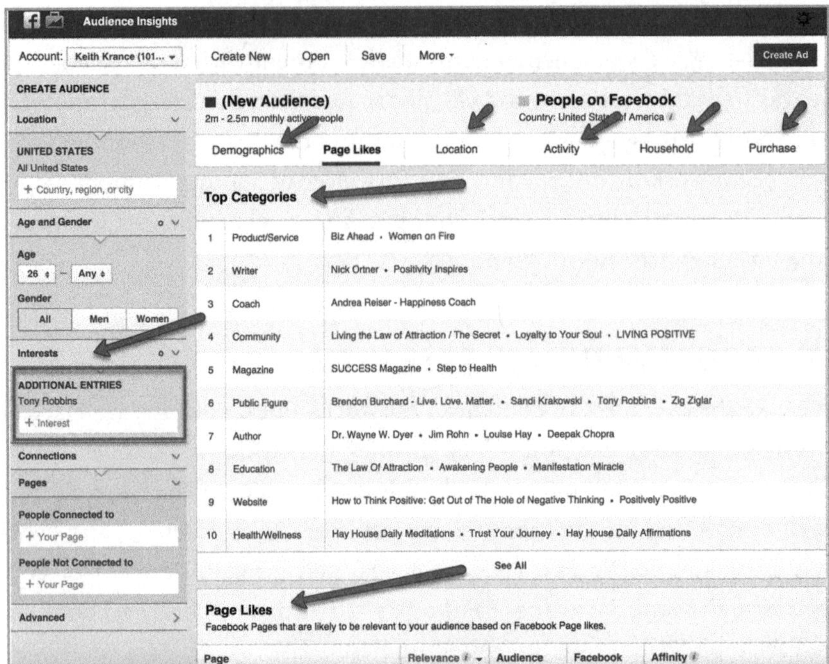

FIGURE 28–11. Audience Insights Delivers Extremely Detailed Information about Who Tony Robbins' Fans Are, What they Buy, What they Read, Who they Like. If You're Targeting Similar People, this Gives You Insight Into Where You Will Find Them.

Page Likes

Facebook Pages that are likely to be relevant to your audience based on Facebook Page likes.

Page	Relevance	Audience	Facebook	Affinity
Brendon Burchard - Live. Love. Matter.	1	584.3K	1.3m	9.4x
Nick Ortner	2	266.7K	412.2K	13x
Sandi Krakowski	3	343K	819K	8.4x
Tony Robbins	4	312.2K	697.1K	9x
Zig Ziglar	5	465.5K	1.6m	5.9x
Dr. Wayne W. Dyer	6	337.5K	1.1m	6.2x
SUCCESS Magazine	7	218.6K	536.6K	8.2x
Victoria Osteen	8	361.6K	1.5m	4.9x
Joel Osteen Ministries	9	842.5K	6.4m	2.7x
Paula White	10	323.1K	1.2m	5.2x

See More

FIGURE 28–12. Which Target Groups Are Most Relevant to Your Desired Audience? The Page Likes Report Tells You.

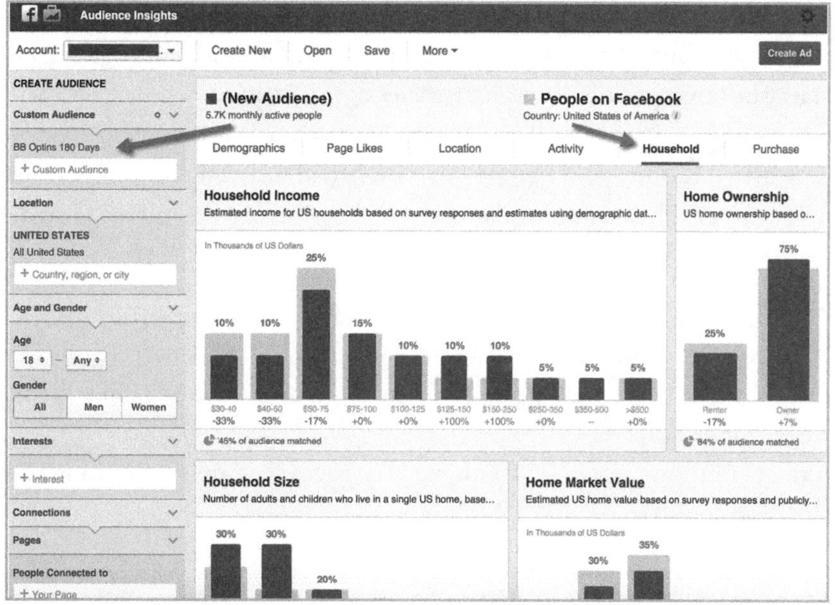

FIGURE 28–13. This Audience Insights Report Gives You Demographic Information on a Specific Group of Fans.

In Figure 28–14, I still have my custom audience selected but now have the "Demographics" tab selected on the right. This gives me more information about my subscribers than I ever knew before.

One important point to understand about local business targeting is that in many cases your customer base may be in a small geo-targeted radius, and if you are not in a

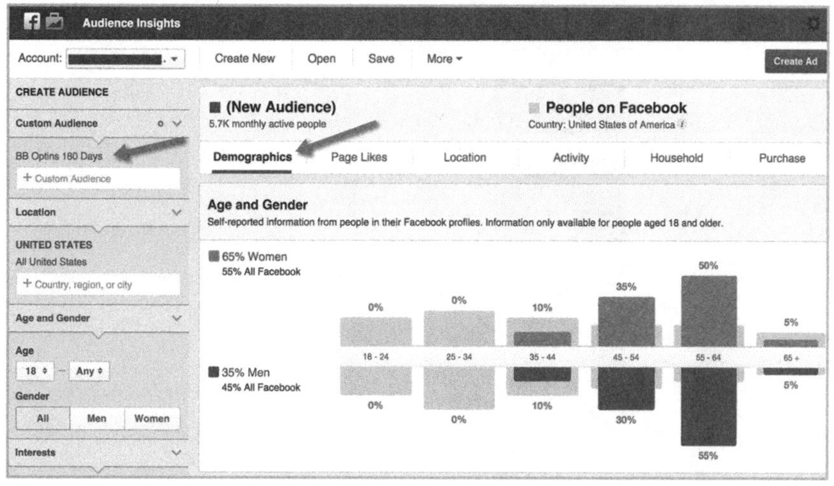

FIGURE 28–14. How Old Are Your Fans? Men vs. Women? Audience Insights Tells You.

densely populated area you may be able to keep your targeting very broad. For example, if you own a local sports bar, you might not use any interest-based targeting at all—you might start out targeting all males and females ages 21 to 55.

Facebook impressions are still very cheap compared to traditional offline advertising, so don't be afraid to start your campaigns with broad targeting as long as your ads are only showing to people in your local area.

Facebook Search

Another great way to find potential target audiences is to use the regular Facebook Search bar. Type in this search phrase: "Pages liked by people who like [your page or your competitor's page]."

Figure 28-15 shows a search I conducted for pages that are similar to my Dominate Web Media Facebook page.

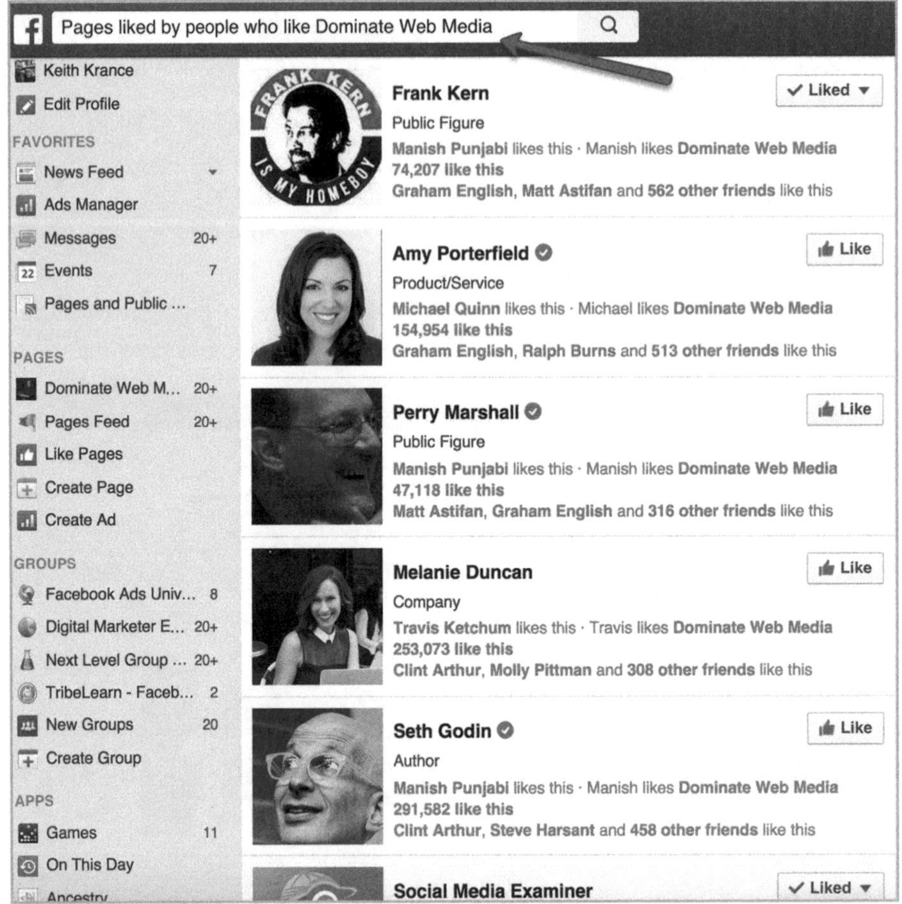

FIGURE 28-15. Pages Liked by People Who Like the Page "Dominate Web Media."

Just understand that Facebook will try and personalize these results, so in some cases they can be a little off. If you have a lot of friends in the same industry as your search then the results will normally be great, but if you are searching about an industry that none of your friends have any interest in, then your results can be way off.

The one thing I like about Facebook Search that's not available in Audience Insights yet is you can search for people who like "Page A" *and* "Page B." At the time of this writing, Audience Insights only gives you results for people who like "Page A" *or* "Page B."

In Figure 28-16, it is showing results for people who like *both* pages. This can be really helpful in your research.

Suggested Interests

Even if you're not quite ready to start running ad campaigns, I still suggest you get inside the Ads Manager and simulate creating an ad campaign. The first reason is that the more

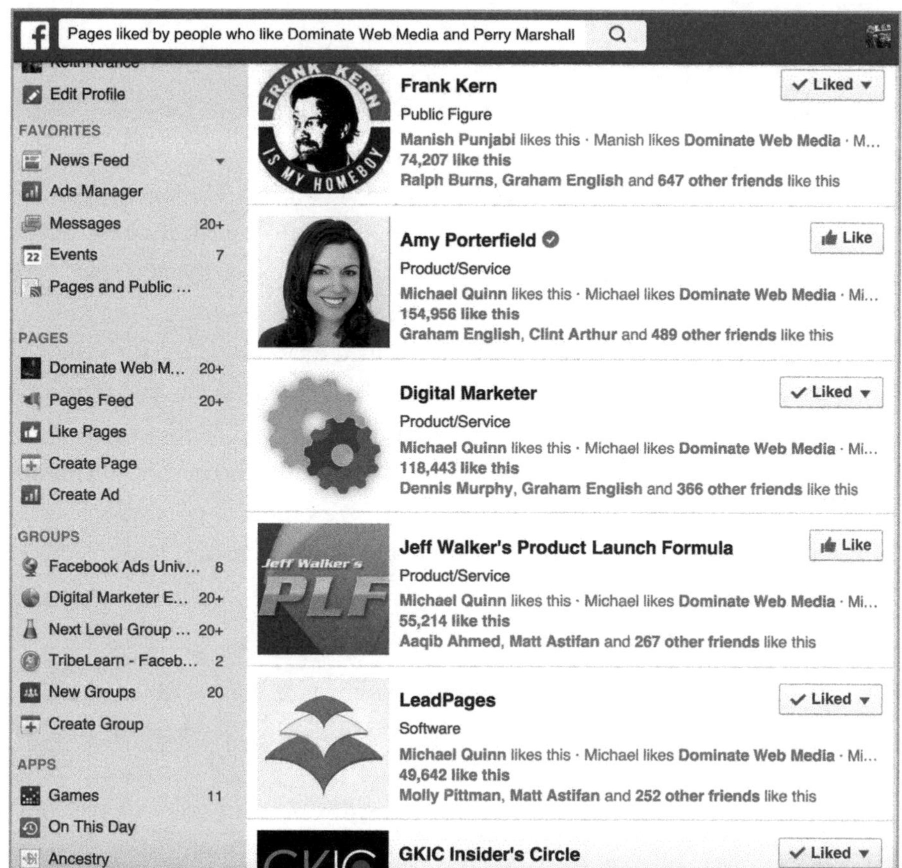

FIGURE 28-16. People Who Like Dominate Web Media and Perry Marshall Facebook Pages Also Like These Pages.

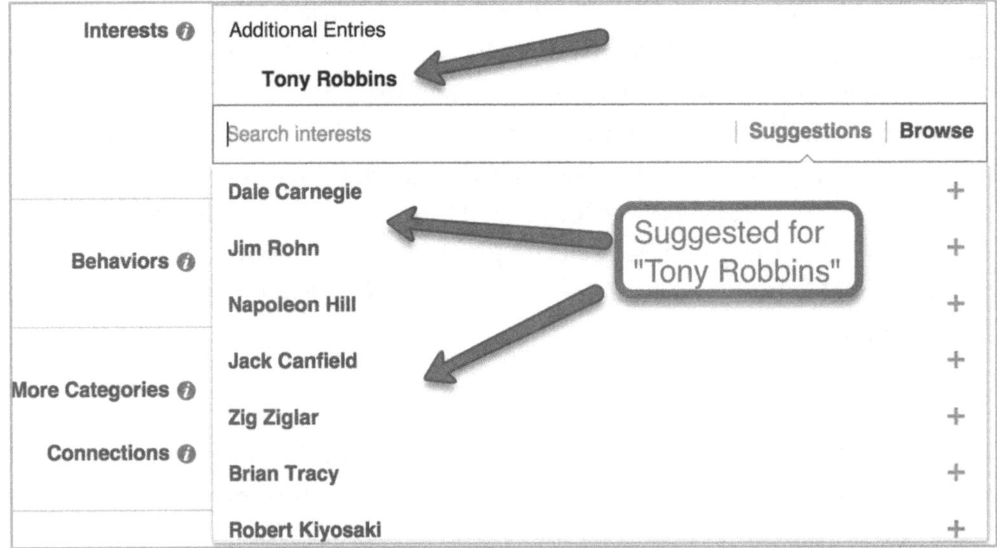

FIGURE 28–17. Who Do Tony Robbins' Fans Say Is a Lot Like Tony? Facebook Knows.

exercise you get using the Ads Manager or the Power Editor, the faster you will learn everything and get comfortable working your way around. The other reason is that you can get some great target audience research done inside the Ads Manager.

Notice in Figure 28–17 that after I select "Tony Robbins" as an Interest, Facebook will list a few suggested related Interests. These suggestions are usually very accurate, as Facebook has so much data on all its users that it is mind-blowing. And notice how some of the suggested interests are slightly different than what Audience Insights lists in their top ten Pages for Tony Robbins. This doesn't mean either one is not accurate, it just means there are a lot of different potential interests for you to choose from!

There are some other resources outside Facebook you can use for your audience research, like Amazon, Google, Similarweb.com, and a few more, but Facebook has more data within its own suite of free tools than any other third-party tool I can recommend.

Interests and Audiences Spreadsheet

When you first begin your target audience research, you will want to open a new spreadsheet to track it all. We use Google Drive and use a Google Sheet for this, so it is easily shared between team members and clients.

At first, think of this spreadsheet as one big brainstorm, where you will just copy and paste every potential interest that comes up in your research. Don't think about it too much–just start filling in your spreadsheet with names. The more names you have, the more ideas that will trigger in your head for more possible Interests.

After you start to fill up your spreadsheet, you can create a few different columns to help organize your data.

While you are doing your target audience research, one important tip is to try and think about what your audience *really* likes. Think about things such as:

- Who are the authority figures, thought leaders, or big brands in your niche?
- What books, magazines, newspapers, TV shows, or movies does your audience read or watch?
- What websites do they visit?
- Where do they live and how old are they?
- What kinds of products do they buy?
- What are some beliefs, opinions, passions, activities, or groups that your customers have in common?

The target audience research phase is a pretty fun exercise, as you will learn quite a bit about your existing subscribers and customers as well as your potential target audiences. This should be an ongoing exercise. As you gather more and more data about your audiences and start to analyze your campaign reporting, you will be able to go back to these tools and add to or organize your target audiences even more!

STEP 3: PUBLISH AND BOOST YOUR FACEBOOK POST

Now that you know your perfect target audience and you have a destination to send them to, it's time to give them a vehicle to get them to your destination. There are several different ways you can create an ad campaign depending on your objective, and there are some seriously ninja ways to optimize your targeting, bidding, and ad placement by using the Power Editor or the Ads Manager. The Power Editor gives you the most targeting options with your Facebook ads. At this time it can only be accessed through the Google Chrome browser. So make sure you are logged in to your Facebook Ads account via Google Chrome or you will not be able to access this awesome tool! However, for the purposes of this chapter we are going to focus on the fastest and easiest way to get traffic to your content: Boosting a post on your Facebook page.

Inside Facebook Ads University over at www.DominateWebMedia.com, we have the entire blueprint on how to run the most successful Facebook campaigns with maximum scalability and profit, via several training videos, checklists, and guides. However, if you are looking to get started now, get some quick wins, and gain some momentum, then you can head over later to Dominate Web Media for more advanced training. For results now, follow these instructions and you will be off to the races generating new fans, leads, and customers, and creating goodwill along the way.

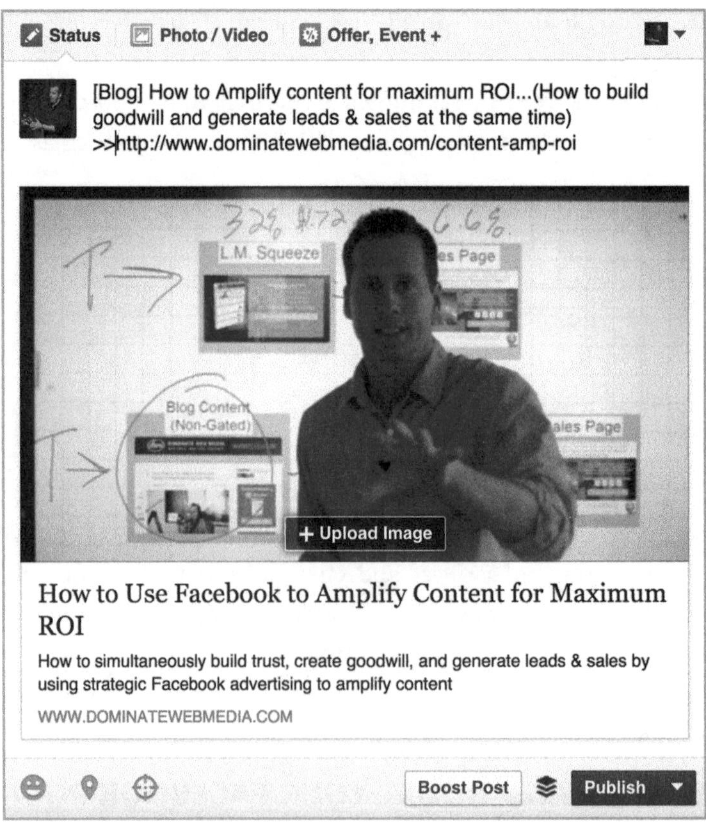

FIGURE 28–18. Page Post Link in Facebook News Feed.

To have your ads show up in the Facebook News Feed, your ad needs to be hosted by a Facebook Page. A News Feed ad is native advertising, which means your ad is in the same form as all the other organic content in the News Feed.

The easiest way to do this is to first publish a Facebook post on your page. When you add the link to your landing page or content page, the post should pull an image from your website. In Figure 28–18, you can see that I am about to publish a page post "link" post on my Facebook page. The reason it is called a "link" post is because I posted a link in the post area and Facebook automatically pulled an image from my website. That image will be a clickable link when it's published. This is the best type of ad if your goal is to get people to click over to your website.

Notice the "Upload Image" button on the lower portion of the image. This lets you upload your own custom image to replace the one that Facebook pulls from your site's meta data. The optimum image size is 1,200 x 627 pixels. However, you will be OK uploading an image as small as 600 x 315 pixels.

You are not allowed to have more than 20 percent of the image covered with text if you are going to boost a post with advertising. You can use Facebook's Grid Tool to

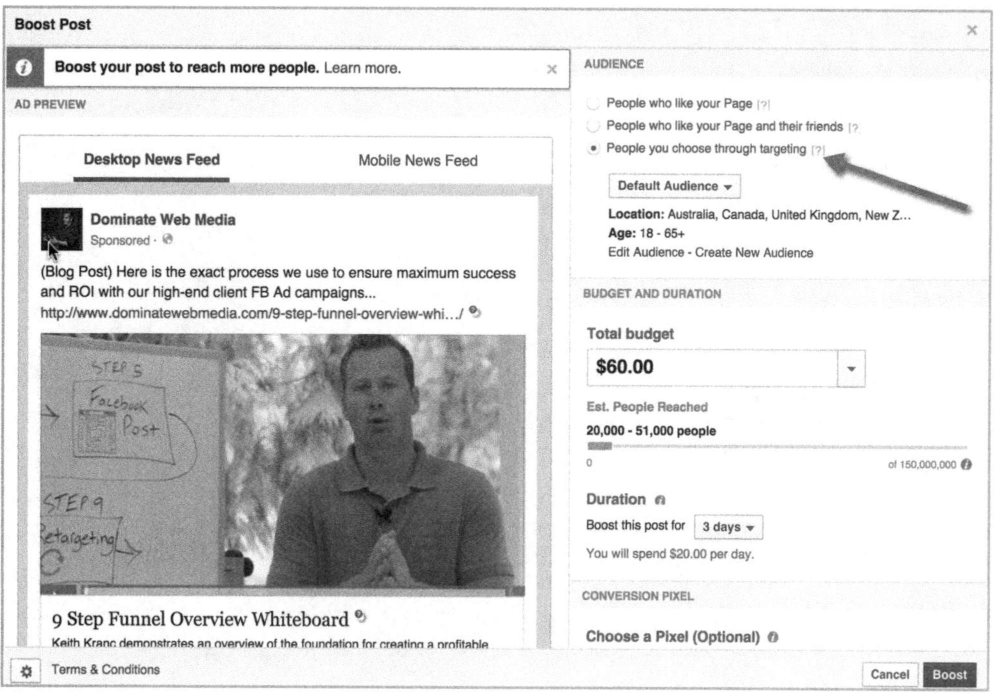

FIGURE 28–19. You Can Boost Your Post Using Ad Spend and Make It Seen by Fans, Friends of Fans, or Any Definable Group.

check if your image will pass the 20 percent text rule at: www.facebook.com/ads/tools/text_overlay.

Once you have published your post, you can now boost your post by clicking the "Boost Post" button. Figure 28–19 shows what happens after you click the Boost Post button. You now have the ability to target people who like your page, friends of people who like your page, or people you choose through Facebook's interest targeting.

Have you noticed that millions of businesses put Facebook's logo on their signs, menus, brochures and windows? They're accumulating fans, but only 10 percent to 20 percent of those fans ever see their news feed posts. You should *expect* to spend a little money to reach those fans, and if you do, you'll reach all 100 percent. You do it with this Boost Post feature.

Because most businesses don't understand this, advertising to your own fans is very inexpensive.

You need to choose a "Total budget" and for how long to boost the post. You can choose between one and seven days. (*Note:* After you Boost Post, you can now go into the Ads Manager or Power Editor and create another campaign with different budgeting options, no end date, and with much more advanced targeting and ad placement options.)

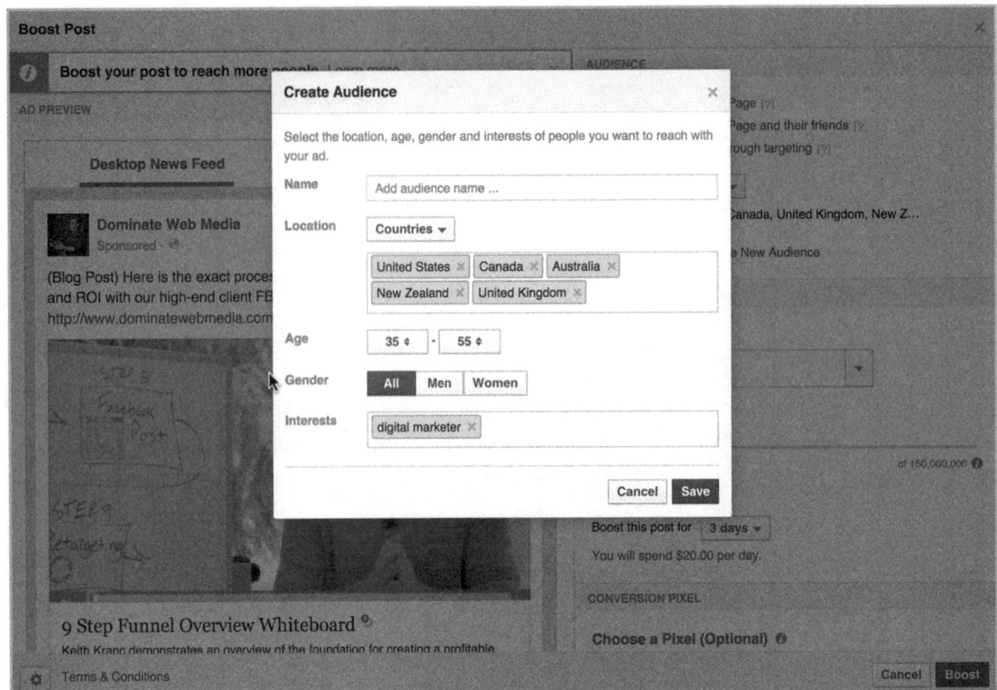

FIGURE 28-20. When You Boost a Post, You Can Create a New Audience Based on All Kinds of Criteria and Show Your Ad to Them.

Figure 28-20 shows what the targeting options look like when you select "People you choose through targeting." You have access to Facebook's Interest Targeting, but you are not able to choose custom audiences or lookalike audiences, or use some of the behavior and category targeting that you see in the Ads Manager and Power Editor.

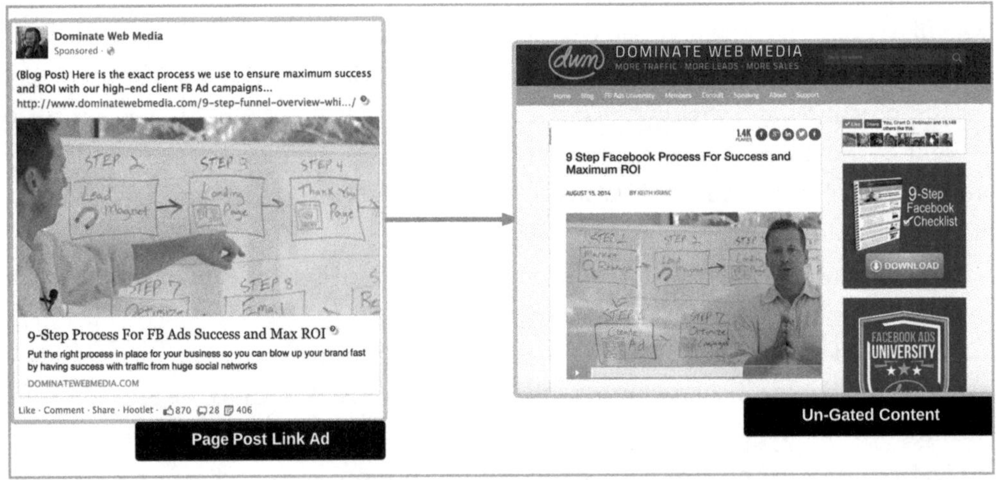

FIGURE 28-21. Here Is The Post That We Boosted and the Page It Is Driving Traffic To.

After you boost your post and confirm that it gets approved, you can go into the Ads Manager to see your campaign. If you want to create a new campaign with the same Facebook post using the Ads Manager or Power Editor but with a different objective (i.e., website conversions or clicks), you can do that now. Just select "Use Existing Post" when you get to the ad creation section.

Even if you are an advanced Facebook advertiser, in most cases, I still recommend initially boosting a post. The main reason is because your ad will typically get approved faster, you will get more organic reach, and you can verify that your ad will get approved before submitting further campaigns and ad sets.

STEP 4: REPEAT WITH CONVERSION-FOCUSED CAMPAIGN

Now that you understand the process of boosting a post to your perfect target audience, it is time to start focusing on generating conversions and maximizing your overall ROI.

As I mentioned earlier, it is best to think about most of your campaigns as a one-two punch, where you are simultaneously running goodwill indoctrination campaigns along with more direct response campaigns focused on getting conversions.

In my earlier example in Step 2, I demonstrated how to drive traffic to ungated goodwill content. Now, let's learn how to drive traffic to a landing page.

The type of landing page offer you drive Facebook traffic to depends on the kind of business you have. (*Note:* Facebook-appropriate landing pages are usually different from Google AdWords landing pages.) In my case, we use free resources people can download in exchange for their email address, like our "Nine-Step Facebook Campaign Checklist" or my "Video Equipment Guide." We also love using webinar registration pages for Facebook traffic.

Figure 28–22 on page 202, shows another page post "link ad," sometimes called "link post ad," that is driving traffic to a webinar registration page. Webinar landing pages are great for Facebook traffic because you have more space to build deeper relationships and more trust, plus they make a good sales vehicle for the product or service.

Local Brick and Mortar Offers

With local businesses, we've seen that more direct offers related to the product or service sometimes work better than education-based offers, like the previous examples. Some successful offers that can work well include "buy one get one free," a free consultation, a free teeth whitening or free teeth cleaning, a discount coupon offer, a fitness challenge, a contest or giveaway, a live event, and many others.

In Figure 28–23 on page 202, the main offer on the landing page for a free consult at a back therapy office has been very successful. However, one of the reasons they

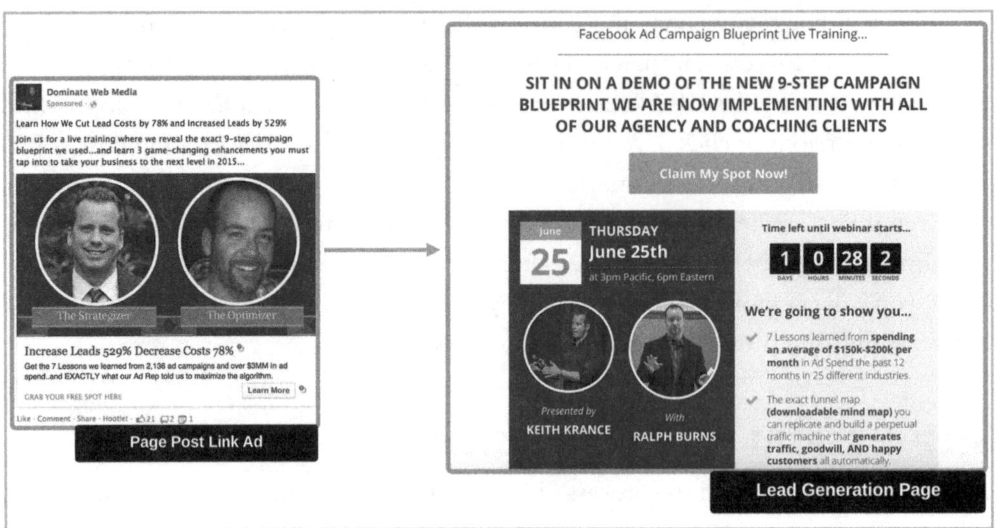

FIGURE 28-22. A Page Post Link Ad Drives People to a Webinar Signup Page.

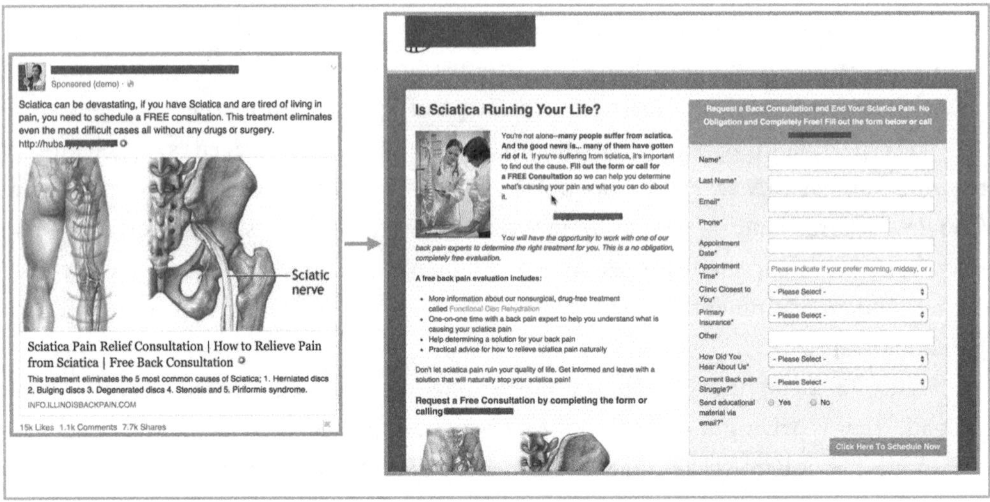

FIGURE 28-23. Ads Drive Warmed-Up Visitors to a Signup Page.

are successful with these lead-generation campaigns is because they are continually amplifying goodwill content and running Facebook Video Ads to build trust and goodwill, and grow their custom audiences so they can retarget warm visitors back into these conversion-focused campaigns.

In most cases, it's OK to run content amplification ads and lead-generation ads to the same target audiences, as different people respond to different touch points, and many people need multiple touch points. Remember, people on Facebook are not actively searching for a solution; they are just hanging out and probably trying to get away from all their problems! So you need to focus on making friends with people first (just like when you meet someone at a party) and also occasionally making offers to the people that might be ready.

If you want to target only "warm" audiences for these lead-generation campaigns, then you must use the Ads Manager or Power Editor to select the correct targeting. It's pretty simple: When selecting your targeting, you choose the appropriate website custom audience as the target audience.

If you want to exclude subscribers or customers, then you "Exclude" the website custom audience page that people land on after they opt-in or purchase. (See Figure 28-24 for an example.) We consider a "warm audience" any audience that has previously been engaged with your brand in some capacity. This could be a Facebook fan, a website visitor, a subscriber, or a video view.

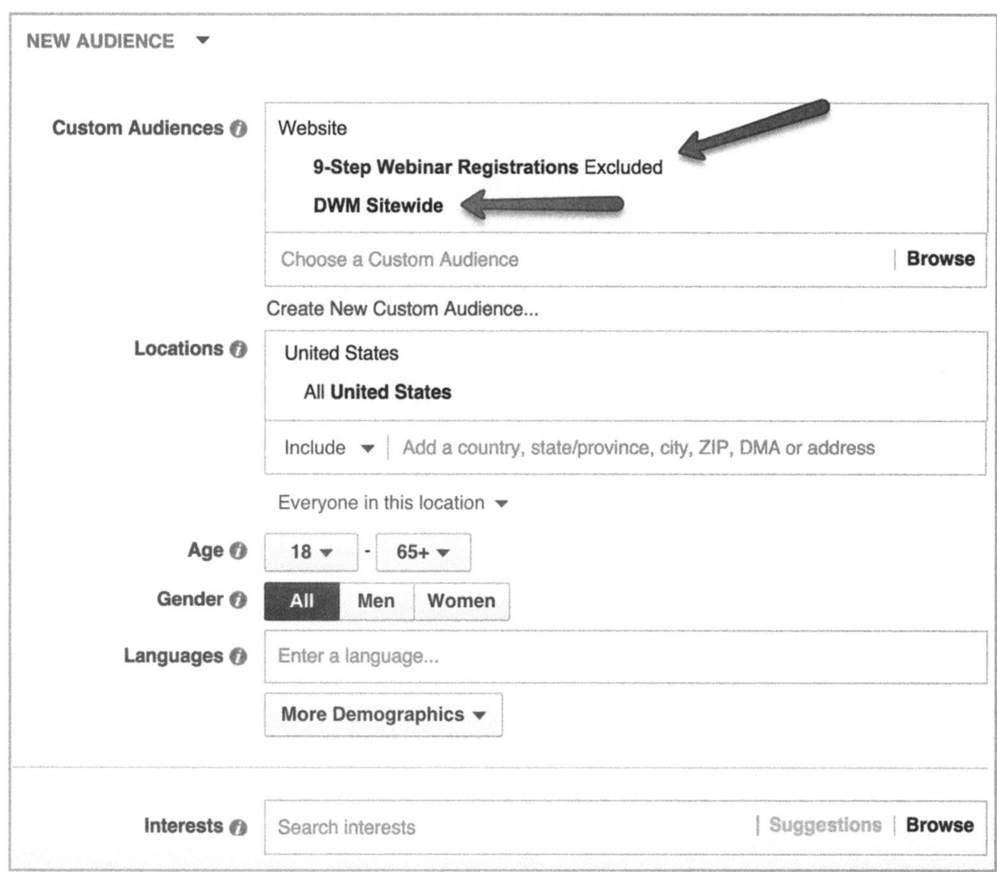

FIGURE 28-24. A Custom Audience Includes a Large Group of People but Excludes Everyone Who Already Signed Up for a Webinar.

After you get your feet wet and start getting some results, there are other types of conversion-focused campaigns you can test. For example, you could run an ad targeting visitors who landed on a sales page but didn't buy. You could run a Video Ad with some testimonial content, hoping to connect with those people who just needed a little more proof that your product or service is awesome. We are doing this exact strategy with several of our clients, and they are working well.

STEP 5: ANALYZE AND OPTIMIZE

As soon as a few hours after your campaigns start running, use Facebook's amazing reporting tool to make important discoveries about your campaigns. This is where you can find which Interests are performing best, which placement is giving you the best ROI (News Feed, right column, desktop, mobile, etc.), which Demographics are performing best, what ad copy is working best, which image is winning, etc.

Once you click into a campaign, you can customize the metrics you want to analyze in the Ads Manager. In Figure 28-25, you will see "Columns: Performance" in the drop-down menu. The exact location or name of these elements may change by the time you're reading this, but the process will still be basically the same.

In the "Customize Columns" (see Figure 28-26 on page 205) section, select the appropriate metrics to measure depending on what the core objectives are with that campaign. Some campaigns may be focused most on optimizing lead costs, some on sales conversions, some on video metrics, some on website clicks and engagement metrics.

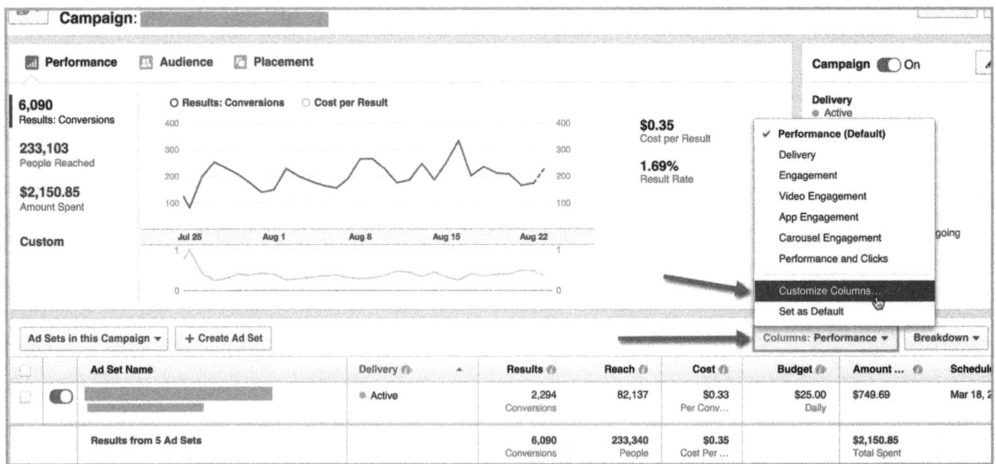

FIGURE 28-25. Do You Need to See Daily Spend? Conversion Rates of Different Campaigns? Customize the Columns in Your Reports.

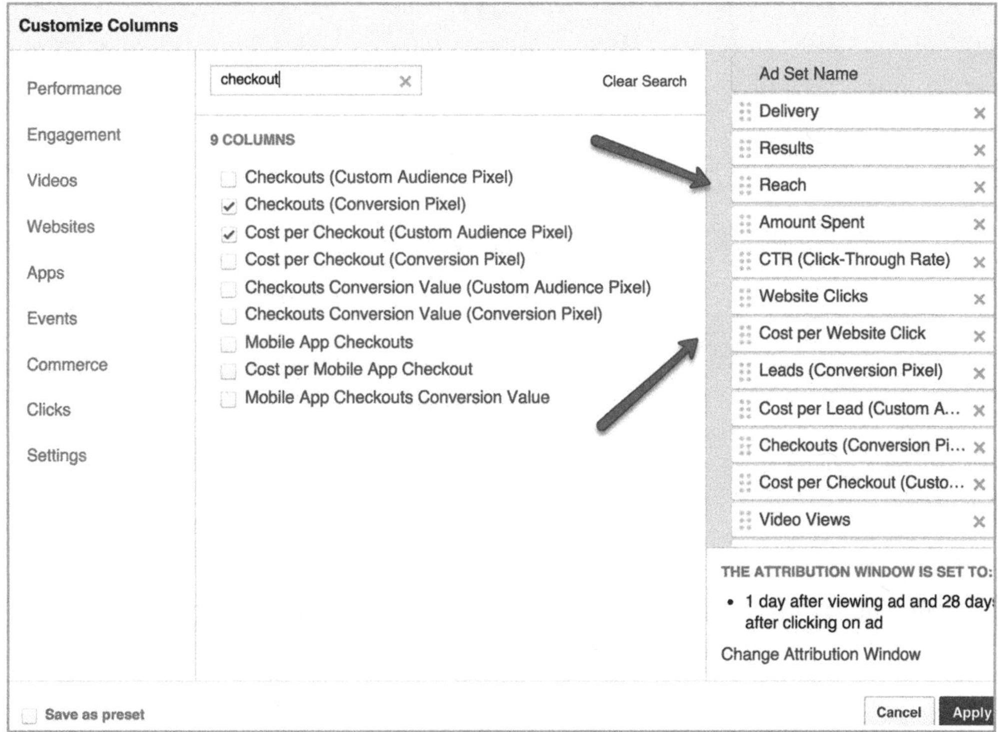

FIGURE 28–26. You Have Considerable Latitude in What Kind of Metrics You See in Custom Columns.

The next most important section in the reporting tool is the "Breakdown" column, as seen in Figure 28–27 on page 206. Take some time to analyze the "Age and Gender" and "Placement and Device" selections. I promise you will find some glaring differences in click costs, conversion costs, etc., when comparing things like desktop and mobile, or News Feed and right column.

One of the keys to winning at Facebook ads is to analyze the reporting data and make adjustments. The most successful coaches in the professional sports world are incredible at making game-time adjustments after analyzing how the other team reacted to their playbook. If you think about your campaigns in the same way, you will win big at Facebook.

THE FACEBOOK FAST START REVIEW

Let's recap the Five-Step Facebook Fast Start system:

- *Step 1:* Publish "Facebook Friendly" Goodwill Content
- *Step 2:* Target Audience Research

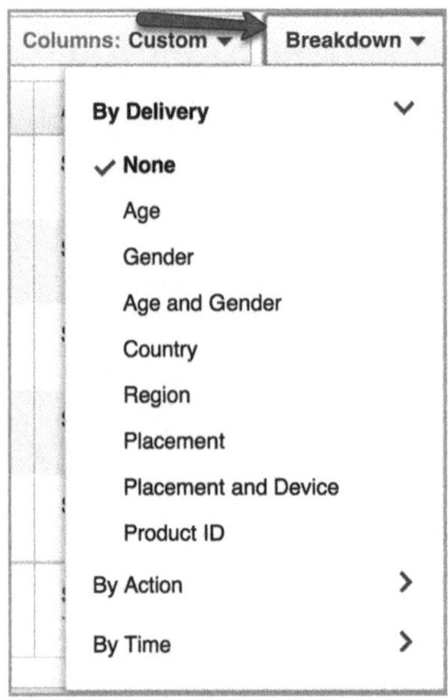

FIGURE 28–27. Further Subdivide Your Data by Other Criteria and Look for Buying Behaviors that Characterize Your Customers.

- *Step 3:* Publish and Boost Your Facebook Post
- *Step 4:* Repeat with Conversion-Focused Campaign
- *Step 5:* Analyze and Optimize

Whether you're brand-new to Facebook advertising or you ample experience running Facebook ads, if you implement this five-step process, you will have a sporting chance of creating successful new campaigns or improving your current campaigns.

My last piece of advice is to think about this the next time you're getting ready to launch a campaign: If you were at a party or event, would you talk to people the same way you do with your Facebook ads? Facebook is an online social gathering, so you should talk to your target audience in the same manner as if you had met them at a party or event.

■ ■ ■

About Keith Krance: After spending six years as an airline pilot for Horizon Air, a subsidiary of Alaska Airlines, and racking up over 4,000 hours in a 70-passenger jet, Keith Krance's entrepreneur spirit finally took over. After leveraging some early real estate success, he started, owned, and operated several brick-and-mortar retail businesses as a part of two franchises. Then after a few years of "grinding" through managing these businesses he dove into direct response online marketing.

He quickly fell in love with Facebook Advertising, as he had never seen any other advertising medium like it in the offline world; similar to billboards and TV advertising yet cheaper to test and implement, and far more targeted.

Keith is now founder and president of Dominate Web Media, which has three core divisions: an online Facebook Ads education company, a Facebook Ads coaching program, and a full-service Facebook Ads agency. His team has managed several million dollars in Facebook advertising spend which has generated hundreds of thousands of new leads and several million dollars in revenue generated directly from Facebook and other online media channels.

Dominate Web Media has helped clients in dozens of markets all over the world, working with both small businesses and large companies. They also manage campaigns and work closely with some of the biggest experts in the online marketing industry, which gives them even more insight and perspective on what really works and what doesn't work. Learn more from Keith at www.DominateWebMedia.com.

Chapter 29

Take Action—and Get Started!

You now have in your hands everything you need to create a highly effective pay-per-click (PPC) campaign for your local business and to be able to accurately track your ROI. The only thing left is to take action!

There is a lot of information to digest in this book, and it is normal to feel overwhelmed. To help make things easier for you to implement what you have learned, we have created a step-by-step process to follow to get your PPC campaign launched.

Simply follow the steps below (and refer back to the appropriate chapter to get the specifics when you need to), and you will end up with a highly effective lead generation campaign.

Step 1: Set up your landing page(s) and post them online (either on your own website or buy a new domain).

Step 2: Create a Google My Business account if you don't have one already (for integration with your location extension).

Step 3: Create a Google AdWords account.

Step 4: Set up dynamic call conversion tracking on your landing page.

Step 5: Get contact form conversion tracking set up on your landing page.

Step 6: Conduct keyword research to identify your best and most targeted keywords.
Step 7: Organize keywords into ad groups and select the appropriate match types.
Step 8: Write your ads and copy for sitelinks and callout extensions.
Step 9: Build your campaign in Google AdWords.
Step 10: Launch your campaign!
Step 11: Monitor conversions and adjust bids up or down depending on results.
Step 12: Add remarketing/retargeting.
Step 13: Decide if the campaign is working and you want to scale things up or down.
Step 14: If you want to scale up, add Bing Ads, increase geo-targeting, add keywords, etc.
Step 15: Split-test ad copy.
Step 16: Grow your local business!

We recommend taking things one step at a time. Right now just focus on getting your landing page done and online, since that is step 1!

80/20: TOP STRATEGIES TO IMPLEMENT NOW

There is a very specific reason why Google PPC using high-converting landing pages is the number-one strategy taught in depth in this book. It's because out of *everything* that we have seen local businesses try in terms of marketing their businesses, we have yet to find *anything* that has consistently yielded such a high return (when done correctly, as taught in this book).

Rather than touching on dozens of smaller, less effective (mostly outdated) marketing strategies that have very little upside potential, we taught you tactics with the newest and greatest ROI, the highest upside potential, and the lowest risk that have the biggest impact on local businesses.

We also went deep into what we truly believe is by far the number-one strategy you should be focusing on right now: Google AdWords. We have seen local businesses more than double their business in a short period of time because of all the new customers they have generated from Google AdWords. And we have clients right now that are doing *millions* of dollars a year in business with over 80 percent of their leads coming from Google AdWords, so we know it works.

We have given you the model; now it's your turn to take action and make it happen. We want to be clear, Google AdWords with high-converting landing pages is the number-one strategy we recommend you at least test right now, because it can *dramatically* grow your business. It has huge upside potential with a very low downside risk (just a couple grand to give it a test).

A Final Call to Arms

Remember, the 80/20 rule is ALWAYS working—either **for** you or **against** you. Twenty percent of your marketing is going to bring in 80 percent of your business.

In this book we have covered the 20 percent that we believe can bring in 80 percent (or more) of your business. Our advice is to LASER focus on this 20 percent and the strategies we have outlined in this book.

Google is going to be around for a LONG time, and even if Yahoo! and Bing were to overtake them as number one, they'll still use the exact same ad platform as Google, so everything you learned in this book applies exactly the same on those platforms.

YES—Google does make updates. That is why we HIGHLY recommend that you go to www.UltimateLocalBook.com and get on the notification list for any and all changes/updates. We will constantly be updating that site with new information, resources, and important supplemental training that will help you.

BEFORE WE GO . . .

Perry Marshall here. From time to time I host a small two-day event at my home office called a Four-Man Intensive. A guy named Steve from the East

Coast came. He was a small local business that sold a very specific service for pets. He wanted to improve his AdWords performance.

We went to work. He was normally showing up around positions four to six. I told him he needed to get into positions one to three, and if he did, his traffic would go up exponentially.

His landing pages weren't tailored to the keywords and he wasn't split-testing. We sat together and made numerous improvements. Then in the following weeks we continued working together over the phone.

Within a few weeks, the improvements palpably kicked in. His traffic doubled, then tripled. He called me in the winter and said, "Perry, this is normally the slowest season of the year but I'm breaking sales records. I'm selling more in November and December than we used to sell in May and June—which is normally our busy season!"

This small niche business was suddenly very profitable. Steve had underestimated how much traffic Google could deliver when you tune the engine right (most people do). Eventually our conversations turned to expanding his business to other locations. He even considered franchising his approach all over the country.

When you're the number-one player in your market, you're automatically in a position to start thinking much bigger than you ever have before.

Don't underestimate what you can do if you laser-focus your efforts and get this done right.

Carpe Diem—Seize the Day!
—Perry Marshall and Talor Zamir

About the Authors

PERRY MARSHALL is one of the world's most expensive and sought-after business consultants. Clients seek him for his capacity to integrate many disparate fields: engineering, biology, chaos theory, mathematics, physics, art and psychology.

He has launched two online revolutions. In pay-per-click advertising, he pioneered many of today's best practices and wrote the world's best selling book on internet advertising, *Ultimate Guide to Google AdWords, Fourth Edition* (Entrepreneur Press, 2014).

More recently, he's applied the 80/20 Principle to more facets of business than any other author, being the first to expand on 80/20 as an infinite fractal law of nature. 80/20 is the central lever for nearly every profitable strategy in sales, marketing, and business. His book *80/20 Sales and Marketing* (Entrepreneur Press, 2013) is required reading in many growing companies.

Works also include the bestseller *Ultimate Guide to Facebook Advertising, Second Edition* (Entrepreneur Press, 2014), *Evolution 2.0: Breaking the Deadlock Between Darwin and Design* (BenBella, 2015), and *Industrial Ethernet, Second Edition* (ISA).

He is referenced in dozens of influential business books by authors like Jay Conrad Levinson, Mark Joyner, Joel Comm, and Mari Smith. He's shared the stage with Barbara Corcoran, Brian Tracy, and Les Brown, having consulted in over 300 industries.

In 2015 he launched the Evolution 2.0 Prize, which seeks an answer for Origin of Information, one of the most fundamental unsolved problems in all of biology.

Direct marketing maverick Dan S. Kennedy says, "If you don't know who Perry Marshall is—unforgivable. Perry's an honest man in a field rife with charlatans."

Perry has a degree in electrical engineering and lives in Chicago.

TALOR ZAMIR is a highly-sought after speaker and consultant in the fields of Internet Marketing, Entrepreneurship, and Personal Development.

Talor made a name for himself in his late 20s by being a "pay-per-performance" marketer and negotiating deals where his clients didn't have to pay unless he got them a huge ROI (which he consistently did).

He has generated tens of thousands of leads for local businesses via his "Local Business Landing Page Template" and unique PPC strategies that have made him an internationally known marketer at age 34.

More recently over 3,000 of the world's top marketing consultants have purchased Talor's trainings and implemented them to attain extraordinary results for their clients.

Talor is widely known as the top local business lead generation and conversion expert in the world and works with some the highest spending local businesses in terms of ad spend.

Index